RACE, GENDER, SEXUALITY, AND THE POLITICS OF THE AMERICAN JUDICIARY

The judicial system in a liberal democracy is deemed to be an independent branch of government with judges free from political agendas or societal pressures. In reality, judges are often influenced by their economic and social backgrounds, gender, race, religion, and sexuality. This volume explores the representation of different identities in the judiciary in the United States. The contributors investigate the pipeline, ambition, institutional inclusion, retention, and representation of groups previously excluded from federal, state, and local judiciaries. This study demonstrates how diversity on the bench improves the quality of justice, bolsters confidence in the legitimacy of the courts, and provides a vital voice in decision-making power for formerly disenfranchised populations.

SAMANTHA L. HERNANDEZ is Director of Strategic Initiatives and Policy Office of San Antonio City Council – Councilwoman Shirley Gonzales. She is the coeditor of *Latinas in American Politics: Changing and Embracing Political Tradition* (2016). Her work has been featured in *Politics and Gender*, the *New York Times*, *Bloomberg News*, and *Chronicle of Higher Education*.

SHARON A. NAVARRO is Professor of Political Science at the University of Texas, San Antonio. Her research interests focus on Latinos – as in American politics; women and politics; and race-ethnic, gender and public policy. She is the coeditor of *Latinas in American Politics* (2016), *The Roots of Latino Urban Agency* (2013), and *Latino Americans and Political Participation* (2004). She is also the coauthor of *Politicas: Latina Public Officials in Texas* (2008) and author of *Latina Legislator: Leticia Van De Putte and the Road to Leadership* (2008).

Race, Gender, Sexuality, and the Politics of the American Judiciary

Edited by

SAMANTHA L. HERNANDEZ

Director of Strategic Initiatives and Policy Office of San Antonio City Council – Councilwoman Shirley Gonzales

SHARON A. NAVARRO

University of Texas at San Antonio

CAMBRIDGE
UNIVERSITY PRESS

CAMBRIDGE
UNIVERSITY PRESS

Shaftesbury Road, Cambridge CB2 8EA, United Kingdom

One Liberty Plaza, 20th Floor, New York, NY 10006, USA

477 Williamstown Road, Port Melbourne, VIC 3207, Australia

314–321, 3rd Floor, Plot 3, Splendor Forum, Jasola District Centre, New Delhi – 110025, India

103 Penang Road, #05–06/07, Visioncrest Commercial, Singapore 238467

Cambridge University Press is part of Cambridge University Press & Assessment,
a department of the University of Cambridge.

We share the University's mission to contribute to society through the pursuit of
education, learning and research at the highest international levels of excellence.

www.cambridge.org
Information on this title: www.cambridge.org/9781108429887

DOI: 10.1017/9781108555500

First published 2019

A catalogue record for this publication is available from the British Library

Library of Congress Cataloging-in-Publication data
NAMES: Hernandez, Samantha L., editor. | Navarro, Sharon Ann, editor.
TITLE: Race, gender, sexuality, and the politics of the American judiciary / edited by Samantha L. Hernandez, Arizona State University [and] Sharon A. Navarro, University of Texas San Antonio
DESCRIPTION: Cambridge, United Kingdom ; New York, NY : Cambridge University Press, 2018. | Includes bibliographical references and index.
IDENTIFIERS: LCCN 2018023530 | ISBN 9781108429887 (hardback)
SUBJECTS: LCSH: Judges–Selection and appointment–Social aspects–United States. | BISAC: LAW / General.
CLASSIFICATION: LCC KF8776 .R33 2018 | DDC 347.73/14–dc23 LC record available at https://lccn.loc.gov/2018023530

ISBN 978-1-108-42988-7 Hardback

For my father, Vidal Navarro

Contents

Figures

Tables

Contributors

Nancy Bays Arrington is Assistant Professor of Political Science at California Polytechnic State University in San Luis Obispo. Her work addresses how judicial selection institutions shape prospects for the inclusion and incorporation of women, minority, and minority women judges. She received her PhD from Emory University in Atlanta, Georgia; master's in International Policy from the University of Georgia; and bachelor's from the University of Texas at Austin. She is the author of "Gender and Judicial Replacement" (*Journal of Law and Courts*, 2018). Current projects include an examination of how institutional changes to constitutional courts affect gender diversity cross-nationally and survey experimental work on how observers learn and make inferences about gender bias in the judiciary.

Shenita Brazelton is a licensed attorney and Assistant Professor of Political Science at Tuskegee University in Tuskegee, Alabama. She earned a BA in political science from Tuskegee University, a JD from Vanderbilt University Law School, and a PhD in political science from Georgia State University. Her research interests include examining decision-making in federal circuit courts. She also explores issues pertaining to race with an emphasis on voting rights litigation and affirmative action. She is coauthor of "Specialization in Judicial Decision-Making: Comparing Bankruptcy Panels and Federal District Court Judges" (*American Bankruptcy Institute Law Review*, 2014). She served as guest editor of the Fall/Winter 2016 issue of *The Journal of Race and Policy*, in which she also authored "A Hollow Hope? Social Change, the U.S. Supreme Court and Affirmative Action."

LaTasha Chaffin-DeHaan is Assistant Professor of Political Science at the College of Charleston in Charleston, South Carolina. She earned her PhD and MA in political science from Western Michigan University. She also holds a master's in public administration and a bachelor's in business administration from Grand Valley State University. Her research interests are in the field of American politics with a particular emphasis on examining public policy and bureaucratic outcomes and their impacts on diverse and vulnerable populations. Her research interests extend to United States and comparative labor, economic, social welfare, judicial, and state and local politics and policy. She is the coauthor (with Maurice Mangum, Anthony D. Greene, and Jason Shelton) of "Aligned or Misaligned? Similarities and Differences between African Americans' and Black Caribbeans' Opinions on Affirmative Action" (*The Journal of Race and Policy*, 2017) and (with Christopher Cooper and H. Gibbs Knotts) "Furling the Flag: Explaining the 2015 Vote to Remove the Confederate Flag in South Carolina" (*Politics & Policy*, 2017).

Patrick Gauding is a PhD candidate in political science at the University of Kansas. His research interests include political behavior, representation, and state and local policy environments.

Barbara L. Graham is Associate Professor of Political Science at the University of Missouri-St. Louis. She teaches and conducts research in the area of judicial politics. Her work on judicial redistricting, judicial diversity and representation on the bench has appeared in *American Politics Quarterly*, *Political Research Quarterly*, *Judicature*, *Michigan Journal of Race & Law*, and *The Book of the States*. She is the author of the forthcoming book *Social Identity and the Law: Race, Sexuality and Intersectionality*.

Donald P. Haider-Markel is Professor and Chair of Political Science at the University of Kansas. His research and teaching is focused on the representation of interests in the policy process and the dynamics between public opinion, political behavior, and public policy. He has more than twenty years of experience in survey research, interviews, and in policy studies. He has authored or coauthored over sixty refereed articles, over a dozen book chapters, and several books on a range of issue areas, including civil rights, politics in the culture wars, criminal justice policy, counterterrorism, and environmental policy.

Samantha L. Hernandez is Director of Strategic Initiatives and Policy Office of San Antonio City Council – Councilwoman Shirley Gonzales. She is the coeditor of *Latinas in American Politics: Changing and Embracing Political Tradition* (2016). Her work has been featured in *Politics and Gender*, the *New York Times*, *Bloomberg News*, and *Chronicle of Higher Education*.

Lisa M. Holmes is Associate Professor of Political Science at the University of Vermont. She received her BA from the University of Vermont and her MA and PhD from the University of Georgia. She specializes in judicial politics, constitutional law, gender and law, and American politics. Her research focusing on various issues surrounding the politics of appointing judges has been published in a variety of journals, including *American Politics Research*, *Political Science Quarterly*, *Judicature*, and *P.S.: Political Science & Politics*. Her current project examines the implications of politicized appointment politics on the careers and attitudes of federal judicial nominees.

Taneisha Nicole Means is Assistant Professor of Political Science at Vassar College in Poughkeepsie, New York. She specializes in judicial politics, and race, ethnicity, and politics. She received her BA from John Carroll University, and both MA and PhD from Duke University. Before joining the faculty at Vassar, she was a 2014–2016 predoctoral fellow in the Carter G. Woodson Institute for African-American and African Studies at the University of Virginia in Charlottesville. Her work has been published in *Politics, Groups, and Identities*, and will soon be published in several edited book volumes. She is currently finishing a book manuscript on black state court judges' identities and decision-making.

Sharon A. Navarro is Professor of Political Science at the University of Texas, San Antonio. Her research interests focus on Latinos – as in American politics; women and politics; and race-ethnic, gender and public policy. She is the coeditor of *Latinas in American Politics* (2016), *The Roots of Latino Urban Agency* (2013), and *Latino Americans and Political Participation* (2004). She is also the coauthor of *Politicas: Latina Public Officials in Texas* (2008) and author of *Latina Legislator: Leticia Van De Putte and the Road to Leadership* (2008).

Adriano Udani is Assistant Professor of Political Science at the University of Missouri-St. Louis, with a joint appointment in the public policy administration program. He specializes in the study of political attitudes toward immigrant groups, voter fraud, and public support for voter restrictions. His research is published in *American Politics Research*; *Politics, Groups, and Identities*; *Social Science Quarterly*; *Policy Studies Journal*; and *State Politics and Policy Quarterly*.

Acknowledgments

Sharon would like to thank Samantha for agreeing to coedit this project. She would also like to thank all of the contributors. This book could not have been completed without them.

Toward the end of this project, Sharon's father passed away. His passing caused her to step away from spearheading this project. Samantha took over, among her many other duties, and saw this book to the end. To her, Sharon is truly grateful. She also thanks her mom, siblings, and Ashley.

Samantha would like to thank Sharon. She has been a rock for Samantha throughout her graduate career and has also been a great mentor and friend. Samantha can never thank Sharon enough for her support. She would also like to thank her parents, siblings, and Carlo.

Introduction

For most individuals and organizations, courts are the "law" for all effective purposes. We know little about who serves on courts – i.e., federal judges, state judges – despite their central and powerful role. This lack of information is especially significant because judges' backgrounds have important implications for the works of courts. The characteristics of those who sit in judgment can affect the internal workings of courts as well as the external perception of courts and judges. In fact, judges' biases are often used to politicize their rulings. The background of judges can influence how they make decisions and impact the public's acceptance of those decisions. The effects of having more minorities in the judiciary is not fully developed; yet the diversification of the bench is something that could affect how the judicial system works. We need to know more about justices.

The number of women, minorities, and LGBT candidates gaining access to positions of power in the United States has grown in recent years and is expecting an unprecedented boom in the coming ones. One important seat of power is on the bench, as the judiciary may be a crucial site of arbitration for nearly every political issue. Therefore, for those interested in women's, minority, and LGBT political power, whether on the grounds of fairness, enhancing the legitimacy of state institutions, or improving representation, their presence on the bench matters.

In order to understand this serious shortcoming in our understanding of America's courts, we have constructed an unprecedented collection of judicial scholarship from top researchers across the country. In this edited collection, we examine the intersectionality of race, ethnicity, gender, sexuality, and the composition of courts. It is our contention that the composition of courts, when compared to the composition of the general population across the country, is not representative of the people whom they serve.

If women and minorities are increasingly taking seats on the bench, under what conditions are they doing so? Why are they more successful in some places than others? Does the method of judicial selection influence their relative success (Alozie 1990; Glick and Emmert 1987)? These questions are of extreme importance given the institutional power of the courts and the status of justices as political elites. Or are the influences on political minorities' success in the judiciary related more to the cultural, political, and social characteristics of their constituencies? If so, we can better understand the representativeness of the bench and how those dynamics affect the courts' decision-making.

POLITICAL MINORITIES IN THE JUDICIARY

Diversity among the ranks of public officials serves a number of important purposes. The perceived legitimacy of government is enhanced when office-holders have similar characteristics to those they represent. A correspondence between political elites and their constituencies brings greater legitimacy and validity to the policy decisions of those representatives (Alozie 1988; Bratton and Spill 2002; Mansbridge 1999; Pitkin 1967; Rosenthal 1995; Uslaner and Weber 1983). While descriptive representation is important to all public institutions, it may be especially important for the judiciary, where normative yet ambiguous concepts such as "justice" and "rule of law" are most often associated with the work of the courts. The judiciary has the power to affect the daily lives of citizens, and it is one of the most direct and frequent points of contact between citizens and their government (Walker and Barrow 1985). Consequently, we need to understand which factors enhance and detract from diversity and descriptive representation on the bench.

Numerous factors have the potential to influence judicial diversity. First, there are structural influences, which arise from institutional variance across the courts. Justices in different states attain their position through varying selection methods, including partisan and nonpartisan election, executive nominations, legislative appointments, and merit selection. In contrast, all Article III judges in the federal court system are appointed by the president, with Senate confirmation.

While we are not the first to study judicial diversity and selection, we are the first to include LGBT justices in the analysis of judicial diversity. We are also the first to provide the most complete analysis of judicial diversity across various levels of the bench. Some authors contend that merit systems, external political interests, and executive appointments influence political minorities' representation (in one direction or another) on the bench (Alozie 1990;

Graham 1990; Henry et al. 1985), and others have found that electoral systems lead to lower minority representation there (Lyon 1981; Warden, Schlesinger, and Kearney 1979). Still others have found that selection methods have no discernible effect on diversity (Alozie 1996; Dubois 1983; Flango and Ducat 1979; Glick and Emmert 1987; Hurwitz and Lanier 2001). The studies in this volume incorporate multimethod analyses to address this issue.

Since justices "can be viewed largely as a product of the political environment in which they are selected" (Brace, Langer, and Hall 2001, 395), we must also consider the political factors that may influence judicial diversity. For example, ideology could affect diversity similarly to merit system (Graham 1990; Hall 2001). Furthermore, political minorities are more likely to win elections in districts where their constituents are more liberal in their policy views, whether because political minorities tend to be more liberal than other candidates (Sigelman and Welch 1984) or because some voters may seek to promote fellow women and minority candidates who bring a unique set of policy views to the bench (McDermott 1997).

Finally, demographic variations among states citizens may affect judicial diversity. In particular, scholars have advanced an eligibility pool theory to explain the ascent of women and minorities to the judiciary (Alozie 1990, 1996; Martin 1987). Since earning a law degree is a necessary condition for becoming a judge, a positive relationship is expected between the number of political minorities earning law degrees and practicing law in a state and the number of political minorities on the bench. The rise in the number of political minorities who are lawyers affords more available and qualified candidates to fill a vacancy on a bench. Yet, Bratton and Spill (2002) found that once a political minority has been selected for a particular bench, the likelihood that another political minority candidate will be chosen for that bench declines, due to the relative scarcity of judicial positions. Thus, the selection of one political minority might work to preclude others from obtaining a seat on that bench, since an acceptable level of diversity on the bench is akin to an unstipulated quota and no additional political capital for the selectors is gained from further diversification (Schroedel and Mazumdar 1998). We now turn to the chapters in this volume to provide a closer look at the intersectionality of gender, sexuality, race/ethnicity, and occupation.

OUTLINE OF THE BOOK

In Chapter 1, Nancy Bays Arrington uses data on the racial and gender identification of women, minority, and minority-women state supreme court judges to uncover potential ways in which women, minority, and especially minority-women state supreme court judges are similar to and different from white and male state supreme court judges. Arrington finds that minority women are more likely to have attended Ivy League law schools than white women but are no more or less likely to have prior judicial experience than white women or minority men. Minority women are not discernibly older or younger than white women or minority men at selection, while white men are, on average, the oldest at time of selection. Minority women are less likely to be elected than white women, but there are no differences in selection method between minority men and minority women. Minority men and women are more likely to be liberal or Democratic than white men or white women, and minority women have shorter average lengths of tenure than white women. Minority women have the highest rate of interim appointment, and they also have the highest rate of nominations to the federal judiciary. Although there have only been fifteen minority women who have left the bench, their vacancies are rarely filled by white men. Instead, vacancies by minority women are most often filled by white women and other minority women.

In Chapter 2, Sharon A. Navarro proposes that with the changing demographics in Texas and the increasing population of Latinos, Texas should experience more Latinos in elected office such as the judiciary. She argues that the intersection of race/ethnicity and gender created avenues of opportunity for Latino men and women to climb to state-level judicial offices in Texas, one of the most conservative states in the country. Utilizing standpoint theory, Navarro contends that political and institutional pressures converge with race and gender to enable diversification of Texas' state level courts. This study is important for understanding how a historically underrepresented group can become politically incorporated into a state's judiciary. The findings suggest that Latino/a judges recognize and use their race/ethnic and gender identities to their advantage in political judicial appointments.

Barbara L. Graham and Adriano Udani's Chapter 3 suggests that for women of color, entry into the state judicial hierarchy is not nearly as open as entry into the legislative hierarchy. Women of color, defined by constitutive features of "otherness," have experienced a long history of discrimination and exclusion from law schools and the legal profession. Unfortunately, this exclusion extends to representation in the state judicial system. To date, only token levels of representation among women of color exist in state appellate courts. These courts are frequently the subject of scholarly attention because state appellate judges have the greatest opportunities to shape state legal policy. In the United States, the process of judicial selection is especially contentious at the state level. Judicial elections, whether partisan, nonpartisan, or retention, exemplify the highly charged political and partisan atmosphere over who will occupy seats on the state bench. Politicians, political parties, and interest groups battle over judicial selection to influence legal policy outcomes most favorable to their interests.

The concept of descriptive representation as applied to state courts views courts as institutions of government where their decision-makers – judges – should mirror the diversity of its citizenry. Scholarly inquiry is warranted in the area of race, gender, and representation in the judiciary because courts, like other institutions, are often evaluated by the presence of women of color in key decision-making positions such as judgeships. Judicial diversity is linked to legitimacy and trust in legal institutions in the eyes of underrepresented groups. Calls for greater representation of women of color in state courts is not incompatible with democratic principles of presentation, participation, and equality.

Women of color make up approximately 6 percent of state appellate courts (intermediate appellate courts and state supreme courts). What accounts for token levels of representation among women of color on state appellate courts? Early studies point to the eligible pool theory, which posits that the lack of race and gender diversity on state courts is directly linked to the underrepresentation of women and minorities in the legal profession. The competing hypothesis, which examines the effects of institutional arrangements such as judicial selection methods, has produced mixed results. The debate centers around whether judicial elections or judicial appointment methods account for gender and racial diversity on the bench.

The objective of this research is to investigate whether judicial selection methods and political party effects present barriers to women of color's ascension to state appellate courts. This data is based on a cross-sectional analysis of all intermediate and state supreme court judges on the bench as of January 2017 (approximately 1,280). These models predict the likelihood that the observed judge is a woman of color for intermediate appellate courts and state supreme courts. Because we are interested in the conditional effects of judicial selection system characteristics, including partisan effects, we will present predicted probabilities that will conceptualize and communicate the nature of the relationships uncovered in this research.

In Chapter 4, Donald Haider-Markel and Patrick Gauding provide a seminal piece on LGBT justices. They explore LGBT representation in the United States through the lens of appointed and elected judges. Their historical analysis and case studies examine where and when LGBT justices have served, their pathways to the bench, and the implications of openly LGBT judges for the LGBT community and LGBT equality. Haider-Markel and

Gauding include data on local, state, and federal judges, showing patterns at each level. Their discussion concludes with speculation about future LGBT representation in the courts.

Taneisha Nicole Means's Chapter 5 provides a front row seat to the challenges intersectionality and occupation bring. At the urging and encouragement of Senators Robert F. Kennedy (D-NY) and Jacob K. Javits (R-NY), Lyndon B. Johnson nominated Constance Baker Motley to the Southern District of New York's court bench on January 26, 1966. While seen as remarkably qualified by many and a watershed moment in federal judicial selection, some wondered whether she would actually be confirmed because President Johnson had already been forced to withdraw his previous nomination of Motley to the Court of Appeals for the Second Circuit due to racial and gender politics.

As anticipated, a number of private groups, conservative federal judges, and southern senators fiercely opposed Motley's nomination to the district court bench. For instance, Senator James O. Eastland (D-MS), chairman of the Senate Committee on the Judiciary during the 1960s, held up her confirmation for months arguing that Motley's past required close scrutiny, and alleging that Motley had been active in a communist organization in the 1940s. To force senatorial action on Motley's nomination, President Johnson refused to nominate any other judges to the federal bench. This strategy worked, because on August 30, 1966, Constance Baker Motley became the first black woman appointed to the federal judiciary.

Motley's nomination and confirmation undoubtedly helped pave the road for other women of color appointed to the federal judiciary between 1966 and 2017. Scholars, however, have largely overlooked the nomination of Motley as a potential starting point to explore and better understand how race and gender fundamentally influence the federal judicial selection process, and therefore, judicial diversity. Here, Means addresses the following questions: How did the politics of race and gender influence the appointment of the first black woman federal judge? What lessons can we learn from the nomination and confirmation of Motley, and how can we apply these lessons to twenty-first century federal judicial selection politics and processes? Using interviews and the growing scholarship on Motley, in addition to the Senate Judiciary Committee's historical documents, Means reveals the politics involved in placing Motley on the federal bench. Her historical and qualitative analysis demonstrates that Motley's appointment is the beginning of a long legacy of racial-minority women being appointed to the federal judiciary, and that her treatment by the Senate, and perception of her by elites, as a (potential) judicial nominee, was deeply influenced by her race and gender.

In Chapter 6, Shenita Brazelton and LaTasha Chaffin examine whether diversity at the federal level mirrors changes in the citizenry. As the U.S. population diversifies, will the federal courts be representative? What determinants lead African-American and Latina women to be nominated and confirmed to the federal judiciary? Using the Federal Judicial Center database, this study qualitatively examines the demographic, political, and economic determinants that influence the appointments of African-American and Latina women to the district and circuit courts since the Carter administration. They additionally interview African-American and Latina women judges who have earned senior status, to assess their perceptions of the changing diversity of federal judgeships. Brazelton and Chaffin anticipate that changing demographics and socioeconomic status will impact the ascent of Latina women to the federal bench, political mobilization will impact the ascent of African-American women to the federal bench, and interest group pressure will influence both.

In Chapter 7, Lisa M. Holmes takes a close look at Supreme Court–worthy nominees. In April of 2013, *The New Yorker* published a short article by Jeffrey Toobin on Sri Srinivasan days before Srinivasan's hearing with the Senate Judiciary Committee (Toobin 2013). The focus of Toobin's article was that Srinivasan's nomination to a seat on the U.S. Court of Appeals for the District of Columbia Circuit was a trial run for his future nomination to the U.S. Supreme Court. Put succinctly and starkly in the article, Toobin predicted that "if Srinivasan passes this test and wins confirmation [to the DC Circuit], he'll be on the Supreme Court before President Obama's term ends."

Toobin's assessment of Srinivasan's nomination to the federal circuit court highlights a largely unexamined problem for women and people of color who seek appointment to U.S. district and circuit courts. Namely, their placement on these lower levels of the judiciary puts them as directly as possible in the pipeline for future appointment to the U.S. Supreme Court. While a seat on the lower federal judiciary is a favored stepping stone for any viable future Supreme Court nominee, for women and people of color, the pedigree that identifies a lawyer as being "Supreme Court–worthy" may be *more* of an impediment to the initial appointment than is the case for highly credentialed white men. Opposing senators may fight harder to keep the most highly qualified women and people of color off the lower courts out of concern that a future position on the Supreme Court may be difficult, if not impossible, to deny someone who has already been confirmed to a federal judgeship. Holmes's chapter examines the treatment of court of appeals nominees who are not white men. Specifically, Holmes examines if "non-traditional" nominees (those who are not white men) are treated less favorably in the confirmation process, especially when they have the kind of education and professional backgrounds that mark a court of appeals nominee as a potential future Supreme Court pick.

This is an important question to consider, especially in the wake of Clarence Thomas's contentious appointment to the Supreme Court in 1991 a mere sixteen months after his relatively easy confirmation to the U.S. Court of Appeals for the District of Columbia Circuit. A preliminary analysis based on limited data found some evidence that minority nominees with the most prestigious educational pedigrees are treated less favorably than non-minority, high-pedigreed nominees in the confirmation process. A fuller assessment is required to determine whether women and people of color with the most impressive educational and professional backgrounds are the targets of more opposition out of concern that their exemplary pedigrees mark them as particularly viable future nominees to the Supreme Court.

And finally, Samantha L. Hernandez discusses Supreme Court Justice Sonia Sotomayor's rise to the highest court in the country in Chapter 8. In a 2017 lecture held at Arizona State University, Justice Sotomayor was asked to reflect on how she made it all the way to the Supreme Court. Her candid discussion highlighted parallels found in women and politics literature focusing on ambition and opportunity. Sotomayor hints towards important changes that can happen when a minority or woman are sitting on the bench. Hernandez delves into potential changes in the judiciary by examining the number of women and minorities in the legal and judicial pipeline. In order to examine the effect of having a Latina on the Supreme Court, Hernandez uses Sotomayor's dissent in *Schuette v. Coalition to Defend Affirmative Action* to highlight differences in case positions.

Our courts must be representative in order to fulfill their purposes. Our laws are premised in part on the idea that our courts will be staffed by judges who can understand the circumstances of the communities which they serve. Our judicial system depends on the general public's faith in its legitimacy. Both of these foundational principles require a bench that is representative of the people the courts serve. A truly representative judiciary would have the same ratio of women and minorities on the bench as it does in the general population. Having justices mirror constituencies would go immeasurably far in chipping away at the stereotype that a minority may possess as a "perpetual foreigner" – that minorities are something other than simply American or heterosexual. As judges break barriers throughout the country, they serve as role models for generations to come.

REFERENCES

Alozie, Nicholas O. 1988. "Black Representation on State Judiciaries." *Social Science Quarterly* 69: 979–86.

1990. "Distribution of Women and Minority Judges: The Effects of Judicial Selection Methods." *Social Science Quarterly* 71: 315–25.

1996. "Selection Methods and the Recruitment of Women to State Courts of Last Resort." *Social Science Quarterly* 77: 110–26.

Brace, Paul, Melinda Gann Hall, and Laura Langer. 2001. "Placing Courts in State Politics." *State Politics and Policy Quarterly* 1: 81–108.

Bratton, Kathleen A., and Rorie L. Spill. 2002. "Existing Diversity and Judicial Selection: The Role of the Appointment Method in Establishing Gender Diversity in State Supreme Courts." *Social Science Quarterly* 83: 504–18.

Dubois, Philip. 1983. "The Influence of Selection System on the Characteristics of a Trial Court Bench." *Justice System Journal* 8: 59–87.

Flango, Victor Eugene, and Craig R. Ducat. 1979. "What Difference Does Method of Judicial Selection Make? Selection Procedures in State Courts of Last Resort." *Justice System Journal* 5: 25–44.

Glick, Henry R., and Craig F. Emmert. 1987. "Selection Systems and Judicial Characteristics: The Recruitment of State Supreme Court Judges." *Judicature* 70: 228–35.

Graham, Barbara Luck. 1990. "Do Judicial Selection Systems Matter? A Study of Black Representation on State Courts." *American Politics Quarterly* 18: 316–36.

Hall, Melinda Gann. 2001. "State Supreme Courts in American Democracy: Probing the Mythos of Judicial Reform." *American Politics Science Review* 95: 315–30.

Henry, M. L., Estajo Koslow, Joseph Soffer, and John Furey. 1985. *The Success of Women and Minorities in Achieving Judicial Office: The Selection Process*. New York: The Fund for Modern Courts.

Hurwitz, Mark S., and Drew Noble Lanier. 2001. "Women and Minorities on State and Federal Appellate Benches, 1985 and 1999." *Judicature* 85: 84–92.

Lyon, Mark A. 1981. *The Proportions of Black Judges to Black Population in Supreme and Appellate Jurisdictions: Elective vs. Appointive Systems of Judicial Selection*. Chicago: Committee on Courts and Justice.

Mansbridge, Jane. 1999. "Should Blacks Represent Blacks and Women Represent Blacks and Women Represent Women? A Contingent 'Yes'." *Journal of Politics* 61: 628–57.

Martin, Elaine. 1987. "Gender and Judicial Selection: A Comparison of the Reagan Carter Administrations." *Judicature* 71: 136–42.

McDermott, Monika L. 1997. "Voting Cues in Low-Information Elections: Candidate Gender as a Social Information Variable in Contemporary United States Elections." *American Journal of Political Science* 41: 270–83.

Pitkin, Hanna. 1967. *The Concept of Representation*. Berkeley: University of California Press.

Rosenthal, Cindy Simon. 1995. "The Role of Gender in Descriptive Representation." *Political Research Quarterly* 48: 559–611.

Schroedel, Jean Reith, and Nicola Mazumdar. 1998. "Into the Twenty-First Century: Will Women Break the Political Glass Ceiling?" In *Women and*

Elective Office, eds. Sue Thomas and Clyde Wilcox. New York: Oxford University Press.

Sigelman, Lee, and Susan Welch. 1984. "Race, Gender, and Opinion toward Black and Female Presidential Candidates." *Public Opinion Quarterly* 48: 467–75.

Toobin Jeffrey. 2013. "The Supreme Court Nominee-in-Waiting."*The New Yorker*. April 8. www.newyorker.com/news/daily-comment/the-supreme-court-nominee-in-waiting.

Uslaner, Eric M., and Robert E. Weber. 1983. "Policy Congruence and American State Elites: Descriptive Representation versus Electoral Accountability." *Journal of Politics* 45: 183–96.

Walker, Thomas G., and Deborah J. Barrow. 1985. "The Diversification of the Federal Bench: Policy and Process Ramifications." *Journal of Politics* 47: 596–617.

Warden, R. T., Schlesinger, and J. Kearney. 1979. *Women, Blacks and Merit Selection of Judges*. Chicago: Committee on Courts and Justice.

1

Qualification, Selection, and Retirement Characteristics of Women, Minorities, and Minority-Women State Supreme Court Judges

NANCY BAYS ARRINGTON

INTRODUCTION

The judiciary – and in particular supreme courts tasked with interpreting law – shapes public policy and stands as a symbol of the state's power. Understanding diversity in the judiciary is therefore important for understanding the diversification of state power. Researchers have long addressed the relationships between descriptive, substantive, and symbolic representation of women and minority elected officials (Pitkin 1967).[1] Increasingly, researchers are also studying the representation of and by women of color under the expectation that gender and race may intersect (e.g., Bejarano 2013; Brown 2014). But while there is an emerging literature on women of color in the legislative context, little is known about women of color in the judiciary.

Until very recently, any assessment of minority women on the bench was constrained by the marked absence of female judges of color.[2] At the state supreme court level, the first minority woman justice was a Latina judge named Dorothy Comstock Riley selected to the Michigan supreme court in 1982.[3] Juanita Kidd Stout was selected to the Pennsylvania supreme court in 1988, becoming the first black female state supreme court justice.[4] A year later, Joyce Luther Kennard became the first Asian-American/Pacific Islander

[1] See, for example, Preuhs (2006); Reingold (2008); Schwindt-Bayer and Mishler (2005).

[2] I identify the minority judges who describe themselves as members of minority racial/ethnic groups or judges who have been identified as members of minority groups by other scholars or news media. When I refer to the "first" members of a racial/ethnic group on the bench, I mean the first member of that racial or ethnic group that I was able to identify.

[3] The Michigan Supreme Court Historical Society identifies Judge Riley as Hispanic, although Martin and Pyle (1999) describe her as "a white Republican" (p. 1207).

[4] Julia Cooper Mack, a black woman judge, was appointed to the DC Court of Appeals – the DC equivalent of a state supreme court – by President Ford in 1975 (Blackburne-Rigsby 2009).

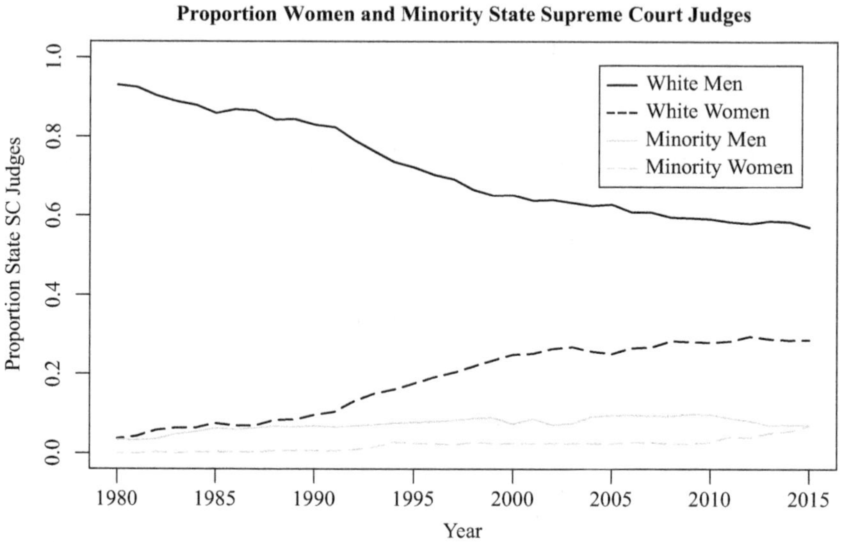

FIGURE 1.1 Proportion of judges selected to state supreme courts over time who are minority women, minority men, white women, and white men. Most judges are white men, and much of the diversity on the bench gained in recent decades is due to the increased presence of white women.

(AAPI) state supreme court judge when she was selected to the California Supreme Court.

Since the early 1980s, thirty-six women of color have been selected to state supreme court benches. The inclusion of women of color on the highest state courts coincided with increases in the presence of white women and men of color as well. Figure 1.1 shows the proportion of state supreme court judges who are white men, white women, minority men, and minority women over time.[5]

Given the newness and relative rarity of minority-women to state supreme court benches, little is known about the characteristics of minority-women judges and the circumstances under which they are selected to states' highest

[5] Data on the gender of judges and whether judges are black/African-American from 1960 to 2010 are from the State High Court and Justice Database (Bratton 2017). Data on the gender of judges selected since 2010 were collected by the author from Ballotopedia and internet searches. Indicator variables for Latinx and AAPI judges were generated through searches of National Association of Latino Elected and Appointed Officials (NALEO) directories and the Asian-American and Pacific Islander Almanacs. In addition, keyword searches of Asian-American, Pacific Islander, and Latino/a judges were used to augment missing directory and almanac years. Finally, when photographs of judges suggested a racial or ethnic identification, electronic newspaper searches or biographies were used to confirm race or ethnicity.

courts. It may be that minority women judicial candidates or nominees are held to a particularly high standard and have to overcome additional hurdles.[6] For example, Goldman et al. (2000) find that among President Clinton's district court judicial appointments, the time between nomination and a Judiciary Committee hearing for women and minority judicial nominees took, on average, forty-three days longer than the time for white male judges (120 days versus 77, respectively). Insights from the intersectionality paradigm (Crenshaw 1989; Hancock 2007; Hawkesworth 2003) suggest that minority women may have experiences that are distinct from both white women and minority men. If minority-women judges face hurdles related to both gender and race, they may be held to a particularly high standard for selection.

This chapter uses a new data set on the racial/ethnic identification of state supreme court judges to describe ways in which characteristics of minority-women state supreme justices are similar to or different from characteristics of women justices and minority men justices. There are myriad ways in which minority women may have different experiences in the accumulation of qualifications, in selection, and in retirement compared to white women or minority men. The characteristics addressed here are by no means exhaustive. This analysis provides a preliminary look at the ways in which minority women are like and distinct from their white and male counterparts on state supreme court benches.

The next sections outline arguments for why the inclusion of women, minority, and minority-women judges is important and compare several characteristics of state supreme court judges across race and gender. These characteristics are organized into sections on qualifications, selection, and retirement. Because multiple comparisons with one limited sample increases the probability of finding a relationship where one does not exist (type I errors), findings should be considered preliminary. That said, I find that for the characteristics assessed here, minority-women state supreme court justices are more similar to minority men than to white women. Across all comparisons, minority-women judges are more similar to their white and male counterparts than they are distinct.

THE IMPORTANCE OF DIVERSITY ON THE BENCH

Although political representation is often addressed in the legislative context, the implications of descriptive, symbolic, and substantive representation are

6 In the legislative context, see Anzia and Berry (2011); Lawless and Fox (2005); Milyo and Schosberg (2000).

particularly important in the context of courts because "judges have a more direct and irrevocable impact in the lives of many Americans than local or even national legislators" (Ifill 2000, pp. 407–08). Indeed, existing research suggests that a diverse judiciary can have important consequences on judicial behavior and outcomes, judicial legitimacy, and judicial discourse.

Latina Justice Sonia Sotomayor, prior to her appointment to the U.S. Supreme Court, said, "Whether born from experience of inherent physiological or cultural differences . . . our gender and national origins may and will make a difference in our judging" (Sotomayor 2002, p. 92). Similarly, Judge Anna Blackburne-Rigsby, a black woman currently serving as Chief Judge of the District of Columbia Court of Appeals, wrote, "I have seen that being both black and female brings an important additional voice to the deliberative process, but that voice is varied because there is no singular 'black woman' perspective" (Blackburne-Rigsby 2009, p. 689).

Although empirical evidence of race and gender differences in judging is mixed, there is some evidence that race and gender identity and experiences may affect judging. For example, Welch, Combs, and Gruhl (1988) find racial differences in decisions to incarcerate and in sentencing decisions at the trial court level. Collins, Manning, and Carp (2010) find that at the district court level, women judges make different decisions than their male counterparts on civil rights and liberties cases and criminal justice cases. Similarly, they find that minority judges decide more liberally than white judges across all issue areas except labor and economics. Gruhl, Spohn, and Welch (1981) find that women judges are more likely to sentence women defendants to prison than male judges, although on other measures men and women judges convict and sentence similarly. Allen and Wall (1993) find that women justices on state supreme courts are more likely to decide pro-woman on women's issues; Songer and Crews-Meyer (2000) find that women state supreme court judges vote more liberally than male judges in death penalty and obscenity cases; and McCall and McCall (2007) find that women state supreme court justices decided more liberally than male judges on search and seizure cases after 1991. Others, however, find no race or gender differences in judging, or find that differences have been overstated (Dixon 2009; Kenney 2008; Segal 2000; Walker and Barrow 1985; Westergren 2003).

Evidence suggests that diversity on the bench can affect the behavior of male judges as well. For example, the presence of women judges on a three-judge U.S. appellate panel affects the behavior of male judges: Farhang and Wawro (2004) find that male judges voted more liberally in anti-discrimination cases when there was a woman serving on the panel. Similarly, Boyd, Epstein, and Martin (2010) find that male appellate judges are more likely to decide in favor of plaintiffs in sex discrimination cases when a woman is serving on a panel alongside them.

Finally, diversity in the life experiences of those on the bench can alter the judicial discourse and the deliberative process (Ifill 2000) and lead to "structural impartiality" (Ifill 1998, p. 99). Ifill (2000) writes, "we should value racial diversity if it brings alternative perspectives and analysis to the process and enriches the legal decision-making" (p. 455). Regardless of the extent to which women or minority judges make different decisions than their white male counterparts, add new perspectives to the deliberative process, or alter the trajectory of judicial decision-making, the presence of diverse judges has important symbolic consequences (Scherer and Curry 2010) and signals that powerful state institutions are open to women, minority, and minority-women individuals. Even in the absence of racial or gender differences in behavior, Kenney (2013) argues that the presence of women on judicial benches is important because the presence of women in the judiciary "normalizes women's authority and power" (p. 175). Understanding characteristics of minority-women judges and the conditions under which they are selected to state supreme courts is an important next step in understanding the role of diversity in the judiciary, but the study of minority-women judges has been minimal.

CHARACTERISTICS OF MINORITY, WOMEN, AND MINORITY-WOMEN JUDGES

Using new data on the race and gender of state supreme court judges, I identified ninety-eight minority-men and thirty-six minority-women state supreme court justices selected between 1970 and 2016. Table 1.1 lists the number of men and women who are black/African-American, AAPI, Latinx, Native American, or white.[7] Of black judges, 25 percent are female. Of Asian judges, 37.5 percent are female. The only Native American judge is female, and 18.4 percent of white judges are female. Of all male judges, just over 9 percent are men of color. Among women judges, almost 15 percent are women of color. Table 1.2 lists the thirty-six identified minority-women state supreme court justices.

In the following sections, I compare characteristics of minority women, minority men, white women, and white men justices on state supreme courts.

7 The "white" category includes all judges not identified as either black/African-American, Latino, AAPI, or Native American. Judges described as Irish-American or Greek-American, for example, were classified as "white."

TABLE 1.1 *Gender and racial/ethnic summary of judges selected between 1970 and 2016*

	Male	Female	(%Female)
Black/African-American	63	21	(25.0)
AAPI	10	6	(37.5)
Latinx	20	9	(31.0)
Native American		1	(100)
White/Not Identified	935	211	(18.4)
(% Minority)	(9.1)	(14.9)	

Gender and racial/ethnic summary of judges selected between 1970 and 2016, with the exception of Lorna Lockwood, a white, female Justice of the Arizona Supreme Court selected in 1961 and the first woman selected to a state supreme court. She is included here for an exhaustive count of women judges selected through 2016.

Reported p-values should be interpreted with caution: because several comparisons are made from one sample, the probability of committing a type I error – inferring a pattern where none exists – increases. The comparisons are of characteristics associated with qualification, selection, and retirement.

QUALIFICATION CHARACTERISTICS

If women, minority, or minority women are held to a higher standard for qualification, then we may see discrepancies in qualification characteristics across race and gender. To test whether minority women are held to a higher standard of qualification, I compare the rates of Ivy League law school attendance, prior judicial experience, and age at selection. If white women, minority men, or minority women are held to a higher standard of qualification, more women and minority judges may have attended Ivy League law schools; more women and minority judges may have had prior judicial experience; and minority and women judges may have been older at the time of selection to allow for the accumulation of qualifications.

Ivy League Law School Attendance Figure 1.2 shows that there are no significant gender differences in Ivy League law school attendance among co-ethnics, although a greater proportion of minority women attended Ivy League law schools than white women ($p = 0.09$). There are no clear differences across race and gender for Ivy League law school attendance.

TABLE 1.2 *Minority-women state supreme court judges that have been identified as female and minority*

Name	State	Year Joined	Race/Ethnicity
Riley, Dorothy Comstock	MI	1982	Latina
Stout, Juanita Kidd	PA	1988	Black/African-Am.
Kennard, Joyce Luther	CA	1989	AAPI
Sears, Leah Ward	GA	1992	Black/African-Am.
Ciparick, Carmen Beauchamp	NY	1993	Latina
Nakayama, Paula Aikko	HI	1993	AAPI
Johnson, Bernette Joshua	LA	1994	Black/African-Am.
Roaf, Andree Layton	AR	1994	Black/African-Am.
Selby, Myra Consetta	IN	1994	Black/African-Am.
Toney-Williams, Felicia	LA	1994	Black/African-Am.
Brown, Janice Rogers	CA	1996	Black/African-Am.
Maes, Petra Jimenez	NM	1998	Latina
Quince, Peggy A.	FL	1998	Black/African-Am.
Baldwin, Cynthia Ackron	PA	2005	Black/African-Am.
Timmons-Goodson, Patricia	NC	2006	Black/African-Am.
Guzman, Eva	TX	2009	Latina
Marquez, Monica M.	CO	2010	Latina
Brown, Yvette McGee	OH	2011	Black/African-Am.
Cantil-Sakauye, Tani Gorre	CA	2011	AAPI
Duffly, Fernande R. V.	MA	2011	AAPI
McKenna, Sabrina S.	HI	2011	AAPI
Powell, Cleo E.	VA	2011	Black/African-Am.
Beasley, Cheri	NC	2012	Black/African-Am.
Wright, Wilhelmina	MN	2012	Black/African-Am.
Abdus-Salaam, Sheila	NY	2013	Black/African-Am.
Espinosa, Carmen	CT	2013	Latina
Rivera, Jenny	NY	2013	Latina
Watts, Shirley Marie	MD	2013	Black/African-Am.
Hines, Geraldine	MA	2014	Black/African-Am.
Yu, Mary	WA	2014	Latina & AAPI
Hotten, Michele	MD	2015	Black/African-Am.
Hudson, Natalie	MN	2015	Black/African-Am.
Kruger, Leondra	CA	2015	Black/African-Am.
Budd, Kimberly	MA	2016	Black/African-Am.
Makamoto, Lynn	OR	2016	AAPI
McKeig, Anne	MN	2016	Native Am.

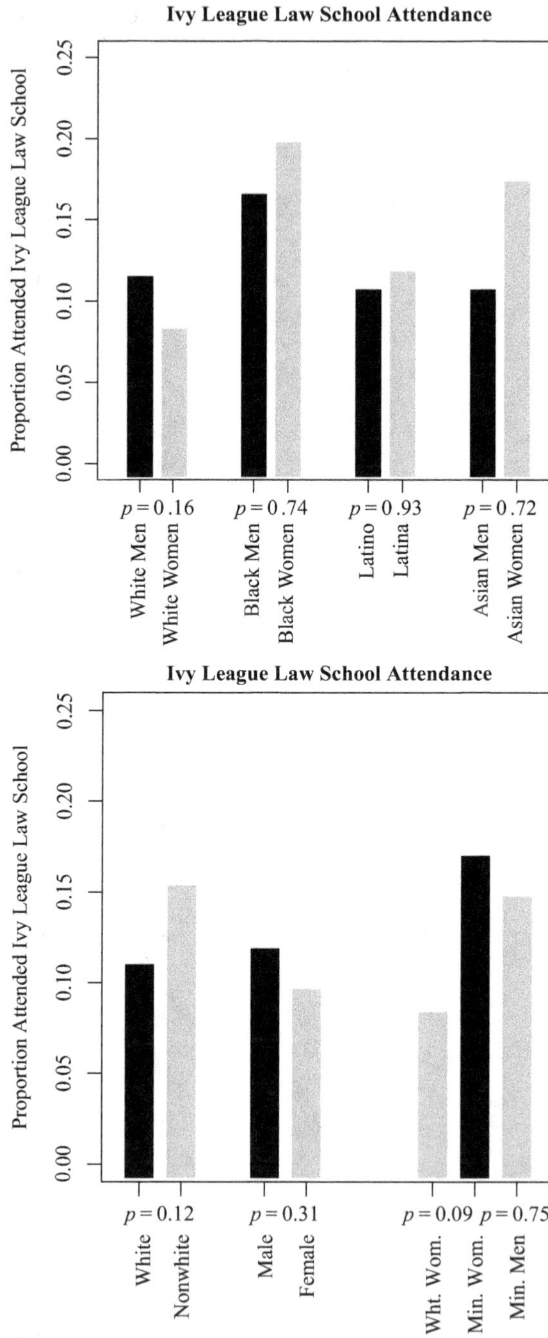

FIGURE 1.2 Proportion of judges who attended Ivy League law schools by identity groups. Small numbers of Latino, black, and Asian/Pacific Islander judges limits statistical significance.

When we measure elite education as Ivy League law school attendance, minority women are not held to a higher standard of education.

Prior Judicial Experience Epstein, Knight, and Martin (2003) argue that the norm of prior judicial experience for U.S. Supreme Court justices may serve to restrict professional, gender, and racial diversity on the Supreme Court. They argue that the disparity of women and minority judges on federal benches restricts prospects for diversity on the Supreme Court. Martin (1987) acknowledges that in the selection of federal judges, both Presidents Reagan and Carter may "have applied a double standard in demanding more judicial experience from women" (p. 141). If women, minority, and minority women are held to a higher standard for qualification, we may observe a greater proportion of nonwhite and non-male judges with prior judicial experience.

Figure 1.3 shows that across all race/ethnic groups, a greater proportion of women had prior judicial experience than men; however, the gender difference among co-ethnics is only statistically significant among white judges ($p = 0.01$). Aggregating to compare white and minority judges, a greater proportion of minority judges had prior judicial experience than white judges ($p = 0.04$) and a greater proportion of women than men had prior judicial experience ($p = 0.003$). However, there are no differences between minority women and white women or minority men.

Age at Selection In the legislative context, female candidates (Burrell 1992) and representatives tend to be older than their male counterparts (Carroll 1983; Dubeck 1976; Moncrief and Thompson 1992). Traditional explanations for this discrepancy suggested that women delayed running for office until after their children were born or were older. Carroll (1983) found, however, that among state legislators, patterns of delaying office due to the number and age of children were consistent between men and women, suggesting that childbirth and rearing was not the explanation for the age difference between men and women legislators. An alternative explanation focuses on gender differences in political ambition among younger potential candidates. In surveys of potential legislative candidates, there was a substantial gender gap among men and women younger than forty in responses to questions about whether they had considered running for office, had seriously thought about a political career, or had discussed the prospect of running for office with party leaders (Lawless and Fox 2005). Delaying candidacy also allows for more time to accumulate qualifications.

In the context of the judiciary, the appointment of (some) judges rather than election may diminish the effect of disparate political ambition among men and women because appointed judges do not need to organize and

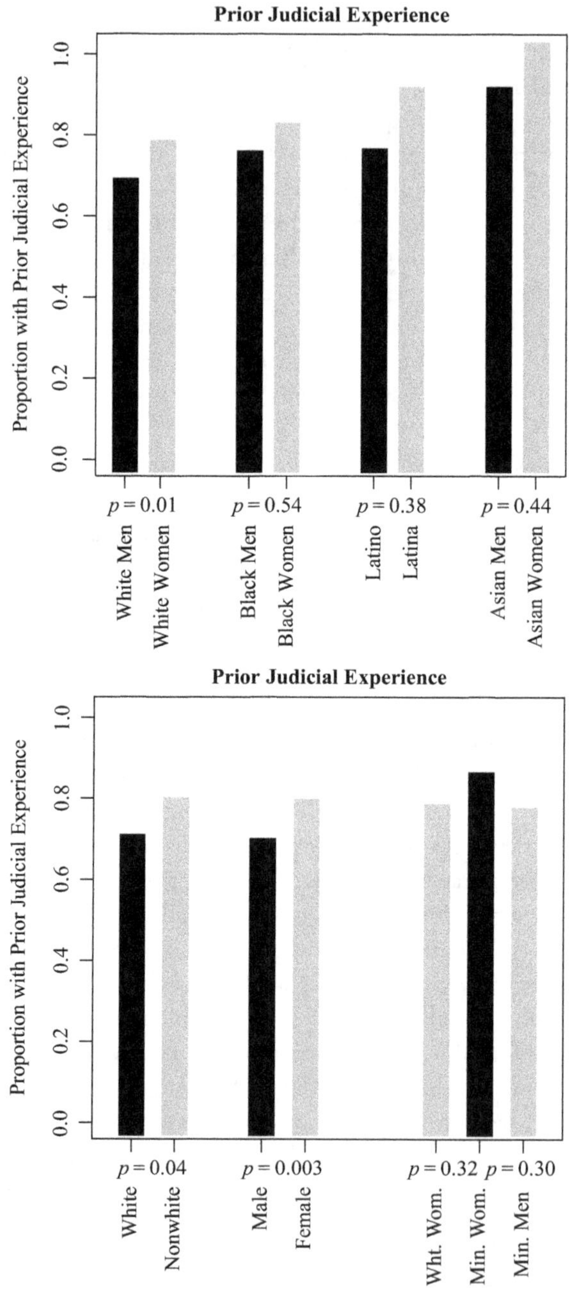

FIGURE 1.3 Proportion of judges with prior judicial experience. The only within ethnicity gender difference is among white judges ($p = 0.01$). Aggregating to all white versus all nonwhite judges, the p-value for the difference in proportions is $p = 0.04$, and the p-value for the difference in proportion between all men and all women is $p = 0.003$. These comparisons indicate that a greater proportion of women state supreme court judges have prior judicial experience relative to men.

undertake a campaign.[8] In addition, differences in the pool of judicial versus legislative candidates may also affect gender differences in aging across context: most states have a formal or informal requirement that judges hold a law degree or are members of the bar. Since graduation rates of women from law schools have increased substantially in the last several years, the candidate pool for female state supreme court judges may be younger than the candidate pool for male supreme court justices, which could serve to cancel out differences in political ambition or time to accumulate qualifications between male, female, white, and minority judicial candidates. Indeed Yoon (2003) finds that women and minority judges on the federal bench between 1945 and 2000 began their judgeships at a younger age than their white male peers. Black judges were, on average, 49.2 years old when then joined the bench. Women were 47.2 years old, while white and male judges averaged 51.3 years.

Figure 1.4 shows the average age of judges at the time of selection. White men are, on average, the oldest at selection (54.1) and white women are the youngest (50.6). On average, white judges are older at selection than nonwhite judges ($p = 0.01$) and men are older than women ($p < 0.001$). The gender difference among all judges is due to the gender difference between white men and white women ($p < 0.001$), as there are no gender differences in age at selection among minority women and men.

If the age difference between men and women stems from an age difference in the candidate pool because women have only relatively recently been graduating from law school at rates commensurate with men, then the age difference ought to decrease over time as the candidate pool of women lawyers for judgeships has gotten larger and has been able to age. Figure 1.5 shows a scatter plot of the ages of women judges selected over time. The black line is the regression of age by year. The grey shaded region is the 95 percent confidence interval. Women have been getting older at selection over time, but the change is slight, suggesting that it may not just be differences in the maturity of the candidate pool that accounts for the age difference between men and women judges.

SUMMARY: SIMILARITIES AND DIFFERENCES IN QUALIFICATIONS

The qualification characteristics of white men, white women, minority men, and minority women are similar in some ways and distinct in others. There are no differences across gender or race/ethnicity in Ivy League law school

[8] This is not to say that appointed judges are not or have not been involved in politics.

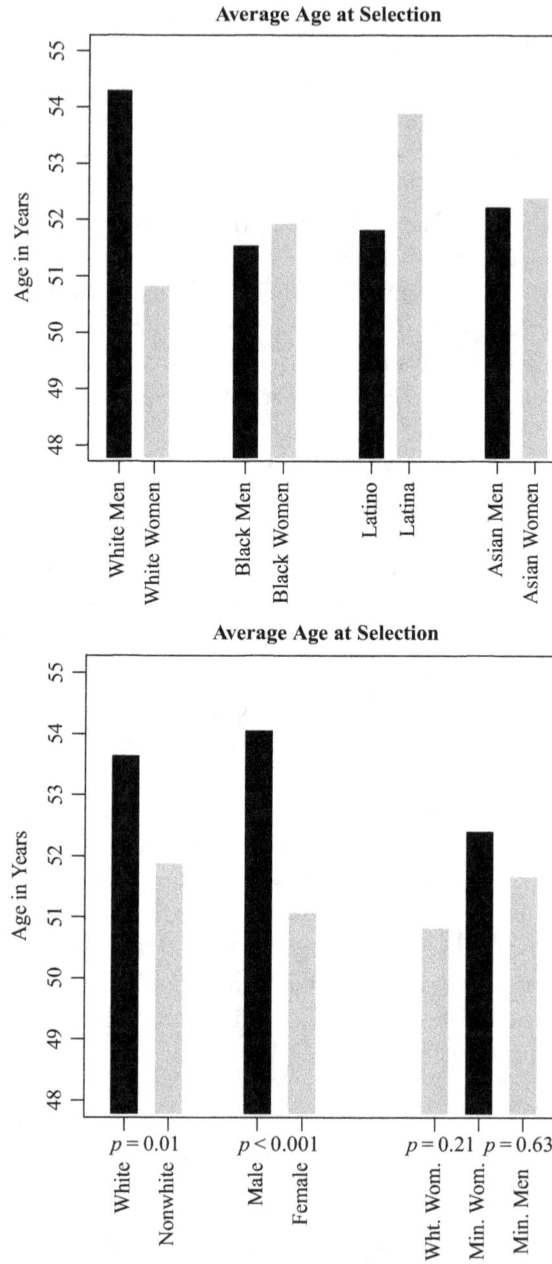

FIGURE 1.4 Average age at time of selection. White judges are older at the time of selection than nonwhite judges ($p = 0.01$) and men are older than women ($p < 0.001$). The gender difference in age is driven by the gender difference among white judges ($p < 0.001$), as there are no gender differences among black, Latina, or Asian-American judges.

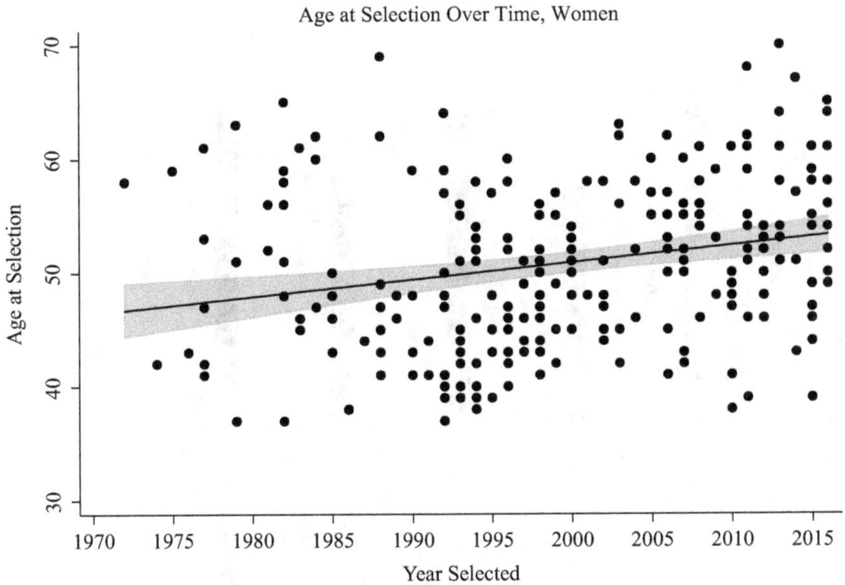

FIGURE 1.5 The average age at selection for women over time. The average age has increased slightly over time. A one-year increase in the appointment year is associated with a .015 increase in average age at selection ($p < 0.001$).

attendance. When it comes to prior judicial experience, across all ethnic categories, a greater proportion of women had prior judicial experience, but the only gender difference among co-ethnics is among white judges. For age at time of selection, white judges and male judges are older – on average – than women and minority judges. The gender discrepancy in age at selection between men and women judges is driven by the age difference among white men and women judges ($p < 0.00$). Among racial minority judges, there are no statistically significant differences in age.

SELECTION CHARACTERISTICS

Moving from qualification characteristics to characteristics of judicial selection, in this section I compare party identification and the method of selection across race and gender.

Appointment versus Election Given the importance of minority and women judges on the bench, scholars have studied the conditions under which minority and women judges are selected to courts. Many explanations focus on differences in selection institutions. Findings on the effect of different selection methods – executive appointment, elections, or merit selection – on

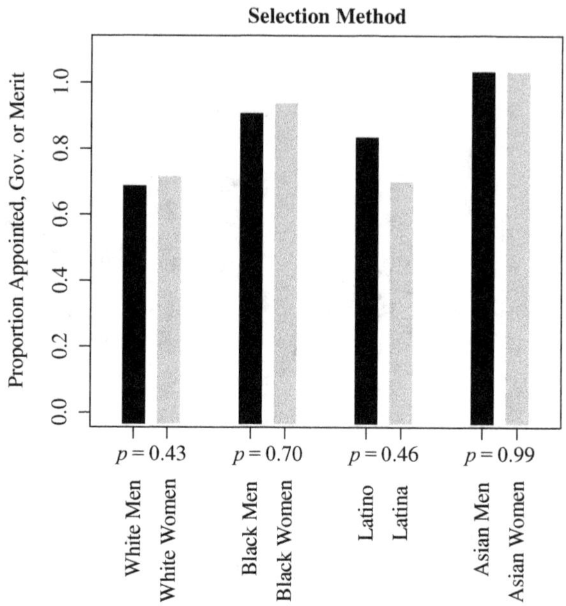

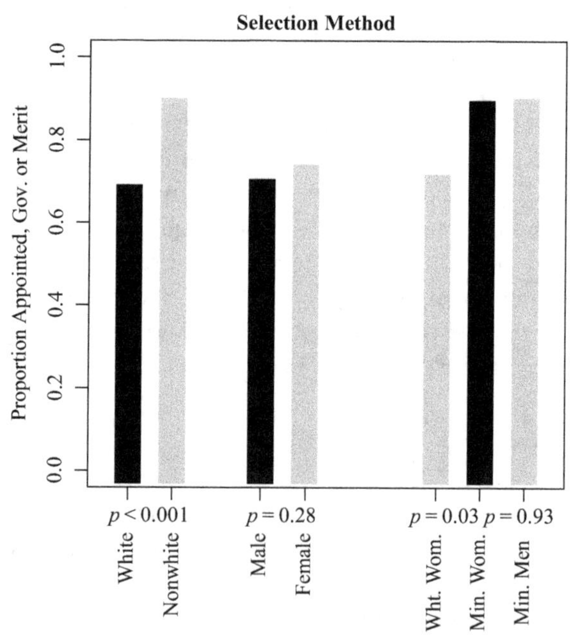

FIGURE 1.6 The proportion of judges selected through gubernatorial or merit selection procedures (including judges selected by the governor to fill a vacancy between elections) by race and gender.

the appointment of women and minority judges are mixed. Some find that the concentration of accountability on elite selectors such as a governor (Bratton and Spill 2002; Carbon, Houlden, and Berkson 1982) or merit commission (Esterling and Andersen 1999; Goelzhauser 2011) leads to greater diversification.[9] However, many scholars find no relationship between selection method and diversity on the bench (Alozie 1988; 1990; 1996; Hurwitz and Lanier 2001; 2003).

Figure 1.6 shows the proportion of judges appointed by elites, either through gubernatorial selection or merit selection. There are no gender differences among co-ethnics or in the aggregate, but there does appear to be a difference between white judges and minority judges; a greater proportion of minority judges were appointed relative to white judges ($p < 0.001$). Among women, a greater proportion of minority women were appointed than white women.

Party In addition to selection institutions, the partisanship of those tasked with selecting judges may shape judicial diversity: liberal selectors are expected to select more women and minority judges (Bratton and Spill 2002), and liberal constituencies may be more likely to elect women and minority candidates, both because diversity has become an issue associated with the Democratic party[10] and because women and minority judges may be more likely to run as Democrats in partisan elections due to gender and racial partisan gaps (e.g., Gay and Tate 1998; Kaufmann 2002). Figure 1.7 shows that there are no gender differences among co-ethnics in party identification, but there is a difference ($p < 0.00$) between white and minority judges.

SUMMARY: SELECTION CHARACTERISTICS

Among selection characteristics, two patterns emerge. First, a greater proportion of minority judges than white judges are appointed by elites. Second, a greater proportion of minority judges are identified as liberal or Democratic than white judges.

9 Likewise, Hall (2001) finds some – albeit weak ($p = 0.06$) – evidence that minority judges fare worse in non-partisan elections than their peers. Goelzhauser (2011) finds that when citizen liberalism is relatively high, partisan election is associated with state supreme courts having their first black justice selected sooner. Glick and Emmert (1986) find that merit selection systems are the least likely to select religious minorities to state supreme court benches.

10 For example, *The 2016 Democratic Platform* states, "Above all, Democrats are the party of inclusion. We know that diversity is not our problem – it is our promise" (DNC 2016).

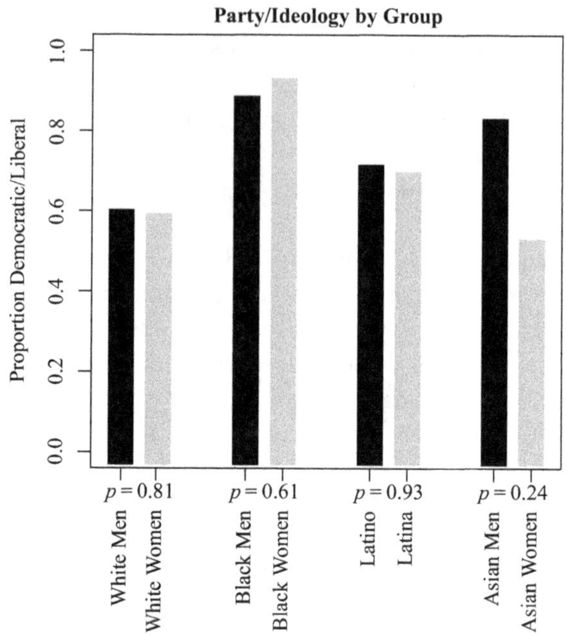

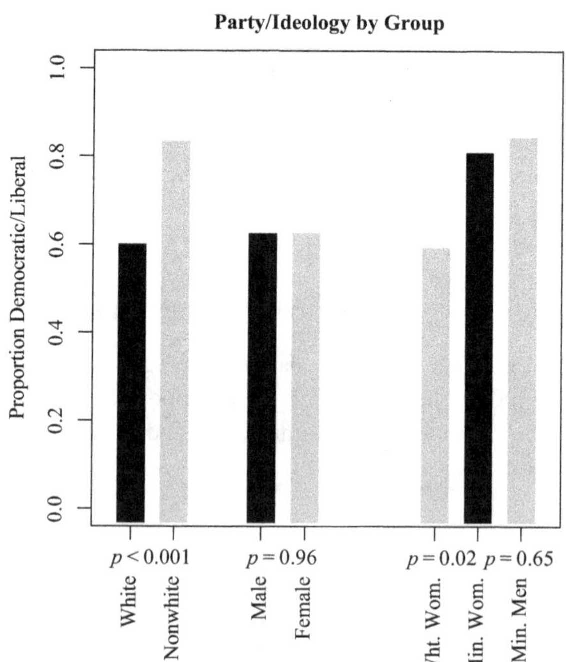

FIGURE 1.7 Proportion of judges who have been identified as liberal or Democratic.

RETIREMENT CHARACTERISTICS

In this final section, I compare characteristics of retirement across race and gender. Specifically, I compare length of tenure and reasons for vacating the bench, and then I describe patterns of replacement for minority-women judges.

Length of Tenure There are a few reasons why we might expect women, minority, or minority women to serve on the bench for a different length of time than white or male judges. Women, minorities, and minority women may be appealing candidates for the federal bench, particularly for presidents who aim to diversify the federal judiciary. If women and minority judges are often nominated to the federal judiciary, their tenures on state supreme court benches may be brief. In addition, experiences of sexism or racism while serving on the bench may lead female and minority judges to retire earlier than their white male colleagues. Finally, differences in the likelihood of winning retention elections or facing electoral opposition may cause discrepancies in tenure length (although Luskin et al. 1993 find no racial differences in retention election vote share). In contrast, limitations in moving up the career ladder outside of the judiciary – that is, less opportunity in the private or academic sectors – may leave women, minority, and minority women delaying retirement and maintaining their seats longer. Yoon (2003) finds that for judges on federal courts between 1945 and 2000, on average, women served 8.5 years less than their male counterparts, while black judges served 3.9 years less than white judges.

Figure 1.8 shows racial and gender differences in length of tenure on state supreme court benches. White women have served longer than white men ($p = 0.09$); black men have served longer than black women ($p = 0.07$), white judges have served slightly longer than nonwhite judges ($p = 0.06$), and minority women serve for a shorter length of time than white women due to short average length of tenure among black women ($p = 0.03$). However, because the multiple comparisons are made from on sample, the probability of committing a type-I error is greater than the reported p-values.

Reasons for Leaving the Bench While length of tenure does not show clear discrepancies across race or gender, there may be patterns across race and gender for the reasons judges leave the bench. Table 1.3 shows the number and percentage of judges who vacated the bench for different reasons. A greater percentage of minority women are selected to temporary, interim appointments than white and male judges, and a greater percentage of

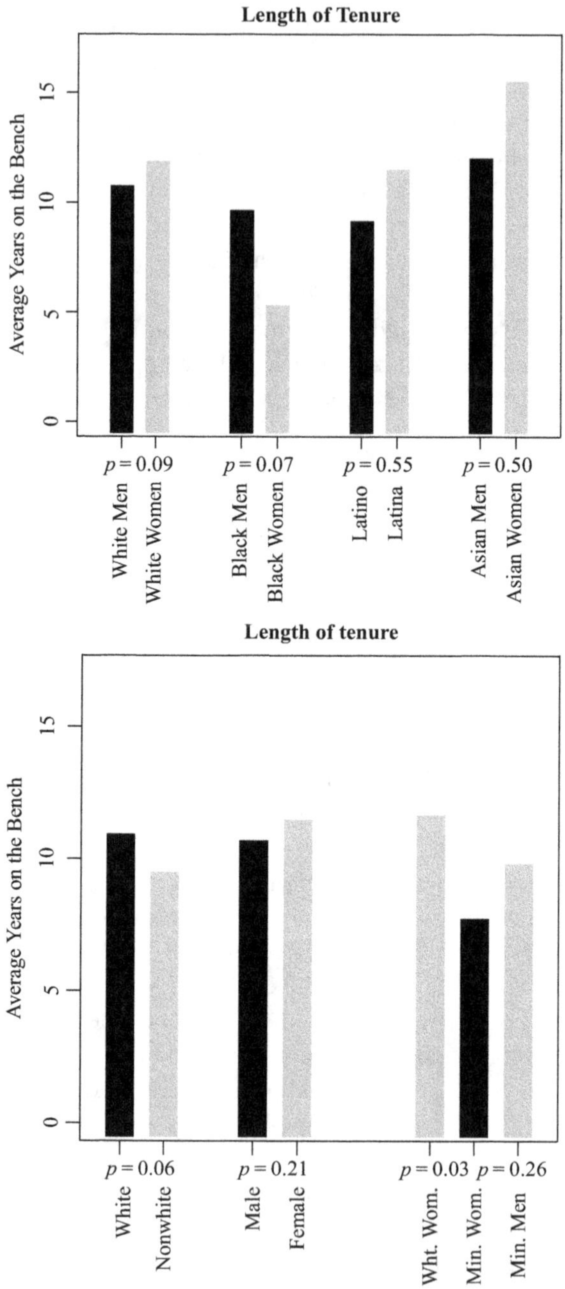

FIGURE 1.8 Average number of years served on the state supreme court by race and gender.

TABLE 1.3 *Reasons for vacating the bench by race and gender*

Reason for Leaving the Bench	White Men	White Women	Minority Men	Minority Women
Mandatory	147	17	15	3
Retirement (%)	22.7	13.8	20.5	18.6
Defeated, Removed	66	18	13	2
Not Re-Nominated (%)	10.2	14.6	17.8	12.5
Retired or	341	68	33	5
Resigned (%)	52.7	55.3	45.2	31.3
Nominated to	35	9	2	2
Federal Judiciary (%)	5.4	7.3	2.3	12.5
Interim	9	6	5	3
Appointment (%)	1.4	4.9	6.8	18.8
Died in	35	5	4	1
Office (%)	5.4	4.1	5.5	6.3
Appointed/Elected	14		1	
to National Office (%)	2.2		1.4	
Total, non-missing	647	123	73	16

Reasons for vacating the bench by race and gender. There have only been 15 judges identified as minority women to serve and leave the bench. Dorothy Comstock Riley of Michigan is counted twice in this table: in 1983 she was removed from office after she was appointed to fill a vacancy by Governor Milliken right before his term ended. In 1984 she was elected to the Supreme Court and served until she retired in 1997. There is substantial missing data for white men ($n = 111$).

minority women are nominated to the federal judiciary than white and male judges.[11]

Replacement Patterns A final analysis addresses the predecessors and successors of minority-women state supreme court judges. Arrington (2018) shows that the gender of vacating judges and replacement judges are interdependent: when a woman judge vacates the bench, she is more often replaced by another woman relative to when a man vacates the bench. Replacing a

[11] See table 1.5 in the Appendix for linear probability regression results that estimate race and gender based on reasons for vacating the bench. Again, because multiple comparisons are made from the same sample, the probability of committing a type-I error is greater than the reported p-values. The only p-values that survive the Bonferroni correction are for interim appointments: both women and minority judges are more likely to be appointed on an interim basis than white and male judges.

TABLE 1.4 *Race and gender characteristics of those who preceded and succeeded minority-women state supreme court justices*

	Predecessors of Minority Women	Successors of Minority Women	All Judges Selected, 1970–2016	All Judges Selected, 2000–2016
White (%)	51.4	15.4	73.3	61
Men	(18)	(2)	(934)	(239)
Minority (%)	22.9	7.7	7.3	8.2
Men	(8)	(1)	(93)	(32)
White (%)	11.3	46.2	16.5	25
Women	(5)	(6)	(201)	(98)
Minority (%)	11.4	30.8	2.9	5.9
Women	(4)	(4)	(35)	(23)

Race and gender characteristics of those who preceded and succeeded minority-women state supreme court justices. Due to the vast number of white judges, I do not have specific information on who succeeded and replaced each white judge.

minority woman justice with a white man justice will decrease both the gender and racial diversity on the bench. Therefore, judicial selectors may face additional pressure to replace a vacating female judge of color with a woman, minority, or minority woman in order to maintain some diversity. Of the fifteen minority women who have left the bench, thirteen have clear successors.[12] Of those thirteen minority-women judges, six were replaced by white women, four were replaced by minority women, one was replaced by a minority man, and two were replaced by white men.

Of the thirty-six identified minority women selected to a state supreme court, thirty-five have clear predecessors.[13] Of the thirty-five minority-women justices selected to the bench, eighteen replaced white men, eight replaced minority men, five replaced white women, and four replaced minority women. In other words, 48.6 percent of minority women were selected to fill seats vacated by nonwhite men. Table 1.4 reports the number and percentage of white men, minority men, white women, and minority women who were the predecessors and successors of minority women alongside the percentage of judges selected in total between 1970–2016 and 2000–2016 as a comparison. Given the high overall

[12] I have not confirmed the successors of Cynthia Baldwin and Felicia Toney-Williams. Both justices were selected on an interim basis.

[13] Bernette Joshua Johnson of Louisiana was selected to fill a new seat on the bench.

proportion of judges who are white men, minority women have low rates of being replaced by white men. Although there are very few minority women who have vacated the bench, only 15 percent of their successors were white men. In contrast, between 2000 and 2016, 61 percent of judges selected to the bench were white men. The pattern of vacancies made by minority women being predominately filled by other women and minorities suggests that selectors face strong incentives to maintain diversity on the bench when women of color vacate.

CONCLUSION: ARE MINORITY-WOMEN JUDGES DISTINCT?

Using data on the racial and gender identification of women, minority, and minority-women state supreme court judges, the goal of this project was to uncover potential ways in which women, minority, and especially minority women are similar to and different from white and male judges. Although statistical significance should be interpreted with caution due to the increased probability of committing type I errors with multiple comparisons, the evidence presented here indicates that there may be a few race and gender differences in characteristics of state supreme court justices.

Minority women are more likely to have attended Ivy League law school than white women but are no more or less likely to have prior judicial experience than white women or minority men. Minority women are not discernibly older or younger than white women or minority men at selection, while white men are, on average, the oldest at time of selection. Minority women are less likely to be elected than white women, but there are no differences in selection method between minority men and minority women. Minority men and women are more likely to be liberal or Democratic than white men or white women, and minority women have shorter average length of tenure than white women. Minority women have the highest rate of interim appointment, and they also have the highest rate of nominations to the federal judiciary. Although there have only been fifteen minority women who have left the bench, their vacancies are rarely filled by white men. Instead, vacancies by minority women are most often filled by white women and other minority women.

Across the six categories where minority women can be directly compared to minority men and white women (Ivy League education, prior judicial experience, age, selection method, party, and length of tenure), minority women are indistinguishable from minority men in all six categories. In contrast, minority women differ from white women across four categories (Ivy League education, selection method, ideology, and tenure). The comparisons presented here suggest that minority-women state supreme court justices may be more similar to minority men than white women.

REFERENCES

Allen, David W. and Diane E. Wall. 1993. "Role Orientations and Women State Supreme Court Justices." *Judicature* 77(3): 156–65.

Alozie, Nicholas O. 1988. "Black Representation on State Judiciaries." *Social Science Quarterly* 69:979–86.

1990. "Distribution of Women and Minority Judges: The Effects of Judicial Selection Methods." *Social Science Quarterly* 71(2):315–25.

1996. "Selection Methods and the Recruitment of Women to State Courts of Last Resort." *Social Science Quarterly* 77(1):110–26.

Anzia, Sarah F. and Christopher R. Berry. 2011. "The Jackie (and Jill) Robinson Effect: Why Do Congresswomen Outperform Congressmen?" *American Journal of Political Science* 55(3):478–93.

Arrington, Nancy. 2018. "Gender and Judicial Replacement: The Case of US State Supreme Courts." Forthcoming: *The Journal of Law and Courts* 1:127–54.

Bejarano, Christina E. 2013. *The Latina Advantage: Gender, Race, and Political Success*. Austin: University of Texas Press.

Blackburne-Rigsby, Anna. 2009. "Black Women Judges: The Historical Journey of Black Women to the Nation's Highest Courts." *Howard LJ* 53:645.

Boyd, Christina L., Lee Epstein, and Andrew D. Martin. 2010. "Untangling the Causal Effects of Sex on Judging." *American Journal of Political Science* 54(2):389–411.

Bratton, K. A. and Rorie L. Spill. 2002. "Existing Diversity and Judicial Selection: The Role of the Appointment Method in Establishing Gender Diversity in State Supreme Courts." *Social Science Quarterly* 83(2):504–18.

Bratton, K. A. 2017. "State High Court Justice Database." www.lsu.edu/faculty/bratton/research.htm.

Brown, Nadia E. 2014. *Sisters in the Statehouse: Black Women and Legislative Decision Making*. New York: Oxford University Press.

Burrell, Barbara. 1992. "Women Candidates in Open-Seat Primaries for the U. S. House: 1968–1990." *Legislative Studies Quarterly* 17(4):493–508.

Carbon, Susan, Pauline Houlden, and Larry Berkson. 1982. "Women on the State Bench: Their Characteristics and Attitudes about Judicial Selection." *Judicature* 65(6):294–305.

Carroll, Kathleen M. 1983. "The Age Difference between Men and Women Politicians." *Social Science Quarterly* 64(2):332–39.

Collins, Paul M., Jr., Kenneth L. Manning, and Roberta A. Carp. 2010. "Gender, Critical Mass, and Judicial Decision Making." *Law and Policy* 32(2):260–81.

Crenshaw, Kimberle. 1989. "Demarginalizing the Intersection of Race and Sex: A Black Feminist Critique of Antidiscrimination Doctrine, Feminist Theory and Antiracist Politics." University of Chicago Legal Forum, p. 139.

Dixon, Rosalind. 2009. "Female Justices, Feminism and the Politics of Judicial Appointment: A Re-Examination." University of Chicago, Public Law and Legal Theory Working Papers.

DNC. 2016. "The 2016 Democratic Platform." www.democrats.org/party-platform.

Dubeck, Paula J. 1976. "Women and Access to Political Office: A Comparison of Female and Male State Legislators." *The Sociological Quarterly* 17(1):42–52.

Epstein, Lee, Jack Knight, and Andrew D. Martin. 2003. "The Norm of Prior Judicial Experience and Its Consequences for Career Diversity on the U.S. Supreme Court." *California Law Review* 91:903–65.

Esterling, Kevin M. and Seth S. Andersen. 1999. "Diversity and the Judicial Merit Selection Process: A Statistical Report." *Research on Judicial Selection, The American Judicature Society*, www.judicialselection.us/uploads/documents/Diversity_and_the_Judicial_Merit_Se_9C4863118945B.pdf.

Farhang, Sean and Gregory Wawro. 2004. "Institutional Dynamics on the U.S. Court of Appeals: Minority Representation under Panel Decision Making." *The Journal of Law, Economics, and Organization* 20(2):299–330.

Gay, Claudine and Katherine Tate. 1998. "Doubly bound: The Impact of Gender and Race on the Politics of Black Women." *Political Psychology* 19(1):169–84.

Glick, Henry R. and Craig F. Emmert. 1986. "Selection Systems and Judicial Characteristics: The Recruitment State Supreme Court Judges." *Judicature* 70:228.

Goelzhauser, Greg. 2011. "Diversifying State Supreme Courts." *Law and Society Review* 45(3):761–81.

Goldman, Sheldon, Elliot Slotnick, Gerard Gryski, and Gary Zuk. 2000. "Clinton's Judges: Summing Up the Legacy." *Judicature* 84:228.

Gruhl, John, Cassia Spohn, and Susan Welch. 1981. "Women as Policymakers: The Case of Trial Judges." *American Journal of Political Science* 25 (2):308–22.

Hall, Melinda Gann. 2001. "State Supreme Courts in American Democracy: Probing the Myths of Judicial Reform." *American Political Science Review* 95(2):315–30.

Hancock, Ange-Marie. 2007. "When Multiplication Doesn't Equal Quick Addition: Examining Intersectionality as a Research Paradigm." *Perspectives on Politics* 5(1):63–79.

Hawkesworth, Mary. 2003. "Congressional Enactments of Race–Gender: Toward a Theory of Raced–Gendered Institutions." *American Political Science Review* 97(4):529–50.

Hurwitz, Mark S. and Drew Noble Lanier. 2001. "Women and Minorities on State and Federal Appellate Benches, 1985 and 1999." *Judicature* 85:84.

2003. "Explaining Judicial Diversity: The Differential Ability of Women and Minorities to Attain Seats on State Supreme and Appellate Courts." *State Politics & Policy Quarterly* 3(4):329–52.

Ifill, Sherrilyn. 1998. "Judging the Judges: Racial Diversity, Impartiality, and Representation on State Trial Courts." *Boston College Law Review* 39(1): 95–149.

Ifill, Sherrilyn A. 2000. "Racial Diversity on the Bench: Beyond Role Models and Public Confidence." *Washington and Lee Law Review* 57:405.

Kaufmann, Karen M. 2002. "Culture Wars, Secular Realignment, and the Gender Gap in Party Identification." *Political Behavior* 24(3):283–307.

Kenney, Sally J. 2008. "Thinking about Gender and Judging." *International Journal of the Legal Profession* 15(1–2):87–110.

Kenney, Sally Jane. 2013. *Gender and Justice: Why Women in the Judiciary Really Matter*. New York: Routledge.

Lawless, Jennifer L. and Richard L. Fox. 2005. *It Takes a Candidate: Why Women Don't Run for Office*. New York: Cambridge University Press.

Luskin, Robert C., Christopher N. Bratcher, Christopher G. Jordan, and Tracy K. Renner. 1993. "How Minority Judges Fare in Retention Elections." *Judicature* 77:316.

Martin, Elaine. 1987. "Gender and Judicial Selection: A Comparison of the Reagan and Carter Administration." *Judicature* 71:136.

Martin, Elaine and Barry Pyle. 1999. "Gender, Race, and Partisanship on the Michigan Supreme Court." *Albany Law Review* 63:1205.

McCall, Madhavi and Michael A. McCall. 2007. "How Far Does the Gender Gap Extend?: Decision Making on State Supreme Courts in Fourth Amendment Cases, 1980–2000." *The Social Science Journal* 44(1):67–82.

Milyo, Jeffrey and Samantha Schosberg. 2000. "Gender Bias and Selection Bias in House Elections." *Public Choice* 105(1–2):41–59.

Moncrief, Gary F. and Joel A. Thompson. 1992. *Changing Patterns in State Legislative Careers*. Ann Arbor: University of Michigan Press.

Pitkin, Hanna Fenichel. 1967. *The Concept of Representation*. New York: Atherton Press, Inc.

Preuhs, Robert R. 2006. "The Conditional Effects of Minority Descriptive Representation: Black Legislators and Policy Influence in the American States." *Journal of Politics* 68(3):585–99.

Reingold, Beth. 2008. *Women as Office Holders: Linking Descriptive and Substantive Representation*. New York: Cambridge University Press, book section 9.

Scherer, Nancy and Brett Curry. 2010. "Does Descriptive Race Representation Enhance Institutional Legitimacy? The Case of the U.S. Courts." *The Journal of Politics* 72(1):90–104.

Schwindt-Bayer, Leslie A. and William Mishler. 2005. "An Integrated Model of Women's Representation." *Journal of Politics* 67(2):407–28.

Segal, Jennifer A. 2000. "Representative Decision Making on the Federal Bench: Clinton's District Court Appointees." *Political Research Quarterly* 53(1):137–50.

Songer, Donald R. and Kelley A. Crews-Meyer. 2000. "Does Judge Gender Matter? Decision Making in State Supreme Courts." *Social Science Quarterly* 81(3):750–62.

Sotomayor, Sonia. 2002. "A Latina Judge's Voice." *Berkeley La Raza LJ* 13(1):87.

Walker, Thomas G. and Deborah J. Barrow. 1985. "The Diversification of the Federal Bench: Policy and Process Ramifications." *The Journal of Politics* 47(2):596–617.

Welch, Susan, Michael Combs, and John Gruhl. 1988. "Do Black Judges Make a Difference?" *American Journal of Political Science* 32(1):126–36.

Westergren, Sarah. 2003. "Gender Effects in the Courts of Appeals Revisited: The Data since 1994." *Geo. LJ* 92:689.

Yoon, Albert. 2003. "Love's Labor's Lost – Judicial Tenure among Federal Court Judges: 1945–2000." *California Law Review*. 91:1029.

Appendix

TABLE 1.5 *Linear probability regression results for comparing men and women judges*

	Dependent Variable			
	(1) Men vs. Women	(2) White vs. Nonwhite	(3) Wht Wom. vs. Min. Wom.	(4) Min. Men vs. Min. Wom.
Mandatory Retirement	Reference Category			
Defeated, Removed, Not re-nominated	0.09 $p = 0.04$	0.05 $p = 0.16$	−0.05 $p = 0.62$	−0.03 $p = 0.81$
Retired or Resigned	0.05 $p = 0.10$	−0.01 $p = 0.6$	−0.08 $p = 0.31$	−0.04 $p = 0.75$
Nominated to Federal Judiciary	0.12 $p = 0.05$	−0.02 $p = 0.75$	0.03 $p = 0.79$	0.33 $p = 0.12$
Interim Appointment	0.28 $p < 0.01$	0.25 $p < 0.01$	0.18 $p = 0.15$	0.21 $p = 0.21$
Died in Office	0.02 $p = 0.7$	0.01 $p = 0.81$	0.02 $p = 0.91$	0.03 $p = 0.87$
Appointed/Elected to National Office	−0.11 $p = 0.26$	−0.03 $p = 0.69$		−0.17 $p = 0.68$
Intercept	0.11 $p < 0.01$	0.1 $p < 0.01$	0.15 $p = 0.04$	0.17 $p = 0.07$
n	859	859	139	89
r^2	0.02	0.02	0.05	0.07

Linear probability regression results for comparing men and women judges; white and nonwhite judges; white women and minority-women judges; and minority-men and minority-women judges, where n = sample size and r^2 = amount of variation in the dependent variable that can be attributed to the variation in the independent variable. For all models, the reference (excluded) category is Mandatory Retirement. Positive coefficients indicate an increased probability that the judge is female in model 1, nonwhite in model 2, minority and female in model 3, and minority and female in model 4.

2

Latinas and the Texas Judiciary

The Intersection of Race, Gender, and Judiciary

SHARON A. NAVARRO

To date, very little has been written on Hispanic[1] women as judges or candidates for judicial office, and the literature that exists is found mainly in law journals.[2] Margaret Williams, in her study of women's representation on trial courts, contends that, "to understand [women's] representation more completely political science needs to examine representation further by exploring individual explanations for it."[3] This same study suggests that appeals courts are important to consider because these "are typically the seats first attained in the judiciary system from trial courts"[4] before women seek higher judicial office. In other words, appeals courts essentially serve as the training ground, and more important, a stepping stone for women's political incorporation into the judiciary at higher levels. This study examines intersections among dimensions of gender and race in the judiciary.

Over the last two decades, Hispanic women have increasingly run for judicial seats, particularly at the appeals court level. In this chapter, I ask under what conditions are they doing so? Specifically, what role does the intersectionality of race, gender, and occupation play in a Hispanic woman's candidacy for the judiciary? I examine the political experience of five Hispanic women who ran for and won positions on the Texas appeals court. A closer look at their personal and political experiences contributes to our understanding of political incorporation of Hispanic women into the judiciary in Texas and nationwide. A feminist

1 Recognizing that the use of a particular label varies with region, politics, and historical context, the term "Hispanic woman" is used interchangeably with "Mexican-American woman," "Latina/Latino," and "Chicana/Chicano." I follow the tradition established by such as Hardy-Fanta 1993; Garcia et al. 2008; and Navarro 2008. These authors use the label interchangeably.

2 Echaveste 2002, pp. 39–42; Johnson 2002, pp. 1–14; Munoz 2002, pp. 29–31; Navarro 2013, pp. 4–20; Sotomayor 2002, pp. 87–93.

3 Williams (2007), 1202.

4 Ibid., 1201–02.

standpoint methodology facilitated the collection of perceptions about gender and race among Latinas who serve as justices.

THE TEXAS COURTS OF APPEALS

The appellate courts in Texas are centralized at the state level. More than one judge presides, citizen participation is virtually absent, and, most important, such courts decide points of law, not points of fact. An appeal of a murder conviction from a trial court to a higher court is not based on points of fact (Is the person guilty?) but on points of law (Were legal procedures followed?). Appellate courts decide whether proper procedures have been followed. For example, in Texas, all death penalty cases are appealed to the Texas Court of Criminal Appeals. The issue is not the person's guilt or innocence, but whether all procedures were properly followed in the trial court and whether the defense presented an adequate defense.

The Texas legislature has divided the state into fourteen courts of appeals districts with a court of appeals in each one. Each court of appeals serves a 17–20 county constituency and judges serve a six-year term with a salary of about $163,000.[5] Each court of appeals has at least three justices (to a maximum of nine) – a chief justice and associate justices. There are currently eighty justices and of those, eleven are of Mexican-American ancestry. Of these eleven, only one is male, a chief justice, who will be retiring at the end of his term on December 31, 2018. Three of the fourteen courts of appeals have sitting Latino/Hispanic justices (the 4th Court of Appeals has four sitting Latina justices, the 8th Court of Appeals has three sitting Latina justices, and the 13th Court of Appeals has six sitting justices). All of the justices of Mexican-American ancestry were solicited for an interview; only five participated. These five women have been given pseudonyms to protect their identity. Their political experience as women and as minorities within the judiciary will be examined. I argue that the intersection of race and gender serve as obstacles that challenge Latino justices' ascension to the intermediate judiciary. This study is important for understanding how a historically underrepresented group has become politically incorporated into one of the most conservative institutions in Texas – the judiciary.

RESEARCH DESIGN, INTERVIEWS, AND CODING CRITERIA

I included questions addressing specific research goals, and whenever possible, used comparable questions from the Latino National Survey and the

[5] Slayton 2016a.

interview instrument used by Garcia et al. (2008) for *Politicas*. (My full questionnaire can be found in Appendix.) Invitation letters were sent to all eleven Latino/a as known to currently serve in Texas's courts of appeals, and five subjects ultimately participated in the study. Some interviews were scheduled at a time and place of the interviewee's choosing, while others were conducted by telephone. The interviews were conducted in English and all were asked the same twenty-four questions in the same order. Each participant was allowed to speak as extensively, or briefly, as she desired, with only occasional interventions by the interviewer. Although minimal guidance was offered to ensure that each question was in fact answered, most of the interviews were subject-driven.

All subjects participated willingly and expressed interest in our research goals. The justices understood that their reflections and experiences would ultimately appear in a book chapter to be read by scholars and practitioners – including other Latina leaders like themselves – and that the ultimate purpose of the project was educational. They were informed that responses would be coded using a pseudonym and thus individual subjects would not be identified during the analysis or in publication. Subjects were also invited to demur on questionnaire items for which they perceived any personal or political risk. All interviews were recorded, with subjects' permission, to facilitate an accurate transcription of responses.

I divided the twenty-four questions into three thematic groups (see Appendix). Questions were posed to the subjects in order, beginning with personal backgrounds (*Personal Background, Identity, and Civic Engagement*), then current empowerment (*Current Position and Experiences*), followed by self-assessment (*Reflections on Leadership Roles in a Social and Political Context*).

For the post-interview analysis, I consolidated the twenty-four responses by combining related items into two distinct themes – gender and race. To better understand the ways in which race and gender intersect the position of the judiciary, we must contextualize these women's experiences through the lens of the standpoint theory.

THEORETICAL FRAMEWORK

Standpoint theory is an interpretative framework that explicates how knowledge remains central to maintaining and changing unjust systems of power.[6] Standpoint theory is premised on the position that any view on experience is

[6] Collins 1997, pp. 375–81.

constructed from a particular location.[7] Standpoint theory's most important concept is that an individual's own perspectives are shaped by his or her social and political experience. Feminist standpoint scholars oppose essentializing the category "woman" but suggest providing a basis for solidarity among women while still maintaining differences.[8] Hispanic women may generally share some perspectives, particularly with regard to race or sex, as they are defined solely by their participation in these categories. The amalgamation of a person's many experienced dimensions form a standpoint – that is, a point of view – through which that individual sees and understands the world. Patricia Hill Collins proposed a form of standpoint theory that emphasized the perspective of African-American women.[9] Collins argued that the matrix of oppression – an interlocking system of race, gender, and class oppression and privilege – has given African-American women a distinct point of view from which to understand their marginalized status. She showed how African-American women have been suppressed by the economic exploitation of their labor, the political denial of their rights, and the use of controlling images that create damaging stereotypes, and suggests that African-American women can contribute something singular to feminist scholarship.

> Each group speaks from its own standpoint and shares its own partial, situated knowledge. But because each group perceives its own truth as partial, its knowledge is unfinished. Each group becomes better able to consider other groups' standpoints without relinquishing the uniqueness of its own standpoint or suppressing other groups' partial perspectives.[10]

The unique perspectives that each of the Mexican-American female justices possess may give us some insight into the present-day challenges that remain in the judiciary.

Standpoint theory supports what theorist Sandra Harding calls strong objectivity,[11] or the notion that the perspectives of marginalized and/or oppressed individuals can help create more objective accounts of the world. Through the outsider-within phenomenon, these individuals are placed in a distinctive position to point to patterns of behavior that those immersed in the dominant group culture are unable to recognize.[12] Standpoint theory gives voice to marginalized groups by allowing them to challenge the status quo as

7 Collins 2000.
8 Allen 2000; Zinn and Dill 1996, pp. 321–31.
9 Collins 2000.
10 Ibid., 270.
11 Tickner 1997, pp. 611–32.
12 Allen 2009.

the outsider within. The status quo is here defined as representing the dominant White male position of privilege.[13] Marginalized groups are socially situated in ways that make it more possible for them to be present and ask questions than for the non-marginalized.

Not all persons or groups experience the predominant political culture in the same way. The views of those who belong to groups with higher social power are validated more than those in marginal groups. Those in marginalize groups must learn to be bicultural, or "pass" in the dominant culture to survive, even though that perspective is not their own.[14] This chapter seeks to reclaim the experience of Mexican-American justices. This reclamation involves discovering, interpreting, and analyzing the ideas and viewpoints of the subgroup justices, who have been overlooked and under-studied within the larger collectivity of Mexican-American women.

THE INTERSECTION OF GENDER AND RACE WITH OCCUPATION

Since 2004, Texas has been a "majority-minority" state, meaning that all racial and ethnic minority groups combined now form a majority of the population and outnumber the non-Hispanic White population.[15] The Hispanic population in Texas is the second largest in the nation. About 10.4 million Hispanics reside in Texas and comprise 18.8 percent of all Hispanics in the United States.[16] Texas's population is 39 percent Hispanic, the third-largest Hispanic statewide population nationally. There are 4.8 million eligible Hispanic voters in Texas – the second-largest Hispanic statewide voter population nationally.[17] California ranks first with 6.9 million. The growing Hispanic population has significant implications for state politics. With this growing population, it would seem logical to assume that Hispanics would have a representative judicial presence on the appellate court. The subjects in this study were asked whether they believe being a woman and/or Hispanic helped or hindered their chances of success in assuming judicial office. They were asked to share their points of view regarding their judicial experience to assist us in understanding why there are so few Hispanic women in the fourteen Texas courts of appeals. Factors that have historically obstructed Hispanic women's paths to public office, such as age, family size and obligations, cultural bias, and

[13] Ibid.
[14] DeFrancisco 2007.
[15] Combs 2008.
[16] Lopez and Stepler 2016.
[17] Ibid.

TABLE 2.1 *Women attorneys: attorney statistical profile (2016–2017)*

	2006–2007(%)	2016–2017(%)
Sex		
Male	69	65
Female	31	35
Race/Ethnicity		
White	73	73
Black/African-American	7	9
Hispanic/Latino	8	10
AAPI	3	5
American Indian/Alaska Native	<1	<1
Two or More Races	–	1
Other Races	1	1

Source: State Bar of Texas. Department of Research and Analysis (2016–2017) at www.texasbar.com/AM/Template.cfm?Section=Demographic_and_Economic_Trends&Template=/CM/ContentDisplay.cfm&ContentID=35996.

marital status, have also continued.[18] The Hispanic women solicited for this study serve on courts that are nestled in the majority-minority Hispanic region (southern part) of Texas.

Over the last forty years, although women have entered law schools and the legal profession in large numbers, they remain underrepresented on the appellate courts. Women comprise roughly 50.4 percent of the Texas population[19] and 47 percent of Texas law schools.[20] According to the Texas Bar Association, there has been a slight increase of female attorneys from ten years ago and a slight decrease of male representation (Table 2.1). Reviewing the composition of women in the Texas Bar Association, it has also changed over the past ten years (Table 2.1). While White women's membership has stayed the same at 73 percent, there was a slight increase of in the numbers of Black/African-American, Hispanic/Latino, Asian-American/Pacific Islander (AAPI), and American Indian/Alaska Native members (Table 2.1). In the state of Texas, minority-women justices are underrepresented on the bench by a ratio of one woman for every three White men.[21]

18 Gutierrez 1999, 181–91.
19 U.S. Census Bureau 2017.
20 State Bar of Texas 2016, pp. 1–6.
21 George and Yoon 2017; Slayton 2016.

Scholarship is limited in understanding the kinds of challenges Hispanic females face as judicial candidates and justices, and as such, this particular analysis is important. It fills the scholarly gap on the political incorporation of Hispanic women in one of the last institutions in Texas – the courts.

INTERSECTIONALITY OF GENDER AND OCCUPATION

Generally, the female justices interviewed for this study believe that being a woman and running for judicial office is viewed positively, particularly in South Texas (which is majority Hispanic). All of the female justices believed that women judges are typically seen as more honest, fair, and less likely to be corrupt or influenced. This is congruent with Frederick and Streb's study on the impact of sex on candidate success in state appellate courts. They found that many voters believe the quite plausible stereotype that female candidates would demonstrate more honesty and integrity if they reached the bench.[22] The justices also believed that being a female, at least in South Texas, is an advantage. Justice Antonia Sanchez went as far as to say that, "being a woman gives them an eight-percentage advantage among voters in South Texas."[23] (No study has been found to support the eight-point advantage claim.) Kelton Morgan, a senior political consultant, does agree that there is a one-to-two-point advantage that women have over male judicial candidates.[24] Another justice pointed out that while being a woman could be a positive attribute, it could also be a negative when it comes to fundraising. Justice Jessica Delgado states that, "females are not financially secure to the point that they can write bigger checks. I can walk into a room full of men and raise $5,000 and then walk into a room full of females and raise $500."[25] Bonneau's study on campaign fundraising and judicial races finds that minority women running in partisan judicial elections may indeed raise less money than their male counterparts.[26]

Once in office, most of the women agreed that being a woman has affected how they are perceived by their peers in the judiciary. According to Justice Sanchez, male colleagues on the court, "tend to think you have less knowledge and experience so you have to prove yourself. They will not give you

22 Frederick and Streb 2008, pp. 937–54.
23 Interview with Antonia Sanchez, September 14, 2017.
24 Interview with Kelton Morgan, November 14, 2017.
25 Interview with Jessica Delgado, October 3, 2017.
26 Bonneau 2017, pp. 68–85.

credit so you must be more aggressive in asserting your thoughts and opinions."[27] Justice Angelica Gutierrez iterated, "I think that more and more male judges are resentful; they think they are smarter or whatever. You still have a few, probably resentful, that think they are smarter and they try to make sure you *really* [interviewee's emphasis] understand what is being argued."[28] (A number of scholars have identified how judicial authority is gendered.) For instance, Rackley notes that, "we have to challenge the notion that the only person who can be taken seriously as a neutral and fair-minded person is the judicial equivalent of a tall man in a suit."[29] The male judge becomes synonymous with the term "authoritative knower." Justice Edith Morales continues, "When I started, as a 30-year-old, you kind of stuck out. The judiciary is dominated by Anglo males."[30] Other justices saw it as being linked to their race.

When it comes to striking a balance between the personal and political, all of the female justices agreed that it was a challenge to balance family with politics. Justice Martinez, Justice Gutierrez, and Justice Delgado contend that the struggle to "have it all" and strike a balance between personal and political/elected office is a "work in progress every day." Sanchez, whose experiences are similar to that of other justices, goes on to say, "Early on in my career it was difficult, it was hard. I gave up a lot of time with my children, as well as vacation and family time in order to get where I am today. The long hours were difficult to maintain with small children."[31] Connell, in his book *Masculinities*, points out that a judge's traditional working day and week was designed to suit men. He continues, "The long hours, culture and competitive ethos of the practicing bar tends to reflect masculine values."[32]

One of the female justices, who was considered a trailblazer in her career, stated, "You know, because of the era I grew up and matured as an attorney and as a public figure, men were not attracted to having someone like me assume the role of partner in a marriage. So, at the time, I thought I had to make a choice between getting married, having children, and being a politician. Now I think that has changed, where men consider women they seek to marry as partners rather than caretakers."[33] When it comes to campaigning,

27 Interview with Antonia Sanchez, September 14, 2017.

28 Interview with Angelica Gutierrez, October 10, 2017.

29 Rackley 2002, pp. 602–24.

30 Interview with Edith Morales, September 18, 2017.

31 Interview with Antonia Sanchez, September 14, 2017; Interview with Angelica Gutierrez, October 10, 2017.; Interview with Jessica Delgado, October 3, 2017.

32 Connell 2005.

33 Interview with Edith Morales, September 18, 2017.

some of the justices believe that gender makes it a little more difficult to raise money. "I think many times women shy away from running because it is hard to ask for money. I hate having to go and ask for money, and for some reason the men are better at it. The men are able to have a golf tournament or a skeet shoot and they raise a ton of money. Certain women try to do that and they don't have the same turnout."[34]

For Justice Sanchez, the obstacle intersected gender and race. She stated,

> I think that traditionally Latinos are coming into a profession where we haven't been in for hundreds of years. That the kind of wealth that we need in our families isn't there… It is not something they are used to doing. My father thought I was crazy when I ran. They asked if "I lost my mind" because it never occurred to any of them to do anything like that. My father said, "I would never do anything politically like that." But, as a businessman, he would take a certain amount of money and risk it in a business adventure and to me, there was no difference. I was taking that money and investing it in myself.[35]

Justice Delgado's assessment of the barriers of Hispanic women in South Texas was threefold: the persistence of a good old boy network, the perceived lack of qualification in running for office, and cultural expectations. She characterizes women running for judicial office this way,

> There was a race where a female was a sitting justice for sixteen years who was running for an open seat and being challenged by someone who had never run for judge and he was out-fundraising her. The only reason was because he was a man and she was a woman. The boys were like, "Well, he is my friend, he is my compadre *y lo va dar dinero*." [he is godfather/friend and I will give money] They hold the purse strings. They are the main wage earners. … If you ask a man, "Do you want to run for office?" "Oh, yes," he replies because he immediately thinks he is more qualified to run for that position. We have been asking more females to run, especially qualified female lawyers and both of them say, "No, I am not qualified to run for that job." So, that is an obstacle that we place on ourselves that we are not qualified. … Last but not least, the Hispanic, Latina, Mexican cultural issue – women stay home and care for their kids, putting their families in front of their careers while men will never put family in front of their careers.[36]

[34] Interview with Angelica Gutierrez, October 10, 2017.
[35] Interview with Antonia Sanchez, September 14, 2017.
[36] Interview with Jessica Delgado, October 3, 2017.

Delgado's viewpoint is similar to the findings in Feenan's study on women running for elected office. Feenan's research on justices highlights that "traditionally the 'old boy's network' denied women access to the flow of information and monies, which are important to maintaining presence and authority. The exclusion of women from such flows may also represent a form of subordination in which women are excluded from significant sources of informal knowledge."[37] In addition, Justice Delgado's understanding of women's perceived lack of qualification to run for office is consistent with Lawless and Pearson's study, which suggests that most women who run have to be better or more qualified than their male colleagues in order to win.[38] Assertiveness in social, public, and political arenas by women of Mexican descent runs counter to those cultural traditions. Sonia A. Lopez writes, "In the Mexican American household, the husband is the main provider in the family ... In Mexican culture, the role of the Mexicana, whether single or married, has been to serve her family, particularly the men: her father, brothers, husbands, and sons."[39] Hardy-Fanta contends that the barriers Latinas face to elected office stem from sexism and cultural traditions.[40] In this one narrative, gender and ethnic cultural expectations intersect.

The Hispanic women justices who sit on the various courts of appeals all shared similar experiences in their motivations and decision to run for the office in which they currently preside. They all agreed that serving as trial attorneys was stressful or they were "burnt out."[41] Making the transition to a justice took away long days and the constant need to meet minimum billable hours. One justice believed that her experience as a trial attorney was the last chapter in a long legal career until she decided to run for a higher office.[42] Another justice mentioned that a male colleague encouraged her.[43] Justice Sanchez knew she wanted to be a judge since she was a little girl. She was initially running for a lower level court seat, but was encouraged to run for a seat on the court of appeals because a friend thought she was qualified and had more to give serving on a higher court. Justice Sanchez took her advice and won a seat on an appeals court. Justice Delgado was a bit more calculating. She waited until the seat was open and her children had grown and left

37 Feenan 2008, p. 497.
38 Lawless and Pearson 2008, pp. 67–82.
39 Lopez 1980, p. 13.
40 Hardy-Fanta 1993.
41 Interview with Patricia Martinez, September 19, 2017.
42 Interview with Edith Morales, September 18, 2017.
43 Interview with Angelica Gutierrez, October 10, 2017.

home.[44] Studies of women candidates in the United States and cross-nationally have shown that political opportunity structures, such as incumbency and access, are factors in more women winning office.[45]

THE INTERSECTIONALITY OF RACE AND POSITION

All of the women interviewed for this study believed that in South Texas it is more advantageous to be of Mexican-American descent and a Democrat than to be a White woman running as a Republican for the same office.[46] In a similar study, Navarro found that Hispanic women running for judicial office in South Texas believed voters to be "partial to Hispanic women judicial candidates."[47] Again, Justice Delgado states that, "Yes, I think there is a stereotype, a perception that female Hispanics are more objective, and more reasonable than White justices when it comes to a majority-minority population."[48] This is similar to the findings of Fraga et al., which suggest that Latina elected officials are positioned to be the most effective advocates on behalf of working-class communities of color.[49] Justice Gutierrez asserts that, "being a woman and Latina gives me extra points; even though I have a male opponent in the ballot box, they will vote for me."[50] The assumption that Latinas have a natural electoral edge over any non-Hispanic candidate or Hispanic candidate is pervasive.

The justices were also asked to address whether they thought their race had any effect on how they were perceived. Justice Gutierrez suggested that since there are few women of Mexican-American ancestry on the Texas court of appeals, they tend to stand out. She purports, "They look at you and don't know how to perceive you and so you have to prove more, show more in order for them to take you seriously."[51]

Justice Delgado believes that people see what they want to see and if you look Mexican or have a Mexican last name, they tend to believe you will be more sympathetic to those who come before you in court. She believes that their Anglo peers do not think minority women are as intelligent as they are.[52]

44 Interview with Jessica Delgado, October 3, 2017.
45 Fowler 1993; Welch and Studlar 1996, pp. 861–74.
46 Navarro 2013.
47 Navarro 2010, p. 74.
48 Interview with Jessica Delgado, October 3, 2017.
49 Fraga et al. 2005.
50 Interview with Angelica Gutierrez, October 10, 2017.
51 Ibid.
52 Interview with Jessica Delgado, October 3, 2017.

This observation is similar to Gutierrez y Muh et al.'s research on the intersecting roles of race and gender in the lives of professional women of color. They write, "It should be no surprise that women of color are presumed to be incompetent."[53]

Both Justice Gutierrez and Justice Sanchez also believe that Mexican-American women face different expectations. Sanchez offers this,

> For example, the woman's bar was the first one I got involved in as a member of the judiciary and a female. You would think they would be more inclusive, but it has taken me three years of standing in front of them, and putting myself in the middle, in order for them to include me and make me part of the group. I had to prove that I was acceptable in their eyes because I was an outsider and Hispanic. If I were White, it would have occurred much faster.[54]

One justice believed that "White voters won't vote for Hispanics. I think everyone votes for their own kind."[55] Justice Gutierrez was the only one who believed that when it came to gender and race, it really did not matter. "At this point, we are sort of lumped together with White women. I think there are different expectation for women in general."[56]

The justices were asked if they felt tension between society's expectations and definitions of being a Latina and their own definition of being a justice. Justice Delgado replied this way, "Not really. I think that society expects me as a Latina to be at the forefront, to be a voice for them and that is what I expect for myself everyday as well. So, their expectation and my expectation is the same—to be a voice for the people that I represent."[57]

Two justices who consider themselves "mature" did not think they had had that struggle. However, if they had been asked this same question twenty years ago, they would have responded "yes." Justice Sanchez claimed that "probably so, people assume that you should always, because of their stereotype of you, you should side with, 'La Raza' [your people]."[58]

In another instance, Justice Gutierrez believed that playing the race card was risky. She put it this way:

> I think we have to be very careful how we play the Latina card because when I ran for the state's highest court I put myself out there on social media. One of my messages was about the importance of electing a Latina to the state

[53] Gutierrez y Muh et al. 2012.
[54] Interview with Antonia Sanchez, September 14, 2017.
[55] Interview with Jessica Delgado, October 3, 2017.
[56] Interview with Angelica Gutierrez, October 10, 2017.
[57] Interview with Jessica Delgado, October 3, 2017.
[58] Interview with Antonia Sanchez, September 14, 2017.

> Supreme Court.... My big deal was why we need a Latina, we never have had a different perspective, different ideology. There was backlash from people in social media saying, "Oh, you should not be elected because you are a Latina." I responded by saying, "I am not asking you to elect me because I am a Latina. I am saying I am a qualified Latina. I think it is important for the reasons I mentioned and to have different perspectives of ideology."[59]

Samantha L. Hernandez's research on Latina candidates' use of social media finds that the types and ways in which certain images are portrayed matter for voter perception and mobilization.[60] Hernandez's research highlights the fact that how a candidate frames their identity can influence electoral behavior. Voters follow and retweet candidates based on shared ideology.

Some of the biggest obstacles to running for and winning judicial office intersect race with position. For instance, all of the justices agreed that money is the biggest obstacle in campaigns. "I think more so for Hispanics trying to raise money in the Hispanic community and as a woman, yeah. I think my answer would be totally different if I were in another demographic," said Justice Morales.[61] These two observations – messaging and campaign fundraising – are consistent with Palmer and Simon's findings, which argue that in order for women to win elected office they have to understand the district in which they choose to run,[62] as well as the obstacles to campaign financing that Latina candidates continue to face.[63]

IMPLICATIONS AND CONCLUSION

It is important that our courts be representative to fulfill their purpose. Our laws are premised in part on the idea that our courts will be staffed by justices who understand the circumstances of the communities that they serve.[64] Our judicial system depends on the general public's faith in its legitimacy. Both of these foundational principles require a bench that is representative of the people. The intuition here is that that because judges inevitably draw upon their own experiences when deciding cases, the judiciary benefits when their experiences draw upon a broader set of the population. Research has shown

59 Interview with Angelica Gutierrez, October 10, 2017.
60 Hernandez 2016, pp. 83–96.
61 Interview with Edith Morales, September 18, 2017.
62 Palmer and Simon 2008.
63 Navarro, Hernandez and Navarro 2016.
64 For a discussion of the challenges of judicial representation, see Segal 2000.

that social background, including race and gender, has measurable individual and group effects on justices.[65]

Second, we need a better process for developing a pipeline of women and minorities to serve as justices. The perspectives from each of these women provide qualitative evidence that challenges to elected office still exist. The issue of the supply of women and minorities to serve as judges is one of labor economics. The bench should not reflect the bar but rather the public. However, lawyers staff the courts, and thus the availability of qualified candidates is a limitation on the ability of states to fill the seats. While the number of judges is small relative to the number of lawyers, it still requires a large pool of candidates.

Increased diversity would contribute to a variety of positive impacts on opinion content and doctrine. Because a wider range of views would be expressed in the decision-making process, legal opinions would be more thorough and incorporate multiple viewpoints when compared to decisions produced by homogeneous groups of judges. An alternative perspective suggests that status differences related to race and gender may produce increased conflict on diverse courts.

Standpoint theory is useful for understanding the experience of the very few Latina justices that sit on the courts of appeals. Despite sitting on different courts, their experiences were similar. Demographics matter for the election of Latina women to intermediate courts. The courts that each of these women represent are nestled in majority Latino districts. Each of the Latina women understood the risk of running for office – that is, the challenge of balancing family and profession, the long, stressful hours working as a private attorney, and the more stable hours serving as a justice. They understood the challenge of running a campaign and raising young children. The Latina justices experienced, in some fashion, the institutional marginalization of working in a White, male-dominated institution. These women also shared their experience about the very different expectations held by their own communities compared to that of their peers.

The lack of women judges on the state appeals courts potentially impacts the development of the law in several aspects. State appellate courts are the forum of last resort for cases that address issues of particular concern to women

[65] Glenn and Sen (2015) found that judges with daughters consistently vote in a more feminist fashion on gender issues than judges who do not have daughters (p. 45); Welch, Combs and Gruhl (1988) found that the presence of Black judges increases equality of treatment between Black and White defendants regarding the decision of whether to incarcerate (p. 131).

and minorities. The appeals courts are also pipelines for the appointment of state supreme court justices.

Appellate justices are public officials who play a vital role in our democracy and in our daily lives. A woman on the bench is important symbolically: it signals to Texans (and to attorneys and non-attorneys) that the government and judicial branch are open and responsive to their needs. A more diverse appeals court would inspire confidence in the Texas judiciary and ensure its legitimacy and success. Additionally, the underrepresentation of Hispanic/minority women on Texas appeals court sends a powerful message about Hispanic/minority women's advancement in society. A Hispanic woman at the top echelons increases a Hispanic woman's sense of belonging to her chosen profession and institution. Women in the judiciary also fight stereotypes by expanding people's notions of who can hold positions of power. As such, it is of great importance that we understand who they are and what they do. The current project hopes to contribute to that effort.

REFERENCES

Allen, B. J. 2000. "'Learning the rope': A Black Feminist Standpoint Analysis." In *Rethinking Organizational & Managerial Communication from Feminist Perspective*, ed. M. Buzzanell. Thousand Oaks, CA: Sage Publications. pp. 177–208.

2009. "A Feminist Standpoint Theory: A Black Woman's Review of Organizational Socialization." *Communication Studies* 47(4): 257–71.

Bonneau, C. W. 2017. "Campaign Fundraising in State Supreme Court Elections." *Social Science Quarterly* 88(1) (March): 68–85.

Collins, P. H. 1997. "Comment on Hekman's 'Truth and Method: Feminist Standpoint Theory Revisited': Where's the Power?" *Signs: Journal of Women in Culture and Society* 22(2): 375–81.

2000. *Black Feminist Thought: Knowledge, Consciousness, and the Politics of Empowerment.* New York: Routledge.

Combs, S. 2008. "Texas in Focus: A Statewide View of Opportunities." www.window.state.tx.us/specialrpt/tif/96-1286.pdf.

Connell, R. W. 2005. *Masculinities*. Berkeley: University of California Press.

DeFrancisco, V. P. 2007. *Communicating Gender Diversity: A Critical Approach.* Thousand Oaks, CA: Sage Publications.

Echaveste, M. 2002. "Brown to Black: the Politics of Judicial Appointments for Latinos." *Berkeley La Raza Law Journal* 13(1): 39–42.

Feenan, D. 2008. "Women Judges: Gendering Judging, Justifying Diversity." *Journal of Law and Society* 35(4): 497.

Fowler, L. 1993. *Candidates, Congress and the American Democracy*. Ann Arbor: University of Michigan Press.

Fraga, L. R., Garcia, J. A., Hero, R., Jones-Correa, M., Martinez-Ebers, V., and Segura, G. M. 2006. *Latino National Survey (LNS) Focus Group Data, 2006*. Ann Arbor,

MI: Inter-university Consortium for Political and Social Research. https://doi.org/10.3886/ICPSR29601.v1

Fraga, L. R., Martinez-Ebers, V., Lopez, Linda, and Ramirez, R. 2005. "Strategic Intersectionality: Gender, Ethnicity, and Political Incorporation." *Institute of Governmental Studies*. http://scholarship.org/uc/item/5r92z54j.

Frederick, B. and Streb, M. J. 2008. "Women Running for Judge: The Impact of Sex on Candidate Success in State Intermediate Appellate Court Elections." *Social Science Quarterly* 89: 937–54.

Garcia, S., Martinez-Ebers, V., Coronado, I., Navarro, S. A., and Jaramillo, P. 2008. *Politicas*. Austin: Texas University Press.

George, T. E. and Yoon, Albert H. 2017. *The Gavel Gap*. American Constitution Society. http://gavelgap.org.

Gutierrez, J. A. 1999. "Experiences of Chicana County Judges in Texas Politics: In Their Own Words." *Frontiers: A Journal of Women Studies*. 20(1): 181–91.

Gutierrez y Muh, G., Niemann, Y. F., Gonzalez, C. G., and Harris, A. P. 2012. *Presumed Incompetent*. Logan: Utah State University Press.

Glynn, A. N. and Sen, M. 2015. "Identifying Judicial Empathy: Does Having Daughters Cause Judges to Rule for Women's Issues?" *American Journal of Political Science*. 59(37): 37–54.

Hardy-Fanta, C. 1993. *Latina Politica, Latino Politics*. Philadelphia, PA: Temple University Press.

Hernandez, S. L. 2016. "Virtually Shaking Hands and Kissing Babies: Congressional Candidates and Social Media Campaigns." In *Latinas in American Politics* , eds. Sharon A. Navarro, Samantha L. Hernandez, and Leslie A. Navarro. Lanham, MD: Lexington Press. pp. 83–96.

Johnson, K. R. 2002. "On the Appointment of a Latina/o to the Supreme Court." *Berkeley La Raza Law Journal*. 13(1): 1–14.

Lawless, J. L. and Pearson, K. 2008. "The Primary Reason for Women's Underrepresentation? Reevaluating the Conventional Wisdom." *Journal of Politics*. (70): 67–82.

Lopez, G. and Stepler, R. 2016. *Latinos in the 2016 Election: Texas*. Washington, DC: Pew Research Center.

Lopez, S. A. 1980. "The Role of the Chicana within the Student Movement." In *Chicana Feminist Thought*, ed. A. M. Garcia. New York: Routledge. pp. 103–07.

Munoz, F. 2002. "Overcoming Barriers: Being Flexible and Creative." *Berkeley La Raza Law Journal*. 13(1): 29–31.

Navarro, S. A. 2008. *Latina Legislator*. College Station: Texas A&M Press.

2013. "Moving on up: the political incorporation of Hispanic women into the federal judiciary of Texas." *Latino Studies*. 11(1): 4–20.

Navarro, S. N. 2010. "Shaking Hands and Kissing Babies: The Intersectionality of Ethnicity, Class, and Gender, and Latina Women's Decision to Run for Judicial Office." *Aztlan: A Journal of Chicano Studies*. 35(2): 74–86.

Navarro, S. N., Hernandez, S. L., and Navarro, L. A., eds. 2016. *Latinas in American Politics: Changing and Embracing Political Tradition*. Lanham, MD: Lexington Press.

Palmer, B. and Simon, D. 2008. *Breaking the Political Glass Ceiling: Women and Congressional Elections*. New York: Routledge.

Rackley, E. 2002. "Representation of the (Woman) Judge: Hercules, the Little Mermaid, and the Vain and Naked Emperor." *Legal Studies*. 22: 602–24.

Segal, J. A. 2000. "Representative Decision Making on the Federal Bench: Clinton's District Court Appointees." *Political Research Quarterly*. 53(37): 137–50.

Slayton, D. 2016a. *Annual Statistical Report for the Texas Judiciary*. Austin, TX: Office of Court Administration.

2016b. *Report on Judicial Salaries and Turnover: For Fiscal Years 2014 and 2015*. Austin, TX: Office of Court Administration.

Sotomayor, S. 2002. "A Latina Judge's Voice." *La Raza Law Journal*. 13(1): 87–93.

State Bar of Texas. 2016. "2015 Population Trends of Women in the State Bar of Texas." 1–6. www.texasbar.com/AM/Template.cfm?Section=Demographic_and_Economic_Trends&Template=/CM/ContentDisplay.cfm&ContentID=33674.

Tickner, J. A. 1997. "You Just Don't Understand: Troubled Engagements between Feminist and IR Theorists." *International Studies Quarterly*. 41(4): 611–32.

U.S. Census Bureau. 2017. "Quick Facts: Texas." www.census.gov/quickfacts/TX.

Welch, S., Combs, M., and Gruhl, J. 1988. "Do Black judges Make a Difference?" *American Journal of Political Science*. 32(126): 126–36.

Welch, S. and Studlar, D. T. 1996. "The Opportunity Structures for Women's Candidacies and Electability in Britain and the United States." *Political Research Quarterly*. 49(4): 861–74.

Williams, M. 2007. "Women's Representation on State Trial and Appellate Court." *Social Science Quarterly*. 88(5): 1201–26.

Zinn, M. and Dill, B. 1996. "Theorizing Difference from Multiracial Feminism." *Feminist Studies*. 22: 321–31.

Appendix

QUESTIONNAIRE FOR LATINA/HISPANIC JUSTICES

As you know, this interview will be used to write a chapter for a book about gender, sexuality, and identity in the U.S. judiciary. With your history and accomplishments, your experiences would be very valuable to our study. The questions have been carefully written to protect your anonymity. Your answers will be confidential, and your name will not be connected to your words. If at any time during this interview you do not wish to answer a question, please feel free to let me know and we will move on to the next question.

Personal Background, Identity, and Civic Engagement

I want to start at the beginning, because I imagine your story begins well before you became a public figure in Texas. So I'm going to start with a few background questions.

1. "'Families' [of Hispanic or Latino] origin or background in the U.S. come from many different countries. From which country do you trace your Latino/Hispanic heritage?" [*Latino National Survey (LNS)* 13]
2. "Where were you born?" [*LNS* 15]
3. "What is your race? Are you White, Black, American Indian, Asian, Native Hawaiian/Pacific Islander, some other race, or more than one?" [*LNS* 53]
4. "[Hispanics or Latinos] can be described based on skin tone or complexion shades. Using a scale from 1 to 5, where 1 represents very dark and 5 represents being very light, where would you place yourself on that scale?" [*LNS* 55, *E* 13, 16]
5. What is your ethnicity identity?

6. What is your educational background?
   a. Please tell me about your educational experience. Did you attend primarily majority-minority schools during your K–12 experience? What was your undergraduate and graduate experience like?
7. "Did you participate in civic activities? If so, can you tell me what kinds of activities you were involved in?" [*LNS* 26]
8. "Many Latinas report that role models have been important to their careers. Were there other women or men who influenced or encouraged you to take on leadership roles in the community?" [*Políticas* I-8]
9. What is your parents' education level? What influence, if any, did they have on you pursuing your education?
10. How many family members do you have?

Current Position and Experiences

11. Thinking about the election/appointment process, do you think being a woman has helped or hindered your chances of success?
12. Thinking about the election/appointment process, do you think your particular identity as a Latina/Hispanic woman influenced the election/appointment process and your chances of success?
13. Once in office, do you believe your identity as a woman has had any effect on how you were received or perceived by your peers in the judiciary?
14. Once in office, do you believe that being a Latina has affected how you were received or perceived by your peers?
15. "Do you believe that all female public officials are held to the same standards, or do Latinas face different expectations as leaders?" [*Políticas* III-6]
    a. Can you expound on these different expectations?
16. Women with demanding careers have varying experiences balancing their personal and professional relationships. How would you describe this balance in your life?
17. Do you ever feel tension between society's expectations of what it means to be a Latina and your own expectation of what it means to be a justice?

Reflections on Leadership Roles in Social and Political Context

18. As a Latina who achieved a position of influence, do you see yourself as a role model for other Latinas? Why or why not?
19. Do you think the political environment has changed in recent years to make leadership/political roles more or less accessible for Latinas?

20. Three-part question:
    a. "Are there obstacles for Latinas running for judicial office?" [*Políticas* I-5]
    b. What are some of the obstacles?
    c. What are the biggest obstacles for women running for judicial office?
21. What was the first elected office you held?
22. The research on Latinas who run for office often mention that Latina or Hispanic women are encouraged to run for office by a colleague. What precipitated your decision to run for the office in which you now sit? (Did someone encourage you?)
23. Research on Latinas who run for office shows that they tend to have the support of their family. Was this the case for you?
24. Research on Latinas who sit on the judiciary has revealed that they experience challenges/obstacles based on their perceived race/ethnicity and gender when dispensing justice. Do you have a similar experience?

3

Structural and Partisan Effects on the Ascension of Women of Color to State Appellate Courts

BARBARA L. GRAHAM AND ADRIANO UDANI

The legal profession is one of the least racially diverse professions in the United States (Rhode 2015). Palmer (2001) observed that "entry into the judicial hierarchy however, is not nearly as open as the entry into the legislative hierarchy" (p. 235). Women and persons of color have experienced a long history of discrimination and exclusion from law schools and the legal profession. Until a few decades ago, this exclusion extended to representation in the state judicial system. George and Yoon (2016) found that more than half of the nation's state judges are white men and less than 30 percent are white women but women of color are the most underrepresented group in state courts (p. 7). When it comes to which conditions, structures, and institutions promote the presence of women of color in state judiciaries, there is a great deal we do not know on a theoretical and empirical level.

White women have made considerable progress in increasing their presence in state courts at all levels; however, women of color have not moved beyond a token presence in state judiciaries. Although prior studies have framed the lack of representation in state courts in the context of race or gender, little scholarly attention has been paid to how the concept of intersectionality informs our understanding of the underrepresentation of women of color in state courts. An intersectionality framework provides an opportunity to shift away from analyzing underrepresentation as discrete lines of inquiry.

Our study examines descriptive representation in state appellate courts. We chose state appellate courts because judges who serve in the upper echelons of the judicial hierarchy have the greatest opportunities to shape state legal policy. For example, state appellate courts have been at the vanguard of progressive policy change in the area of same-sex marriage by expanding rights beyond those expressed and implied in the Bill of Rights and the Fourteenth Amendment. Judges who serve on state supreme courts often have the final say on a range of civil and criminal cases because a very small percentage of state cases are successfully appealed to the U.S. Supreme Court. Although state high courts have greater prestige, intermediate appellate courts hear 71 percent of the total appellate caseload.[1] By expanding our analysis beyond state supreme courts, we are able to offer greater analytical insights on the problem of underrepresentation at the appellate level.

One of the most tested relationships in the study of descriptive representation in state courts concerns the effects of selection arrangements. Prior studies examined the effects of selection arrangements in the context of race or gender but not in the context of intersectional identities. To date, no empirical research exists that systematically examines the effects of state selection arrangements with regard to women of color. Building from the theoretical contributions of Crenshaw (1989; 1991) and the judicial representation literature, our research tests whether selection arrangements and partisan effects account for the presence of women of color in state appellate courts compared to men of color and privileged identities. We collected individual-level data on all judges serving on state supreme courts and intermediate appellate courts in the United States as of October 2017. We employed multilevel mixed models with logistic regression to test the effects of selection arrangements and partisanship on intersectional identities. The results provide strong evidence that Democratic party affiliation of the governor and partisan elections help women of color ascend to the appellate bench, but their routes are more limited compared to other intersectional identities.

To answer our research question, we first provide an overview of the current state of descriptive representation in state appellate courts. Next, we present our categorization of appellate selection arrangements, followed by a review of the relevant literature that seeks to explain racial and gender underrepresentation in state courts. Then, we offer our hypotheses and provide an overview of the data and methods used in this research. Finally, we present the results and conclude the study by discussing the implications of our research findings.

DESCRIPTIVE REPRESENTATION IN STATE APPELLATE COURTS

A considerable body of research exists in the political science literature on representation of women and persons of color in political officeholding and in

[1] See the National Center for State Courts, Court Statistics Project, www.courtstatistics.org/. The naming conventions of appellate courts vary considerably in state court systems. In this study, "state supreme court" is a generic phrase used to designate the court of last resort in the state. Second tier courts in the state appellate hierarchy are referred to as "intermediate appellate courts."

various bureaucratic contexts. Pitkin's (1967) classic work on representation provides the analytic lens to assess the nature of underrepresentation of intersectional identities in state appellate courts. Scholars have advanced arguments to explain why the concept of descriptive representation should extend to the courts (Slotnick 1984; Ifill 1997, 2000). Descriptive representation matters both to what the bench looks like and to what it decides substantively for the following reasons: The sustained growth of the nonwhite population in the United States is expected to increase demands for meaningful representation in legal institutions. In the face of rapid demographic change, the argument for descriptive representation in courts is that a representative judiciary is a connected one – one that looks like multiracial America (Ifill 1997, 2000). Like other political institutions, courts are evaluated by the presence of women and persons of color at the federal and state levels (Phillips 1995). Descriptive representation is linked to legitimacy and trust in legal institutions in the eyes of underrepresented groups (Scherer and Curry 2010).

Are state appellate courts descriptively represented? Based on the proportion of women and persons of color in the population and lawyer population surveys, state appellate courts lack meaningful descriptive representation. The data reported in Table 3.1 describe the current state of descriptive representation in state appellate courts broken down by intersectional identities. White men hold a majority of state supreme court and intermediate appellate seats (56.7 percent) compared to 29 percent of white women. African-American males hold more seats on state supreme courts, followed by Latino men; however, African-American women fare better on intermediate appellate courts compared to other groups. Asian-American and South Asian American representation remain below 1 percent. In 2016, the first Native American judge was appointed to a state supreme court, and she was the first Native American female to serve on any high court.[2] The findings reported in Table 3.1 show that women of color and men of color are equally represented at 7 percent in state appellate courts.[3]

There is some variation between men and women judges of color. Between 1976 and 2017, more women than men of color were selected for the appellate courts. The median year selected among women of color is 2010 compared to

[2] In 2016, Associate Justice Anne K. McKeig was appointed by Governor Mark Dayton to the Minnesota Supreme Court.

[3] We recognize that race and gender are not the only intersectional identities worthy of scholarly attention. The importance of LGBTQ status is highlighted by the presence of Justice Mary I. Yu, who self-identifies as the first Asian, the first Latina, and the first member of the LGBTQ community to serve on the Washington State Supreme Court.

TABLE 3.1 *Race and gender representation by state appellate court, 2017*

Race and Gender	State Supreme Court[1](%)	Intermediate Appellate Court[2](%)	Total(%)
White Men	58.7 (199)	55.9 (533)	56.6% (732)
White Women	29.0 (98)	29.0 (277)	29.0 (375)
African-American Men	4.4 (15)	3.7 (35)	3.9 (50)
African-American Women	1.7 (6)	4.7 (45)	3.9 (51)
Latino	2.4 (8)	2.2 (21)	2.2 (29)
Latina	1.7 (6)	2.6 (25)	2.4 (31)
AAPI Men	0.6 (2)	0.8 (8)	0.8 (10)
AAPI Women	1.2 (4)	0.6 (6)	0.8 (10)
Native American Men	0	0	0
Native American Women	0.3 (1)	0	0.1 (1)
South Asian Men	0	0.2 (2)	0.1 (2)
South Asian Women	0	0.2 (2)	0.1 (2)
Total	339	954	1,293

Notes: Figures reported for October 2017. Percentages may not total to 100 due to rounding errors. The table does not include Justice Mary I. Yu on the Washington State Supreme Court, who is coded as multi-raced and female.

[1] Oklahoma and Texas have two state supreme courts.

[2] Alabama and Tennessee have two intermediate appellate courts. Ten states lack intermediate appellate courts: Delaware, Maine, Montana, Nevada, New Hampshire, Rhode Island, South Dakota, Vermont, West Virginia, and Wyoming. North Dakota has a temporary intermediate appellate court, but no cases were assigned to it during this study's period of investigation.

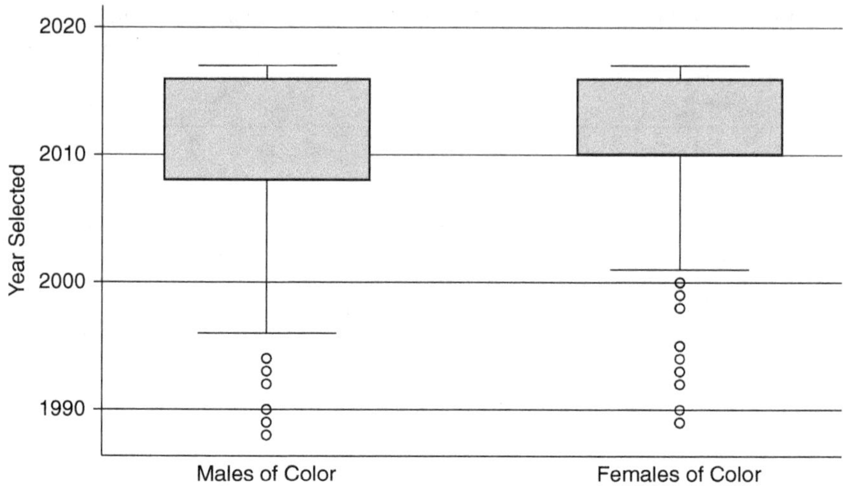

FIGURE 3.1 Distribution of year in which person of color selected to the court

2008 for men of color. Yet, Figure 3.1 also denotes much variation in selection between the two groups. Most of the men of color were selected for judgeships between 1997 and 2017, while women of color experienced a relatively shorter timespan between 2001 and 2017. Men of color comprise a larger proportion of Democrats than women of color. Among all Democrats, there are 11.64 percent men of color compared to 7.96 percent women of color. Judges of color are somewhat more balanced among Republicans (5.07 percent males of color vs. 4.35 percent females of color). More women of color comprise a higher proportion of positions in state supreme courts (4.16 percent vs. 2.26 percent, respectively), although there is a higher proportion of men than women of color in the intermediate appellate court system (11.91 percent vs. 7.23 percent respectively). Lastly, men and women of color comprise similar percentages of appointments (7.94 percent vs. 6.32 percent respectively), but more women than men of color are elected to judgeships (5.23 percent vs. 2.6 percent respectively).

APPELLATE SELECTION ARRANGEMENTS

An important piece of the puzzle in determining the effects of structural and partisan effects on descriptive representation in appellate courts is the complex nature of state judicial selection. The literature identifies five structural arrangements used to select judges to their full-term positions: partisan elections, nonpartisan elections, judicial nominating commissions, executive appointment, and legislative elections (Sheldon and Maule 1997, p. 21). A closer examination of the actual operation of formal methods of selection reveals the existence of mixed systems of selection for state supreme court and intermediate appellate court judges and important variations among certain types of selection mechanisms. If selection mechanisms are thought to inhibit descriptive representation, then systematic attention must be paid to how we classify them because they could significantly affect the conclusions reached (Epstein, Knight, and Shvetsova 2002, p. 204). To account for this complexity, we classify appellate selection into seven categories: partisan election, nonpartisan election, judicial nominating commissions, judicial nominating commissions with legislative approval, gubernatorial appointment, gubernatorial appointment with legislative approval, and legislative elections.

Partisan and nonpartisan judicial elections share a common element – voters have a direct opportunity to choose their candidates for judicial office in primary and general elections. In partisan election systems, the names of judicial candidates on the primary and general election ballot are accompanied by their partisan affiliation. Nonpartisan judicial elections were designed to remove the influence of partisan politics and party labels off ballots, but in reality, they are nonpartisan in spirit only (Streb 2007). In nonpartisan election states, judicial candidates are listed on the primary and general election ballot without designating party affiliation. Nonpartisan judicial elections provide an excellent example of how their actual operation varies in important ways among states. For example, in Ohio judicial candidates run in partisan primaries, but in Michigan, judicial candidates for the state supreme court are selected at party nominating conventions. Based on strong empirical arguments, we classify Michigan and Ohio as partisan election states (Nelson, Caufield, and Martin 2013). Fourteen states are classified as using nonpartisan elections to select appellate judges.

In actual operation, judicial election is a hybrid arrangement because in most instances the governor is authorized to fill vacancies that are created by the unexpired terms of judges leaving office due to strategic retirements, resignation, or death. Interim appointment is an important means by which the governor can maintain partisan control of the appellate bench in judicial election states (Sheldon and Maule 1997, p. 47; Martin and Pyle 2002, p. 5). Prior studies have established the linkage between interim appointments and incumbency in judicial elections (Baum 1983; Streb and Frederick 2009). Holmes and Emrey (2006) found that more than half of all judges placed on state supreme courts between 1964 and 2004 were interim appointments. The frequency of interim appointments varies considerably in judicial election states. Consistent with prior research, our study documents high levels of interim appointments in nonpartisan election states (Dubois 1980, pp. 105–06). For 91.7 percent of women of color in nonpartisan election states, the initial path to the appellate bench was by appointment, compared to 73.3 percent of men of color. In contrast, white men (57.7 percent) and white women (58.8 percent) were more likely to be initially appointed in nonpartisan election states. Given the important differences between partisan and nonpartisan judicial elections, we treat them as separate electoral systems.

Sixteen states use judicial nominating commissions or merit selection to select appellate judges. Judicial nominating commissions, consisting of lawyers and laypersons appointed by the governor, screen applicants for judgeships and then forward a list of names to the governor, who makes the appointment. The governor's choice for the judgeship is limited to the names submitted by the nominating commission. Seven states use a variation of merit selection, which requires the governor's appointee to be confirmed by one or both houses of the state legislature. Merit selection that requires legislature approval is considered a separate category because the legislature acts as an additional constraint on the governor's choice for the judgeship.

Two types of executive appointment of appellate judges are used in a few states: gubernatorial appointment with or without the approval of the legislature. We distinguish between pure appointment systems and those that require legislative confirmation because in pure appointment systems, governors have a freer hand in making judicial appointments. In two states, California and Massachusetts, the governors lack formal constraints in making appointments to the appellate bench.[4] Five states require the governor's choice for the appellate bench be approved by the state senate. This form of executive appointment is similar to the federal model of judicial selection. The full legislative assembly must approve the governor's choices in Connecticut and Rhode Island.

In two states, Virginia and South Carolina, state legislators cast their vote for nominees to the appellate bench. In Virginia, the governor is authorized to make interim appointments to the state appellate bench if the general assembly is not in session when the vacancy occurs; however, in South Carolina, all vacancies are filled by legislative election. As a route to the appellate bench, legislative election is considered a separate category of

[4] In California, the governor's appointees must be confirmed by a commission on judicial appointments, but the governor is not bound by the commission's recommendations. In Massachusetts, the governor's appointees must be approved by the governor's council, but it operates in an advisory capacity.

judicial election because there is no public accountability – voters are not permitted to cast a ballot for state judges.

Data presented in Table 3.2 show appellate selection distribution by race and gender of the judge. We find that partisan election is the only type of selection arrangement where women of color outperform white men, white women, and men of color in obtaining seats on appellate courts in proportion to their numbers. This finding is important when considering that only eight states use partisan elections to select appellate judges, compared to fourteen states that use nonpartisan elections and sixteen states that use judicial nominating commissions. White women outperform women of color, men of color and white men in states that use nonpartisan elections. White men and men of color have an advantage in obtaining appellate judgeships in states that use judicial nominating commissions. Men of color outperform the other groups in states that use gubernatorial appointment. Whereas white men fare better in states where the governor's choice must be approved by the legislature, the differences among the other categories are nominal.

EXPLAINING EFFECTS OF RACE AND GENDER IN STATE JUDICIAL SELECTION

Although there is a lack of scholarly consensus about what accounts for underrepresentation on state courts, two structural accounts stand out in the literature. The first centers on discriminatory election schemes that promote racial homogeneity of the bench (Ifill 1997). Judicial elections are viewed favorably among Blacks and Latino/as, especially in the South, where litigation brought by voting rights advocates pressed the courts to apply the Voting Rights Act of 1965 to judicial elections (Champagne 1988, p. 152; Graham 1991; Sheldon and Maule 1997, pp. 76–79). The use of gerrymandered judicial districts or at-large judicial elections are viewed as attempts to dilute the voting strength of racial groups and Democrats.[5] Although Alozie (1988) found no significant relationship between judicial selection methods and Black representation in state courts, Graham (1991) found that executive appointment and legislative election increased Black representation in state trial courts. For racial minorities, Hurwitz and Lanier (2008) found that Black males and females did not fare well under executive appointment and Hispanic males

[5] The North Carolina legislature is attempting to institute reforms, including gerrymandered judicial districts, that would give Republicans an edge in electing Republican judges to the state bench (Gabriel 2017).

TABLE 3.2 *Full-term methods of appellate selection by race and gender, 2017*

Selection System	White Men(%)	White Women (%)	Men of Color(%)	Women of Color(%)
Partisan Election	29.5 (216)	32.3 (121)	17.4 (16)	40.0 (38)
Nonpartisan Election	17.8 (130)	21.3 (80)	16.3 (15)	12.6 (12)
Judicial Nominating Commission	32.5 (238)	25.3 (95)	29.3 (27)	26.3 (25)
Judicial Nominating Commission with Legislative Approval	5.2 (38)	5.6 (21)	10.9 (10)	8.4 (8)
Gubernatorial Appointment	6.8 (50)	8.5 (32)	18.5 (17)	8.4 (8)
Gubernatorial Appointment with Legislative Approval	5.7 (42)	4.5 (17)	4.3 (4)	2.1 (2)
Legislative Election	2.5 (18)	2.4 (9)	3.3 (3)	2.1 (2)
Total	732	375	92	95

Notes: Percentages may not total to 100 due to rounding errors. Appellate selection methods: (1) Partisan elections: Alabama, Illinois, Louisiana, Ohio, Michigan, New Mexico, Pennsylvania, and Texas. (2) Nonpartisan elections: Arkansas, Georgia, Idaho, Kentucky, Minnesota, Mississippi, Montana, Nevada, North Carolina,[1] North Dakota, Oregon, Washington, West Virginia,[2] and Wisconsin. (3) Judicial nominating commission: Alaska, Arizona, Colorado, Florida, Indiana, Iowa, Kansas (state high court), Massachusetts (intermediate appellate court), Missouri, Nebraska, New Hampshire, New York (intermediate appellate court), Oklahoma, South Dakota, Tennessee,[3] and Wyoming. (4) Judicial nominating commission with legislative approval: Connecticut, Hawaii, Maryland, New York (state high court), Rhode Island, Utah, and Vermont. (5) Gubernatorial appointment: Massachusetts (high court) and California. (6) Gubernatorial appointment with legislative approval: Delaware, Kansas (intermediate appellate court), Maine, New Jersey,[4] and Tennessee. (7) Legislative election: South Carolina and Virginia.

[1] In 2016, North Carolina changed its method of appellate selection from nonpartisan election to partisan election, effective with the 2018 election cycle.

[2] In 2016, West Virginia changed its method of appellate selection from partisan elections to nonpartisan elections.

[3] In 2015, Tennessee changed its method of appellate selection from judicial nominating commission to gubernatorial appointment with legislative approval.

[4] In New Jersey, the governor appoints trial court judges (superior) and state supreme court justices with legislative confirmation. The chief justice of the New Jersey Supreme Court elevates trial court judges to the intermediate appellate bench (appellate division). The method of selection for appellate division judges is coded the same as the state supreme court.

were more likely to reach the bench under merit selection, but Black females fared better in electoral systems (pp. 53–54, 66).

A second account suggests that judicial nominating commissions decrease descriptive representation in state appellate courts. Prior studies show that white men fare better in states that use judicial nominating commissions (Graham 1991, p. 330; Martin and Pyle 2002, p. 48). A study of Florida's reforms to its merit selection process found that the post reforms mattered for increasing the presence of women on the appellate courts, but no comparable patterns were found for Black or Hispanic appointments (Salokar, Berggren, and DePalo 2006). The lack of a relationship between merit selection and descriptive representation is supported by other studies (Hurwitz and Lanier 2008).

Studies examining the effects of state selection methods on gender representation indicate that they are not necessarily identical to those of race (Bratton and Spill 2002; Hurwitz and Lanier 2003, 2008; Martin and Pyle 2002; Williams 2007). Early studies by Alozie (1990, 1996) found that judicial selection methods alone did not explain the distribution of women, Black, and Hispanic judges, although larger court sizes produced gender-diverse courts. Similarly, Hurwitz and Lanier (2003) reported no association between selection effects on descriptive representation in state appellate courts; but larger court sizes increased representation for women and nonwhites. When taking existing gender diversity into account, Bratton and Spill (2002) found that women had a substantially higher chance of being appointed to a vacancy on a state supreme court but once diversity was achieved, the chances of women being appointed dropped. Unlike prior studies, Bratton and Spill (2002) found that the appointment method of selection served to diversify all-male courts. Williams (2007) reported that selection effects on gender diversity worked differently at the trial and appellate levels – nonpartisan elections affected women's representation in trial courts, while merit selection affected women's representation in appellate courts. Goelzhauser (2011) found that states were more likely to seat their first Black and female justice under the following conditions: (1) when there were more frequent openings on the courts, (2) partisan election systems tended to seat Black justices sooner in states with liberal citizens, and (3) judicial nominating commissions tended to seat Black justices sooner.

A third account, the eligible pool theory, posits that women and persons of color have been subjected to a history of discrimination in the legal profession; therefore, the candidate pool of licensed attorneys in the state who are eligible to meet the requirements for judicial office explains the presence of women and persons of color on state courts. The eligible pool hypothesis has produced mixed results in the literature. Alozie (1990) found support for the relationship between Black and Hispanic judges' presence in state courts relative to their share of lawyers in the state; however, this relationship was not substantiated for the presence of women judges in state supreme courts (Alozie 1996, Hurwitz and Lanier 2003). Graham's (1991) study found a significant but weaker relationship between the presence of Black trial judges in state courts and the percentage of Black attorneys in the state. Martin and Pyle's (2002) findings supported the eligible pool explanation for the increase in women on state supreme courts, and comparable results were reported for women judges in state trial and appellate courts (Williams 2007). Alternatively, Bratton and Spill's (2008) findings did not comport with the eligible pool explanation when examining existing gender diversity in state supreme courts.[6]

Despite the similarities in the research questions investigated in prior studies, the resulting findings are quite mixed and have distinct empirical implications. The difficulty in drawing causal inferences from these studies is that they vary considerably in the: (1) state court under investigation (trial versus appellate), (2) research designs and methods used to investigate the hypotheses, and (3) important distinctions in how selection arrangements are categorized. We are less interested in offering a critique of extant work, but rather how prior research findings might inform our research design that focuses on a previously unexplored approach to the problem – using an intersectional framework to investigate judicial selection effects.

HYPOTHESES, DATA, AND METHODS

Our account of state appellate representation is grounded in Crenshaw's (1989, 1991) critical race theory legal scholarship and pathbreaking work that coined the concept of "intersectionality." Intersectionality examines overlapping systems of subordination that women of color face on a number of different dimensions. As applied to this research, intersectionality is an analytical lens used to examine how women of color are situated within two systems of subordination: racism and sexism. Consistent with Crenshaw's (1991) framework, women of color can experience discrimination in ways that are both similar to and different from those experiences of white women and men of color; yet women of color experience double-discrimination – the combined effects of practices which marginalize, discriminate, and subordinate on

6 We did not test for eligibility pool effects in our models due to the lack of reliable data at the state level.

the basis of race and sex (pp. 149–50).[7] Intersectional approaches seeking to advance our understanding of women of color as political actors and participants in the political process are becoming more visible in political science scholarship (Brown 2014; Hardy-Fanta et al. 2006; Hancock 2007; Lien 2015; Smooth 2006). Swain and Lien (2017) adopted an intersectional framework to explain the impact of a political institution's structural design on representation of women of color at the subnational level.

Because of the invisible status of women of color in the state judicial representation literature, far less is known about how the structural and institutional environment shape their ascension to the state bench. In addition, the extent to which structural arrangements influence women of color's ascension to the state appellate bench cannot be so easily deduced from studies which focused more generally on women judges or other groups. Despite these shortcomings, we argue that appellate descriptive representation will vary systematically by privileged identities and structural arrangements. A *structural arrangement hypothesis* expects that the presence of women of color in appellate courts will be higher in states that use methods of judicial selection designed to promote judicial accountability. Proponents of judicial accountability selection arrangements argue that electing judges is more democratic (Bonneau and Hall 2009). We expect partisan elections to bolster the representation of women of color in state appellate courts, whereas nonpartisan elections are expected to disadvantage women of color who benefit from party affiliation on the ballot and campaign support.

Descriptive representation is a product of both statewide and district-level constituencies in which candidates for appellate judgeships are appointed and run for election. In Table 3.3, we present data on the geographical basis for selecting appellate judges broken down by type of court. Examining the data at the aggregate level, 47 percent of the appellate judges were selected statewide, whereas 53 percent were selected in judicial districts. When we examined the data by type of court, we found that most state supreme court justices were selected statewide (77 percent), but intermediate appellate court judges are more likely to be selected in states using judicial districts. When we examined the data by race and gender, we found that women of color are more likely to be selected statewide (83 percent) to state supreme courts

7 The experiences of women of color examined in our analysis are nuanced and complex; therefore, important variations among African-American, Latina, Asian-American, South Asian American, and Native American women may affect their ability to obtain seats in state appellate courts. In our study, we do not examine intergroup differences due to the lack of a critical mass among women judges of color.

TABLE 3.3 *Geographic basis for selecting appellate judges by court type*

Geographic Basis of Selection	White Men(%)	White Women(%)	Men of Color(%)	Women of Color(%)
State Supreme Court				
Statewide	75.9	79.6	72.0	83.3
	(151)	(78)	(18)	(15)
District	24.1	20.4	28.0	16.7
	(48)	(20)	(7)	(3)
Intermediate Appellate Court				
Statewide	34.1	37.9	41.8	40.3
	(182)	(105)	(28)	(31)
District	65.9	62.1	58.2	59.7
	(351)	(172)	(39)	(46)

Note: Data on the geographic basis for selecting state appellate court judges is taken from the National Center for State Courts website, Judicial Selection in the States, www.judicialselection.us.

compared to the other categories. At the intermediate appellate court level, men and women of color are more likely to ascend to the bench using statewide selection compared to the other categories.

In partisan election states, Black and Latino voters argue that statewide races for appellate judgeships dilute their voting strength and deny them the opportunity to elect judges of their choice (Graham 1991). We expect that women of color will be less constrained by district-level selection in obtaining seats in appellate courts, whereas statewide selection will advantage privileged identities.

Structural arrangements designed to promote judicial independence include judicial nominating commissions (Tarr 2012). Prior studies found that judicial nominating commissions decrease descriptive representation in appellate courts (Bratton and Spill 2002; Champagne 2009, p. 557; Williams 2007). We expect that selection systems that add more vetting processes with nominating commissions and require legislative approval of judicial nominees will introduce both racial and gendered biases to the kinds of judges that serve in a particular state.

Judicial selection arrangements do not operate in isolation of the political culture of the state. A *partisan selection hypothesis* asserts that Democratic governors are more likely to appoint women of color to state appellate courts.

It is well documented that Democratic governors are more likely to make judicial appointments based on race and gender compared to their Republican counterparts (Bratton and Spill, 2002; Holmes and Emrey 2006; Salokar, Berggren, and DePalo 2006). Governors make cross-party appointments to appeal to certain segments of the electorate (McLeod 2012). Even in nonpartisan election contests, Lovrich, Sheldon, and Wasmann (1988) found a close association between attitudes favoring more minorities on the bench and partisan affiliation (p. 816). To this end, we expect that partisan effects are important for the ascension of women of color to the appellate bench.

We posit that state selection systems and partisan forces inherently not only bias certain judicial identities over others, but also can present opportunities for intersectionally marginalized groups to become appellate judges. To examine the state selection structures that are associated with each type of identity, we use four logistic regression models of the following intersectional identities: (1) white men, (2) white women, (3) men of color, and (4) women of color. That is, we are interested in ascertaining the conditions under which each group serves as appellate judges. To test our hypotheses, we use individual-level data collected by the authors on all judges serving on state courts of last resort ($N = 340$) and intermediate appellate courts ($N = 954$) in the fifty states as of October 2017 (1,294 cases for analysis). Biographical and judicial selection data were obtained from a variety of sources, including official state court websites, the National Center for State Courts judicial selection data, online newspapers, and judicial directories.

To explore the effects of structural arrangements on descriptive representation, we control for a state's method to select an appellate judge based on the full-term method of selection (Goelzhauser 2011; Hurwitz and Lanier 2003, 2008). We indicate whether a state has partisan elections, nonpartisan elections, gubernatorial appointment with or without legislative approval, judicial nominating commissions with or without legislative approval, and legislative elections.

To test the partisan selection hypothesis, we recorded the political party of the governor for each state and every year (1976–2017). For each year, we indicate whether a state has a Democratic governor (1) or otherwise (0). Observations coded as "otherwise" are mostly Republican governors, as only 0.14 percent of the total state-years were Independents.

To explore institutional effects, we control for the total number of seats in a state's appellate system. The number of judges on appellate courts is a function of state size – the "big" states will always have more appellate seats than the "small states." In this study, court size ranges from 5–9 seats for state supreme courts and 3–100 seats for intermediate appellate courts. Several studies found court size influenced judicial diversity (Alozie 1996,

Hurwitz and Lanier 2003, Bratton and Spill 2002, Williams 2007, Goelzhauser 2011). Smaller court sizes make selection more competitive, thus reducing opportunities to diversify the courts. We expect to find that women of color are more likely judges in states that have more court seats than fewer court seats.

Previous studies have explored the influence of state political culture on judicial diversity. Of particular significance is the state's overall political climate measured in terms of ideology. More liberal states were found to have higher levels of gender and racial representation (Bratton and Spill 2002, Goelzhauser 2011). States that are politically liberal tend to lean Democratic. The Berry et al. (2010) citizen ideology scores are used as a directional measure of state ideology. Higher scores on a 0–100 scale indicate more liberal states, while lower scores indicate more conservative ones. We posit that more liberal states are more likely to increase descriptive representation, especially with regards to women of color. We input a state's ideology score each year between 1976 and 2017. State ideology scores of Berry et al. (2010), though, are only publicly available until 2013. To account for this, we calculate a five-year average of each state's ideology from 2009 and 2013 and input the average into each year between 2014 and 2017.

Lastly, judges of color are relative newcomers to the state appellate bench, especially at the state supreme court level (Martin and Pyle 2002). Bratton and Spill (2002) found support for the newcomer effect in the context of gender diversity on state supreme courts. The newcomer effect suggests that the entry of judges of color into the upper echelons of the state judicial hierarchy is more recent compared to privileged identities and it takes longer for them to overcome obstacles to obtaining appellate judgeships. We measure the newcomer effect by the year the judge was initially selected to the appellate bench – from 1976 until 2017. We expect that women of color are more likely to have obtained their appellate positions in later years.

Our statistical models assume that judges are influenced in part by the state partisan and selection structures in which they are nested. Due to the multilevel structure of the data, we use multilevel mixed models with logistic regression to compute unbiased standard errors for model coefficients (Raudenbush and Bryk 2002, Steenbergen and Jones 2002). We use a random effects model that estimates separate intercepts for each state, which are permitted to vary.

RESULTS

Table 3.4 provides the results from multilevel models of the conditions under which state appellate judges serve. Coefficients are estimated using

TABLE 3.4 *Results from multilevel models of structural, partisan, and institutional conditions under which appellate judges serve*

	White Men	White Women	Men of Color	Women of Color
	coef. (s.e.)	*coef. (s.e.)*	*coef. (s.e.)*	*coef. (s.e.)*
Governor Appoints	1.11 (1.02)	7.73 (1.17)	0.13 (0.84)*	4.74 (1.33)
Nominating Commission	0.54 (0.45)	3.02 (0.54)*	0.69 (0.68)	1.03 (0.65)
Nonpartisan Election	0.73 (0.34)	3.58 (0.39)**	0.21 (0.57)**	1.25 (0.59)
Partisan Election	0.38 (0.36)**	5.22 (0.43)***	0.34 (0.63)	3.95 (0.57)*
District System	1.32 (0.29)	0.75 (0.33)	0.74 (0.65)	1.22 (0.51)
Governor is a Democrat	0.30 (0.17)***	2.15 (0.16)***	2.52 (0.30)**	2.43 (0.31)**
State Ideology	1.01 (0.01)	0.99 (0.01)	1.01 (0.02)	1.02 (0.02)
Year Selected	1.00 (0.01)	0.98 (0.01)	1.01 (0.02)	1.05 (0.02)*
Court Size	1.00 (0.00)	1.00 (0.01)	1.00 (0.01)	1.00 (0.01)
cut1	4.10 (19.64)	-33.28 (20.14)	21.01 (42.36)	95.55 (38.80)*
Wald X^2	59.00***	52.92***	33.75***	30.44***
Level 1 Observations	2793	2793	2793	2793
Level 2 Observations	50	50	50	50

Notes: Exponentiated coefficients; bootstrapped standard errors in parentheses. The base group, represented by the constant term, includes states that have Republican governors, select judges statewide, and in which the legislature either confirms appointments of the governor or nominating commissions, or in which there are legislative elections.
$^{*}p < 0.05$, $^{**}p < 0.01$, $^{***}p < 0.001$.

bootstrapped standard errors and expressed as odds ratios. Coefficients larger than one indicate an increasing likelihood that an appellate judge serves in a state while coefficients lesser than one indicate a decreasing likelihood. The base group, represented by the constant term, includes states that have Republican governors, select judges statewide, and in which the legislature either confirms appointments of the governor or confirms nominating commissions appointees, or in which there are legislative elections.

The results provide strong evidence for our partisan selection hypothesis. Compared to states that involve the legislature in judicial selection, women of color are more than three times more likely to become judges in states with partisan elections (b = 3.95, s.e. = 0.57, $p < 0.05$). They are also more than twice as likely to become appellate judges in states with Democratic governors (b = 2.43, s.e. = 0.31, $p < 0.01$). In contrast, white men are more likely to become appellate judges in states with Republican governors (b = 0.30, s.e. = 0.05, $p < 0.001$). They are also more likely to become judges in states that involve the legislature in judicial selection in comparison to states that have partisan elections (b = 0.38, s.e. = 0.14, $p < 0.01$). Lastly, we find support for the newcomer effect, as females of color are more likely to become judges more recently than in the past (b = 1.05, s.e. = 0.02, $p < 0.05$).

While the results provide evidence that partisan forces are associated with the ascension of women of color to the appellate bench, they also indicate that their window of opportunity is relatively smaller than the other groups of judges. White women and men of color have other routes to the bench. White women (b = 2.15, s.e. = 0.16, $p < 0.001$) and men of color (b = 2.52, s.e. = 0.30, $p < 0.01$) are also more likely to become judges in states with Democratic governors. What is more, white women are more likely to become appellate judges in states with not only partisan elections, but also other states with nonpartisan elections (b = 3.58, s.e. = 0.39, $p < 0.001$) and nominating commissions (b = 3.02, s.e. = 0.54, $p < 0.05$). Lastly, appellate judges who are men of color are also afforded an opportunity to benefit in states that involve the legislature in judicial selection in comparison to states with gubernatorial appointments and partisan elections.

The presence of judges in appellate courts is unaffected by state ideology. This finding accentuates the structural and partisan thesis since citizen ideology does not capture partisan control of political institutions. We contend that liberal forces – as they give rise to Democratic governors – help the ascension of women of color to the appellate bench. Contrary to our expectations, court size did not matter for race or gender. This finding may be explained in part by examining the differences in the geographic basis of selection for state supreme courts and intermediate appellate courts. State supreme court judges are disproportionately selected statewide (77 percent), whereas 63 percent of intermediate appellate judges are selected using judicial districts. Another factor to consider is whether appellate judicial districts are drawn in such a way that dilute the voting strength of district-level constituencies.

CONCLUSION

The models of descriptive representation presented in this study demonstrate the utility of an intersectional approach to the study of race and gender in state judicial selection. Having tested the assumption that intersectional analyses matter, the results support our hypotheses about the interplay between structural and partisan effects in state appellate selection. Mainly, our results show that partisan effects are important for the ascension of women of color to the state appellate bench. However, our results should be interpreted to mean that preexisting structural conditions narrow their window of opportunity. Clearly, partisan forces have helped more men of color and white women to become appellate judges; however, these groups are also afforded more routes to become appellate judges compared to women of color.

Our research provides much-needed insights on the effects of structural arrangements on descriptive representation in state courts. Previously considered to be an open question, our results provide strong evidence that formal, full-term methods of state appellate selection influence descriptive representation when examined from an intersectional perspective. Structural arrangements that reflect democratic accountability values such as partisan elections are more likely to increase the presence of women of color in state appellate courts, whereas structural arrangements that promote judicial independence or require additional vetting by state legislatures decrease the opportunities for women of color to become appellate judges. Given the complex nature of state judicial selection arrangements, we contend that scholars must define selection mechanisms in theoretically defensible categories.

This study raises more scholarly interest in the relationship between structural and political effects on the ability of persons of color to attain seats in the state judicial hierarchy. One line of future inquiry could examine the systematic effects of structural and partisan forces in state judicial selection and intersectional theorizing from an inter-group perspective, since we do not assume that important differences do not exist among the paths taken by women of color to the state bench. A similar intersectional approach could be applied to descriptive representation at the state trial court level. Given the importance of partisan elections as a path to the appellate bench for women of color, more research is needed to understand the relationship between money in judicial elections and underrepresentation in state courts.

REFERENCES

Alozie, Nicolas O. 1988. "Black Representation on State Judiciaries." *Social Science Quarterly* 69 (4): 979–86.

1990. "Distribution of Women and Minority Judges: The Effects of Judicial Selection Methods." *Social Science Quarterly* 71 (2): 315–25.

1996. "Selection Methods and the Recruitment of Women to State Courts of Last Resort." *Social Science Quarterly* 77 (1): 115–26.

Baum, Lawrence. 1983. "The Electoral Fates of Incumbent Judges in the Ohio Court of Common Pleas." *Judicature* 66 (April): 42–50.

Berry, William D. et al. 2010. "Measuring Citizen and Government Ideology in the U.S. States: A Re-appraisal." *State Politics & Policy Quarterly* 10 (2): 117–35.

Bonneau, Chris W., and Melinda Gann Hall. 2009. *In Defense of Judicial Elections*. New York: Routledge.

Bratton, Kathleen A., and Rorie L. Spill. 2002. "Existing Diversity and Judicial Selection: The Role of Appointment Method in Establishing Gender Diversity in State Supreme Courts." *Social Science Quarterly* 83 (2): 504–18.

Brown, Nadia. 2014. "Political Participation of Women of Color: An Intersectional Analysis." *Journal of Women, Politics & Policy* 35 (4): 315–48.

Champagne, Anthony. 1988. "Judicial Reform in Texas." *Judicature* 70 (3): 146–59.

2009. "Parties, Interest Groups, and Systemic Change." *Missouri Law Review* 74 (3): 555–62.

Crenshaw, Kimberle. 1989. "Demarginalizing the Intersection of Race and Sex: A Black Feminist Critique of Antidiscrimination Doctrine, Feminist Theory and Antiracist Politics." *University of Chicago Legal Forum* 1989 (1): 139–67.

1991. "Mapping the Margins: Intersectionality, Identity Politics, and Violence against Women of Color." *Stanford Law Review* 43 (6): 1241–99.

Dubois, Philip L. 1980. *From Ballot to Bench: Judicial Elections and the Quest for Accountability*. Austin: University of Texas Press.

Epstein, Lee, Jack Knight, and Olga Shvetsova. 2002. "Selecting Selection Systems." In *Judicial Independence at the Crossroads: An Interdisciplinary Approach*, eds. Stephen B. Burbank and Barry Friedman. Thousand Oaks, CA: Sage Publications.

Gabriel, Trip. 2017. "In North Carolina, Republicans Stung by Court Rulings Aim to Change the Judges." *The New York Times*, October 18.

George, Tracey, and Albert H. Yoon. 2016. *The Gavel Gap: Who Sits in Judgment on State Courts?* Washington, DC: American Constitution Society for Law and Policy.

Goelzhauser, Greg. 2011. "Diversifying State Supreme Courts." *Law and Society Review* 45 (3): 761–81.

Graham, Barbara L. 1990. "Do Judicial Selection Systems Matter? A Study of Black Representation on State Courts." *American Politics Quarterly* 18 (3): 316–36.

1991. "Federal Court Policy-Making and Political Equality: An Analysis of Judicial Redistricting." *Political Research Quarterly* 44 (1): 101–17.

Hancock, Ange-Marie. 2007. "When Multiplication Doesn't Equal Quick Addition: Examining Intersectionality as a Research Paradigm." *Perspectives on Politics* 5 (1): 63–79.

Holmes, Lisa M., and Jolly A. Emrey. 2006. "Court Diversification: Staffing the State Courts of Last through Interim Appointments." *Justice System Journal* 27 (1): 1–13.

Hurwitz, Mark S., and Drew Noble Lanier. 2003. "Explaining Judicial Diversity: The Differential Ability of Women and Minorities to Attain Seats on State Supreme and Appellate Courts." *State Politics & Policy Quarterly* 3 (4): 329–52.

2008. "Diversity in State and Federal Appellate Courts: Change and Continuity across 20 Years." *Justice System Journal* 29 (1): 47–70.

Hardy-Fanta, Carol, Pei-te Lien, Dianne M. Pinderhughes, and Christine Marie Sierra. 2006. "Gender, Race, and Descriptive Representation in the United States: Findings from the Gender and Multicultural Leadership Project." *Journal of Women, Politics & Policy* 28 (3/4): 7–41.

Ifill, Sherrilyn A. 1997. "Judging the Judges: Racial Diversity, Impartiality and Representation on State Trial Courts." *Boston College Law Review* 39 (1): 95–149.

2000. "Racial Diversity on the Bench: Beyond Role Models and Public Confidence." *Washington and Lee Law Review* 57 (2): 405–95.

Lien, Pei-te. 2015. "Reassessing Descriptive Representation by Women and Men of Color: New Evidence at the Subnational Level." *Urban Affairs Review* 51 (2): 239–62.

Lovrich, Nicholas P., Charles H. Sheldon, and Erik Wasmann. 1988. "The Racial Factor in Nonpartisan Judicial Elections: A Research Note." *Western Political Quarterly* 41 (4): 807–16.

Mansbridge, Jane. 1999. "Should Blacks Represent Blacks and Women Represent Women? A Contingent 'Yes.'" *Journal of Politics* 61 (3): 628–57.

Martin, Elaine, and Barry Pyle. 2002. "Gender and Racial Diversification of State Supreme Courts." *Women and Politics* 24 (2): 35–52.

McLeod, Aman. 2012. "The Party on the Bench: Partisanship, Judicial Selection Commissions, and State High-Court Appointments." *Justice System Journal* 33 (3): 262–74.

Nelson, Michael J., Rachel Paine Caufield, and Andrew D. Martin. 2013. "OH, MI: A Note on Empirical Examinations of Judicial Elections." *State Politics & Policy Quarterly* 13 (4): 495–11.

Palmer, Barbara. 2001. "'To Do Justly': The Integration of Women into the American Judiciary." *PS: Political Science and Politics* 34 (2): 235–239.

Phillips, Anne. 1995. *The Politics of Presence*. New York: Oxford University Press.

Pitkin, Hanna F. 1967. *The Concept of Representation*. Berkeley: University of California Press.

Raudenbush, Stephen W., and Anthony S. Bryk. 2002. *Hierarchical Linear Models: Applications and Data Analysis Methods*, Volume 1. Thousand Oaks, CA: Sage Publications, Inc.

Rhode, Deborah L. 2015. *The Trouble with Lawyers*. New York: Oxford University Press.

Salokar, Rebecca Mae, D. Jason Berggren, and Kathryn A. DePalo. 2006. "The New Politics of Judicial Selection in Florida: Merit Selection Redefined." *Justice System Journal* 27 (2): 123–42.

Scherer, Nancy, and Brett Curry. 2010. "Does Descriptive Race Representation Enhance Institutional Legitimacy? The Case of U.S. Courts." *Journal of Politics* 72 (1): 90–104.

Sheldon, Charles H., and Linda S. Maule. 1997. *Choosing Justice: The Recruitment of State and Federal Judges*. Pullman: Washington State University Press.

Slotnick, Elliot E. 1984. "Judicial Selection Systems and Nomination Outcomes: Does the Process Make a Difference? *American Politics Quarterly* 12 (2): 225–40.

Smooth, Wendy. 2006. "Intersectionality in Electoral Politics: A Mess Worth Making." *Politics & Gender* 2 (3): 400–14.

Steenbergen, Marco R,. and Bradford S. Jones. 2002. "Modeling Multilevel Data Structures." *American Journal of Political Science* 46 (1): 218–37.

Streb, Matthew J. 2007. "Partisan Involvement in Partisan and Nonpartisan Trial Court Elections." In *Running for Judge: The Rising Political, Financial and Legal Stakes in Judicial Elections*, ed. Matthew J. Streb. New York: New York University Press.

Streb, Matthew J., and Brian Frederick. 2009. "Conditions for Competition in Low–Information Judicial Elections: The Case of Intermediate Appellate Courts." *Political Research Quarterly* 62 (3): 523–37.

Swain, Katie E. O., and Pei-te Lien. 2017. "Structural and Contextual Factors Regarding the Accessibility of Elective Office for Women of Color at the Local Level." *Journal of Women, Politics & Policy* 38 (2): 128–50.

Tarr, G. Alan. 2012. *Without Fear or Favor: Judicial Independence and Judicial Accountability in the States*. Stanford, CA: Stanford University Press.

Williams, Margaret. 2007. "Women's Representation on State Trial and Appellate Courts." *Social Science Quarterly* 88 (5): 1192–204.

4

LGBT Judges in the United States

DONALD P. HAIDER-MARKEL AND PATRICK GAUDING

The past thirty years have witnessed a remarkable expansion of descriptive and substantive representation for LGBT people in American politics (Haider-Markel 2007, 2010). A significant literature has developed analyzing the rise of LGBT candidates and office-holders, particularly in legislative races and offices (Bailey and Nawara 2017; Button, Wald, and Rienzo 1999; Casey and Reynolds 2015; Corrales 2017; Everitt and Camp 2014; Golebiowska 2001, 2002; Golebiowska and Thomsen 1999; Haider-Markel 2000, 2010; Haider-Markel and Bright 2014; Haider-Markel, Joslyn, and Kniss 2000; Haider-Markel et al. 2017; Herrick and Thomas 1999; Perry and Manley 2017; Reynolds 2013; Snell 2017). However, the study of LGBT representation in the United States has, to date, largely neglected the presence of LGBT judges on the bench (but see Clendinen and Nagourney 2001; Smith and Haider-Markel 2002). With this in mind, we seek to explore the history of LGBT representation in the American judicial system. We ask: How have LGBT judges come to occupy judicial seats? What are the substantive effects of LGBT judges? What do LGBT judges mean for LGBT representation more broadly?

To answer these questions, we first outline our theoretical perspective on the representation of marginalized groups in government. We then examine systemic data on where and how LGBT judges have served. We turn to case studies to explore how LGBT judges have obtained their offices, highlighting some particularly notable judges. Finally, we conclude with a prospective on the future of LGBT representation on the bench.

GROUP REPRESENTATION IN GOVERNMENT

The representation of groups in society and their interests within government matters for both governments and citizens. For a representative democracy to function effectively, its populace must trust that its public servants, both elected and appointed, act in accordance with the preferences of the mass public, or in the interest of the rule of law (Pitkin 1967).

Much of the representation literature is focused on descriptive representation among elected officials. Simply put, this literature examines whether elected representatives share similar characteristics with the general citizenry, including race, sex, gender identity, ethnicity, religion, and sexual orientation (Hayes and Lawless 2016; Thomas and Wilcox 2014). For example, if the percentage of women in a legislature is similar to the percentage of women in the population, the legislature can be said to be descriptively representative of the population. Likewise, constituents that have an elected representative that shares important characteristics with them can be said to be descriptively represented. The implication is that a group's interest will be best (substantively) represented in government by a member of that group (Bratton and Ray 2002).

Research does suggest that increased descriptive representation of a group does have positive consequences for group interests in government (Haider-Markel 2010; Preuhs 2006) and in how members of the group view government and government policy (Gay 2002). Likewise, increased representation for a group in non-elected government positions is also associated with more positive outcomes for the group and a greater perception of legitimacy for government actions (Riccucci, Van Ryzin, and Lavena 2014; Rocha and Hawes 2009).

Of course, courts play an especially important role in the American system of representative democracy; judges can descriptively represent a group in the population but must also adhere to the rule of law. Existing research has explored the impact of descriptive representation on the bench in regards to gender, race, and ethnicity. The findings of these studies are not consistent, but frequently find that the characteristics of judges shape their decision-making and the composition of courts influences judicial behavior and court rulings (Boyd, Epstein, and Martin 2010).

For example, increased female representation in the courts does have a notable impact (Haire and Moyer 2015; Hoekstra 2010; Kenny 2013). Allen and Wall (1993) examine the decision making of female judges and find that female judges more frequently act as outsiders (holding extreme positions on issues relative to the majority of the court) as opposed to being tokens, who moderate their votes in an effort to align with the majority. They find that female justices rule in a liberal direction on women's issues. On criminal rights and economic issues, the pattern was more nuanced; female Democratic judges were more liberal than their male counterparts, but female Republicans were more conservative than their male colleagues. The authors concluded that female judges take an outsider position in reaching decisions, which may be a reflection of ambition and previous struggle in a male-dominated field, but is also likely the result of female judges perceiving a need to educate their male colleagues as to how their decisions affect women (Allen and Wall 1987, p. 243).

The substantive effects of increased gender representation extend behind the presence of a single female judge. McCall and McCall (2007), for example, observe that the increased presence of female judges on a court liberalizes decisions in Fourth Amendment cases across all female judges. Building on critical mass theory, which suggests that increased descriptive representation only leads to increased substantive representation when the proportion of members reaches a particular level, they argue that female state supreme court justices significantly influence court decisions only once a certain number of female judges are present (McCall and McCall 2007, p. 68; see also Collins, Manning, and Carp 2010).

Similarly, increased racial and ethnic representation on the bench can have substantive effects on decisions when nonwhite judges are involved (Haire and Moyer 2015). Kastellec (2013) demonstrates that the presence of a Black judge on an appellate panel all but ensures that the panel will rule for the plaintiff in affirmative action cases. He compares rulings in cases with and without the presence of Black judges, finding substantive differences in the direction of the ruling when Black judges are on panels. Kastellec (2013) argues that the observed effect is likely the result of Black judges liberalizing the opinions of non-Black judges in deliberation. The institutional effects of panel ruling at the panel level force the interaction of judges in deciding opinions, thus forcing the presence of representation into decision rendering. However, Kastellec (2013) observes stronger effects with only one Black judge on a panel as opposed to two. This finding supports the perspective that a token representative of a group might have more impact than the critical mass suggested by the gender representation literature.

However, other research is less consistent in finding that the race or ethnicity of judges influences outcomes (Farhang and Wawro 2004). For example, Morin (2014) finds mixed results on the effects of minority judges: while Black judges are more likely to rule in favor of Black claimants, the impact of Latino judges is less consistent. Similarly, Farhang and Wawro (2004) find gender effects similar to Kastellec (2013), wherein a single woman on a panel will liberalize panel decision more than two or more women. However, they find no effects for race.

Beyond the influence of diversity on judicial decision-making, there is also evidence to suggest that diversity on the bench can enhance confidence in court decisions and institutional legitimacy. Schere and Curry (2009) use an experiment to manipulate the race of judges in a case. Black participants in the experiment perceived the federal courts as more legitimate if more African-Americans were judges. Interestingly, the influence of racial diversity on the perceptions of white participants was conditioned by ideology.

Our brief review of the literature on representation in the courts suggests two points to highlight. First, the influence of group representation on decision-making and policy is likely conditional on a number of factors, including whether descriptive representation in an institution is one person or several. Additionally, increased gender, racial, or ethnic diversity on the bench will likely influence judicial decision-making, but the institutional constraints of the office and the processes by which judges achieve their posts (appointment or election) can dramatically reduce variation across judges (Haire and Moyer 2015). Second, even if increased representation on previously marginalized groups has limited substantive impact on the behavior of judges or courts, the evidence strongly suggests that increased diversity does shape citizens' perception of the institution and its legitimacy.

Informed by research on judicial diversity, we can turn to representation of LGBT people in government. Previous work has documented the rise of LGBT representation at the local, state, and national levels (Button, Wald, and Rienzo 1999; Haider-Markel 2000, 2007, 2010; Haider-Markel and Bright 2014; Haider-Markel, Joslyn, and Kniss 2000; Perry and Manley 2017; Rayside 1998; Smith and Haider-Markel 2002). In addition, the qualitative and quantitative evidence suggests that an increased number of LGBT elected officials is associated with substantive policy impact and favorable policy outcomes for the LGBT community (Haider-Markel 2007, 2010; Haider-Markel and Bright 2014; Haider-Markel, Joslyn, and Kniss 2000). Part of the increased substantive representation occurs through the advocacy of LGBT officials, but another portion occurs indirectly – the presence of openly LGBT officials as role models changes the behavior of other officials within government (Haider-Markel 2010; Haider-Markel and Bright 2014) and may change the attitudes and perception of citizens.

Given the pattern of outcomes observed in research on openly LGBT elected officials, as well as the findings in research on judicial diversity, we should expect that appointing and electing more LGBT judges would better ensure that the concerns of the LGBT community are reflected in judicial decision-making and the rulings of courts. However, we know very little about LGBT judges, including how many there are, where they are present, and whether or not an increase in LGBT representation on the bench leads to different outcomes relative to non-LGBT judges. Moreover, we know little about what the public might think of LGBT judges or how institutional features of courts or the judicial selection process might inhibit LGBT representation on the bench, or shape the decision-making of LGBT judges once in office. As such, our effort here is to provide a foundational understanding of LGBT judges in the United States. We also suggest that institutional mechanisms for selecting judges (appointment vs. election) might play a role in LGBT representation on the bench.

We do note that judicial selection, although substantively important for citizens, is viewed as less salient than elections of officials for other offices. Some research, such as Brace and Boyea (2008), suggests direct linkages between judicial choices on the bench and the prospect of election or re-election, but this does not actually measure how voters respond to judges in elections. Moreover, the morass of varying judicial appointment processes (governor appointment, state senate confirmation of recommended candidates, etc.) or elections (direct elections, nonpartisan elections, retention elections) leads to an inability to generalize attitudes about judicial elections versus other elections. However, it is important to consider that potential LGBT judges may face more hurdles if the process of selection for office occurs through an election versus appointment.

PUBLIC ATTITUDES ON LGBT JUDGES

So what does the public think about appointed or elected LGBT judges? Our knowledge of attitudes towards LGBT judges is limited, but we do know that a solid majority of Americans would likely vote for an LGBT political candidate who shared their views in city council, state legislature, gubernatorial, and congressional races; support for transgender candidates averaged about 7 percent lower (Haider-Markel et al. 2017). Likewise, in 2008, 70 percent of likely voters in a national poll said they would support the nomination of a gay or lesbian candidate for a cabinet position in the national government (Haider-Markel 2010). These patterns at least suggest that most Americans would support the nomination of LGBT judges and perhaps vote for them in electoral contests.

We were able to locate one publicly available national poll that asked respondents about gay and lesbian judges. A 2011 national poll of American adults conducted for the Public Religion Research Institute asked respondents: "Now please tell me how comfortable you would be with a gay or lesbian person in the following roles in your community? Not at all comfortable (14%), Not too comfortable (12%), Somewhat comfortable (31%), Very comfortable (39%)"; about 3 percent of respondents didn't know or refused to

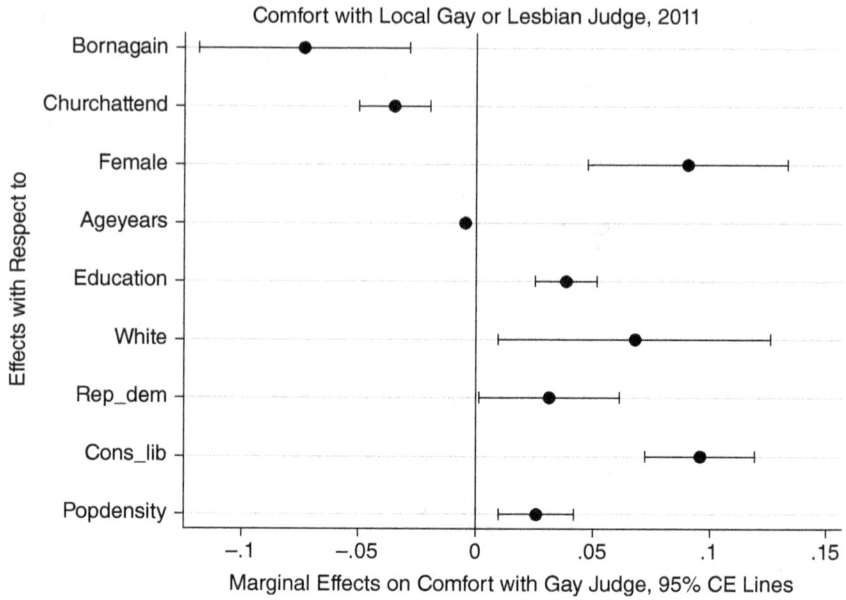

FIGURE 4.1 Comfort with local gay or lesbian judge, 2011

answer (Jones, Cox and Cook 2011). With 70 percent of respondents feeling at least somewhat comfortable, the poll results suggest that most Americans are not opposed to LGBT judges.

Since judges are viewed differently than politicians and appointed bureaucrats in the American system, we conducted a multivariate statistical analysis of responses to the survey question to see who is more likely to be comfortable with a gay or lesbian judge. Following analyses that examined support for LGBT candidates (Haider-Markel 2010; Haider-Markel et al. 2017), we controlled for respondent race (white), sex, education level, partisanship (rep_dem), political ideology (cons_liberal), being a born again Christian (born again), frequency of church attendance (churchattend), and whether the respondent lived in a rural or urban place (popdensity). For simplicity, we collapsed the question responses into two categories, uncomfortable (0) or comfortable (1).

We graphically display the results of this analysis with a post-estimation graph following a logit regression model displaying the average marginal effects of each variable (with lines for confidence intervals at the 95 percent level) in Figure 4.1. The positive side of the x-axis is the comfortable response and the negative side is the uncomfortable response. All of the variables in the model were statistically significant at the $p < 0.05$ level and the number of respondents was 1,321.[1] The results indicate that female, white, more educated, Democrats, liberals, and those living in urban areas are more likely to be comfortable with gay and lesbian judges. Frequent churchgoers, born again Christians, and older people are less likely to be comfortable. These results are very similar to those found for support for LGBT candidates (Haider-Markel 2010; Haider-Markel et al. 2017), and mirror the results for analysis we conducted of comfort with gay and lesbian candidates and police officers in the same survey.[2] In short, we have a fairly predictable profile of citizens more likely to support LGBT judges and those likely to oppose them.

SCOPE OF REPRESENTATION

At the national, state, and local level, at least some judges are appointed to the bench by officials in executive offices. The first appointment of an openly LGBT judge in the United States (and perhaps worldwide) was in 1979. California Governor Jerry Brown, against the advice of his advisors, appointed Stephen M. Lachs to the Los Angeles County Superior Court. Brown also appointed the first lesbian judge in 1981 and is credited for the appointment of three other openly gay or lesbian judges (Clendinen and Nagourney 2001).

Since 1979, many openly LGBT judges have been appointed or elected to office. To compile a database of LGBT judges, we began with data compiled for Haider-Markel (2010) and Haider-Markel and Bright (2014). We supplemented this data with media searches in *Associated Press Collections Online* and *Newspaper Source Plus*.[3] We only count judges that have been identified as LGBT in open-source news media. Our data represent the first attempt to build a comprehensive database of LGBT judges in the United States. The data are summarized in Figure 4.2.

We found 142 unique judges across 177 instances. Among these judges, twenty-six were appointed or elected to a separate judicial office.[4] A governor or a nominating commission initially appointed approximately 58 percent of these judges to the office, with the remaining 42 percent being elected straight to the bench. State judicial systems use a variety of selection mechanisms, including direct election, appointment with confirmation, and appointment

1 For the original logit model results, data, and replication files, contact Haider-Markel.

2 The results of the additional analysis can be obtained by contacting Donald Haider-Markel at dhmarkel@ku.edu.

3 Search terms included "judge AND gay," "judge AND lesbian," "judge AND bisexual," "judge AND transgender," and "judge AND LGBT."

4 One, Jonathan Lack, held a position in Alaska from 2008 to 2013 before resigning and moving to Washington to take a similar position.

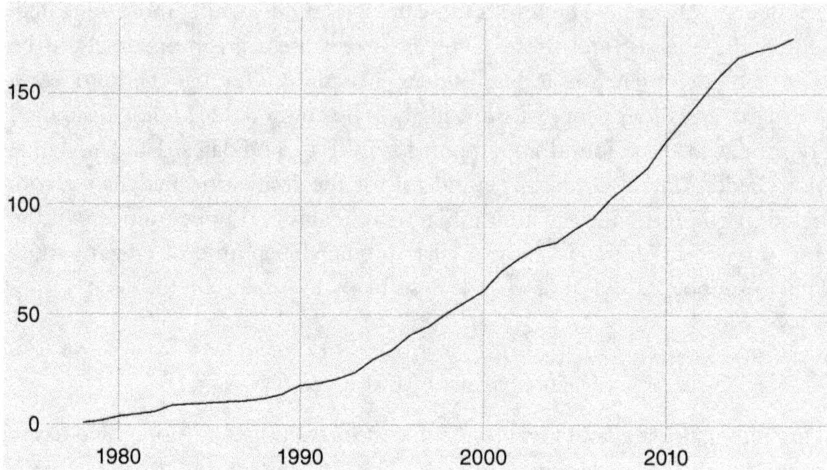

Notes: Compiled by the authors based on news media sources and elements of Haider-Markel (2000, 2010), Haider-Markel and Bright (2014), and Thompson (1994).

FIGURE 4.2 Cumulative appointments/elections of LGBT judges, 1979–2017

with retention elections. Because each state system varies, it is not likely that one could draw a useful comparison between the appointment to election ratios of LGBT judges as compared to judges generally. However, the initial appointment of LGBT judges is important in that it bypasses public opinion and provides the benefit of incumbency to the judge. In addition, we do know that incumbent LGBT officials are more likely to retain their positions in future elections (Haider-Markel 2010).

Figure 4.2 shows the cumulative number of LGBT judicial appointments and elections in the United States from 1979 forward. The slow but steady rise in positions through the 1980s into the mid 1990s tracks with the growing acceptance of LGBT persons in official government positions broadly (Haider-Markel 2010). As public approval of LGBT officials increased over time, it is possible that governors felt pressure to appoint LGBT judges, and that LGBT judicial candidates were more likely to run for office, at least in parts of the country that lean more liberal and are more urbanized.

Our database only includes two transgender judges, Phyllis Frye and Victoria Kolakowski. Frye was appointed to the Houston Municipal Court in 2010 by openly lesbian mayor Annise Parker and unanimously confirmed by the Houston City Council. Kolakowski was elected to the Alameda, California County Superior Court in 2010 and took office in 2011 (Sontag 2015). She is well known within the transgender legal community for her

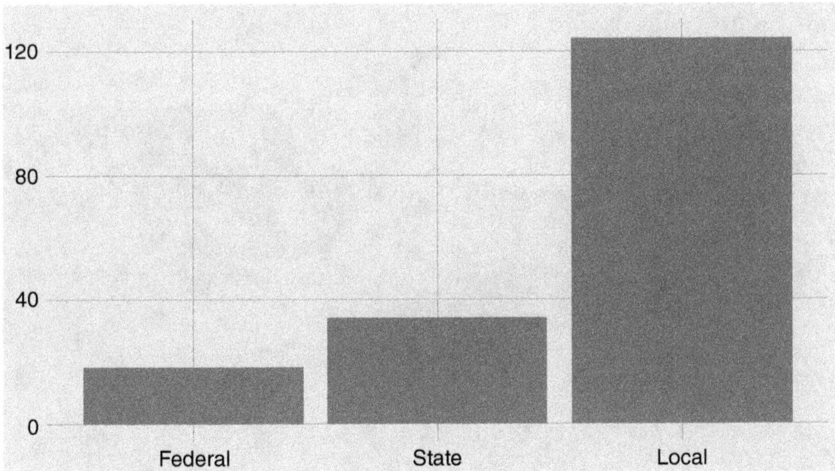

Notes: Compiled by the authors based on news media sources and elements of Haider-Markel (2000, 2010), Haider-Markel and Bright (2014), and Thompson (1994).

FIGURE 4.3 Number of openly LGBT judges by level of government, 1979–2017

organization and advocacy work on behalf of transgender individuals. She was initially prevented from sitting for the Louisiana Bar due to her transgender status, and sued to be able to take the exam. That there are so few transgender judges is perhaps not surprising, given that less than 0.6 of the U.S. population is transgender.[5] However, the ascendance of these two judges represents a major breakthrough for LGBT representation on the bench.

Because most judicial positions in the United States are at the local and state level, it is not surprising that this is where most LGBT judges have served, with the bulk at the local level (see Figure 4.3). However, there has been a notable increase in LGBT judges at the national level as well. In 1994, Deborah A. Batts became the first openly LGBT federal judge when she was nominated for U.S. District Court for the Southern District of New York by President Bill Clinton. From 1994 to 2009, Deborah Batts was the only openly LGBT judge on the federal bench, with Bill Clinton having declined to appoint any more LGBT judges, and George W. Bush having appointed none. The election of Barack Obama in 2008 led to the

[5] For estimates of the size of the transgender population see studies at the Williams Institute: http://williamsinstitute.law.ucla.edu/wp-content/uploads/How-Many-Adults-Identify-as-Transgender-in-the-United-States.pdf.

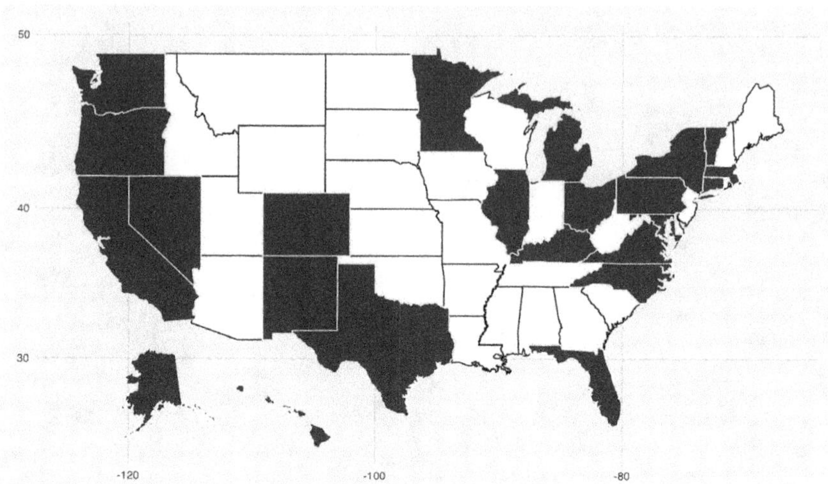

FIGURE 4.4 States with at least one LGBT judge, 1979–2017

appointment of eleven more LGBT judges (Grunwald 2016). In 2013, the Senate confirmed Obama nominee Todd M. Hughes to the Federal Circuit Court of Appeals, making Hughes the first openly LGBT federal appeals judge (Savage 2013).

Given political and social differences across the United States, it is not surprising that the distribution of LGBT judges across the country is uneven. Figure 4.4 shows states in which at least one LGBT judge has been appointed or elected at the local or state level. States that lean liberal and tend to vote for Democratic candidates in statewide and presidential races are clearly more likely to have had LGBT judges. However, there are some surprising exceptions, including Alaska, Kentucky, and South Carolina. In addition, there are two instances of LGBT individuals serving as territorial judges in socially conservative jurisdictions, with Benjamin Cruz serving on the Guam Supreme Court from 1997 to 2001, and Maite Oronoz Rodríguez serving on the Puerto Rico Supreme Court since 2014, and as Chief Justice since 2016.

It is notable that the dispersion of LGBT judges across the states was not always apparent. In New York and Chicago, a mixture of appointments and elections allowed the LGBT community to gain a foothold on the bench, but for much of the rest of the country, there was little progress. Indeed, the first openly LGBT judge outside of California, New York, Illinois, or Massachusetts did not take the bench until 1991, when Janice Wilson was appointed to a seat on an Oregon district court (Wilson 2015).

PATHS TO THE BENCH: MINI CASE STUDIES

The systematic data on LGBT judges can only go so far towards understanding LGBT representation on the bench. In this section we provide several mini case studies to illustrate how LGBT people have reached the bench, and the implications of LGBT representation.

Deborah A. Batts. As noted in the previous section, the first appointment of an openly LGBT judge at the national level was Deborah A. Batts, who was appointed to the U.S. District Court for the Southern District of New York by President Bill Clinton in 1994 (Reske 1994). Judge Batts's appointment also marks the first appointment of an African-American LGBT judge to a federal seat. Batts received her law degree from Harvard in 1972. After serving as a law clerk for the same court she would later serve on, Batts was an Assistant U.S. Attorney, an Associate Professor of Law at Fordham University, and a special associate counsel in New York City.[6]

The Southern District seat had been left open since 1989 and Senator Daniel Patrick Moynihan (D-NY) recommended Batts for the seat to President Clinton. Her nomination received a Unanimously Qualified rating from the American Bar Association. Resistance to her appointment from conservative groups was relatively light, and focused primarily on the judge's qualifications; her sexuality, while noted, was a lesser issue.[7] Batts was confirmed by voice vote in the Senate on May 6, 1994, and sworn into office on May 9, 1994. Judge Batts went on to oversee a number of high-profile cases and married her partner in 2011. She took senior status in 2012 (Neumann 2015).

Jerry Birdwell. After receiving a law degree from Baylor, Jerry Birdwell practiced criminal defense law in Dallas. When a vacancy opened on the Dallas County 195th Judicial District Court in 1992, Texas Governor Ann Richards appointed Birdwell, making him the first openly gay judge in Texas (Nash 2008). A group of Dallas County Republicans was angered by the appointment, and as Birdwell put it: "They held press conferences practically every day asking that I resign because they said I was committing a crime every night when I went home . . . they were talking about sodomy, of course" (Nash 2008).

6 A basic bio for Judge Batts can be accessed at www.fjc.gov/history/judges/batts-deborah-.

7 The lack of controversy on Batts's nomination is notable. In 1993, Roberta Achtenberg was the first openly gay or lesbian person nominated to a federal post and confirmed by the Senate when Clinton nominated her for Assistant Secretary of Fair Housing and Equal Opportunity, but her nomination was strongly challenged on the basis that she was a gay activist (Neumann 2015).

During the controversy, Birdwell pointed to his courtroom experience and said, "I can be fair and impartial . . . I have fought for the rights of individuals, and in my court, everyone will receive a fair trial" (UPI 1992). His critics claimed he was inexperienced and that "Richards' appointment of a gay activist is clearly a political payback to one of the many liberal interest groups who supported her" (UPI 1992). Governor Richards had met with gay and lesbian activists about Birdwell's appointment, and her office released a statement saying that sexual orientation is not a factor in her appointments and, "we appointed him (Birdwell) based on his qualifications as an attorney and what we perceived as his qualifications as a judge.... He came highly recommended to us from members of the Dallas bar and sitting judges" (UPI 1992).

Birdwell served on the bench for several months with regular harassment. However, he said that the fellow judges treated him very well and spoke words of encouragement (Buhrke 1996, p. 196). During his retention election campaign, which began almost immediately, the cars of his campaign workers were vandalized and Birdwell had to receive police protection at his home (p. 196). In the November 1992 election for the seat, Republican John Nelms defeated Birdwell as a wave of Republicans came into office (Nash 2008). In an interview, Birdwell said that he received a higher proportion of the vote in that election than most Democrats did, leading him to suspect that being a Democrat hurt him more in that election than being gay did (Buhrke 1996, p. 197). Birdwell stepped down in December 1992. He returned to private practice and later moved to South Lake Tahoe, California. In 2006, he was elected to the city council. The council elected him to be mayor for one year in December 2008 (Nash 2008).

Victor Carlson.[8] Pioneer LGBT judges were sometimes outed while in office, and some were forced out. Victor Carlson had always wanted to live in Alaska and moved there in the 1960s after completing his law degree. Carlson first worked as a prosecutor in Fairbanks, later moving to Anchorage. He started a public defender agency and became the first borough attorney, before Anchorage was a city. In that position he earned enemies in development fights about the city. In 1970, Carlson was appointed to a Superior Court judge slot and his enemies began public defamation efforts against him.

By 1984, the fact that Carlson was gay leaked out before his retention election, but he was still retained in office. Carlson outed himself further by working with the AIDS Assistance Foundation, and opponents, including

8 Material on Carlson is primarily drawn from Wohlforth 2016.

claimants that were not satisfied with his rulings, became emboldened. Some men organized a smear campaign against him on talk radio and engaged in pickets at the courthouse to highlight the fact that Carlson was gay. In court, Carlson says he was challenged because of his sexual orientation; he recalled:

> It gave some people license to say, "I don't have to follow what you just said, judge, because you're a faggot. ... I would look incredulously at them, because I was the one who had the gavel." One man even put signs on his vehicle calling Carlson a "faggot judge" and another man, unhappy with the outcome of his divorce case, was convicted of hiring a man to kill Carlson, saying it was "because he was queer." (Wohlforth 2016)

Following the very public trial of a police officer in which the defense attorney tried to smear Carlson in 1989, Carlson decided that he would retire in 1991 rather than face what looked to be a difficult retention election. He returned to his first position as a public defender and finished out his career.

Rives Kistler.[9] After serving as a clerk for Justice Lewis Powell on the United States Supreme Court, Rives Kistler went to work for a private law firm in Portland and then moved to an assistant attorney general position in the Oregon Department of Justice office, where he defended the state in appellate courts. In that position he was openly gay and has said it did not create any problems for him in the 1990s. However, when Kistler first applied for a seat on an Oregon appellate court, he was worried that being openly gay would be a problem. His first few applications did not make it far. Based on a later application, he received an interview with the governor's staff and told them that he was gay. Following a fourth application, he was again interviewed but did not bring up his sexual orientation, even though the governor would have known. In 1999, the Democratic governor appointed him to the Oregon Court of Appeals. He was then elected to a full-term shortly after, and Kistler says that his sexual orientation was not a factor in the election.

In 2003, Kistler was appointed to the Oregon Supreme Court, and became the first openly LGBT person to serve on a state supreme court in the United States. Judge Kistler ran for a full six-year term in a contested nonpartisan primary election (Position 4) in 2004 and received about 60 percent of the vote. In an extended interview, Kistler discussed the role of his sexual orientation in the 2004 race:

> The election I had to run in was in May 2004. That was probably the worst timing I could have had being a gay person having to stand for election to the

[9] Material on Kistler is primarily drawn from Kacprowski 2015.

> Supreme Court. Around September 2003, Massachusetts issued its same-sex marriage opinion. Soon after that, San Francisco started issuing marriage licenses. The deadline for someone to file against me in the May 2004 election was March 13, 2004, and the week before that Multnomah County … started issuing marriage licenses without any authority from the state. In the wake of Multnomah County's decision, there was a huge pushback politically, right at the time my election was coming up, and an opponent filed to run against me. (Kacprowski 2015)

In discussing the 2004 campaign Kistler said it was very stressful.

> My sexuality became an issue. There were people opposing me and issuing campaign literature that said things like I was morally unfit to be a judge. On the other hand, there were people who were incredibly supportive in the legal community and throughout the state, and I found that support very heartening … [but] right after my opponent filed we did a poll where we asked one group of voters who they would vote for and did not reference my sexuality at all. In that poll, I was winning by 20 percent. Then we asked the other group who they would vote for, and worked into the poll questions the fact that I was gay, and with that group I was losing by 4 percent, so we knew we had a challenge. Six weeks later, in the May election, I ended up winning by about 20 percent. (Kacprowski 2015)

In 2010 and 2016, he ran for the seat again and was unopposed. Kistler says that his sexual orientation has not been an issue in the elections since 2004. Kistler was joined on the court in 2007 by lesbian Virginia Linder. Currently, Kistler is one of twelve openly LGBT state supreme court justices in the United States.

Although we know little about the political leanings of LGBT judges, considering the fact that most LGBT politicians run as Democrats and lean liberal, we might expect LGBT judges to have similar leaning. In the case of Kistler, this is accurate. Based on an ideological scoring system for state supreme court justices developed by Adam Bonica and Michael Woodruff, Judge Kistler scores a −1.14, which is even more liberal than the rest of the liberal Oregon state supreme court.[10]

Stephen M. Lachs. As noted previously, in 1979, California Governor Jerry Brown, against the advice of his advisors, appointed openly gay Stephen M. Lachs to the Los Angeles County Superior Court (Clendinen and Nagourney 2001; Smith and Haider-Markel 2002). Lachs may have been the first openly gay judge worldwide. Brown's appointment of Lachs may have been an

[10] Information is from Ballotpedia: https://ballotpedia.org/Rives_Kistler.

attempt by Brown to move to the left of President Jimmy Carter prior to the 1980 presidential primaries, in which Brown intended to challenge Carter (Clendinen and Nagourney 2001; Thompson 1994). At the same time, the LGBT community in Los Angeles had long lobbied for the appointment of gay and lesbian judges, partly because of the discrimination and harassment gays faced in the criminal justice system (Smith and Haider-Markel 2002; Thompson 1994).

Lachs was an important part of LGBT activism in Los Angeles in the 1970s, helping to organize the Municipal Elections Committee of Los Angeles (MECLA), which sought to elect gay officials (Faderman and Timmons 2006). Lachs's and MECLA's fundraising work helped support Brown's efforts to run for reelection in 1978 and for the Democratic presidential nomination in 1980, and Lachs's appointment to the bench was a reward both for this support and the persistent efforts of gay political advocates in the LA area (Thompson 1994).

Lachs's appointment was both controversial and inspiring. He faced resistance from court staff and pushback from socially conservative groups. However, Lachs also received letters from gay men who found his success a source of motivation, and his presence on the bench helped accelerate the normalizing of LGBT people in public spaces. In 2014 he recalled the experience, stating, "The more people came out, the more change there was." (Desert Sun 2014). Brown continued to appoint LGBT judges through the end of his second term, including appointing the first lesbian judge, Mary C. Morgan, to the San Francisco Municipal Court in 1981 (Thompson 1994). These appointments helped pave the way for successful elections as well – local electorates in the Los Angeles and San Francisco areas saw fit to elect LGBT judges in 1981 and 1983 respectively.

William J. Thom. Early LGBT judges facing election endured a steeper climb than those relying on appointment. Openly gay William Thom had been a practicing lawyer in New York and helped found the Lambda Legal Defense and Education Fund in 1973, which has become one of the most distinguished LGBT litigation groups in the country. At Lambda, Thom and colleagues initially focused on litigation to overturn anti-sodomy laws, which had been increasingly been used against gay men in the 1970s. Thom ran a campaign for a seat on the Third District of Manhattan Civil Court in 1979. However, he did not win the approval of the local Bar Association and lost to his endorsed opponent ("For Judges" 1979).

Thom was appointed to fill an unexpired term for the New York City Criminal Court in 1984 by Mayor Ed Koch, but was defeated in a primary election to fill the seat's ten-year term in September 1984. Just after his term concluded at the end of 1984, he was reappointed in 1985 for an additional year by Mayor Koch (Anderson and Dunlap 1985). But as Thom ran again for a full term in the seat in 1985, he was again defeated in the primary election in September even though he had the endorsement of *The New York Times* (Freiberg 1985).

Vaughn Walker. One judge not included in our database is Vaugh Walker, who is often noted as a gay federal judge, but he did not come out as openly gay until after leaving the bench. Judge Walker was appointed by George H. W. Bush to the District Court for Northern California in 1989. Walker is noteworthy for having ruled in *Perry v. Brown* (also known as *Perry v. Schwarzenegger*), a precursor case to *Hollingsworth v. Perry*, decided in 2013 by the Supreme Court. *Perry* concerned Proposition 8, the 2008 amendment to the California state constitution that outlawed same-sex marriage. Walker had ruled to overturn Proposition 8, effectively legalizing same-sex marriage in the state.

Walker's sexuality became an issue on appeal, with supporters of Proposition 8 arguing that the judge's sexuality constituted a personal interest in the case and biased his ruling (Wood 2011). The motion to vacate Walker's decision on this basis was denied, with the judge writing: "The fact that a federal judge shares a fundamental characteristic with a litigant, or shares membership in a large association such as a religion, has been categorically rejected by federal courts as a sole basis for requiring a judge to recuse her or himself."[11]

Our mini case studies of LGBT judges highlight the historically difficult path to office for LGBT people hoping to serve, whether though appointment or election. Even today, allegations sometimes surface of bigotry when LGBT people are nominated for the bench. A recent example is the nomination of Connecticut Supreme Court Associate Justice Andrew McDonald to the chief justice position (Vigdor 2018). However, dramatic changes in public opinion and public policy now make the path to office smoother for many, with sexual orientation a non-issue in most appointments and elections. Nevertheless, we still know little about the extent to which LGBT representation might influence case outcomes or public policy.

Certainly increased LGBT descriptive representation in the courts could improve LGBT attitudes towards the courts and the criminal justice system. As Gay (2002) notes, seeing members of your group in government positions is a form of symbolic representation that can improve attitudes towards institutions and perceptions of legitimacy (see also Schere and Curry 2009).

[11] *Perry v. Schwarzenegger* 2011.NO. C 09–02292 JW.

Moreover, we do know that LGBT people currently do not have favorable views of the courts or criminal justice system (Lambda Legal 2014).

Likewise, overall increased diversity in the courts, including LGBT representation, will likely ensure better protection of LGBT rights. In the only empirical study of the impact diversity has on LGBT rights, Lesh et al. (2016) find that less diverse state courts are less favorable towards LGBT rights. In addition, their study finds that in states where judges are elected to the state's highest court, rulings are less favorable towards LGBT rights and the rights of people with HIV; the negative outcomes for LGBT people are most likely in states with partisan judicial elections. And given the increased attention and spending on judicial races (Gibson and Nelson 2017), this bias towards LGBT rights is likely to continue.

CONCLUSION

Our chapter establishes a foundation for understanding LGBT representation on the bench, but the lack of work on LGBT judges represents a notable hole in the descriptive representation literature. We developed and explored a unique database of all openly LGBT judges in the United States since 1979. We also examined the public's level of comfort with LGBT judges and examined the paths to the bench of several LGBT judges.

Our analysis finds that LGBT representation in the courts has become more common over time and is enhanced when judges are nominated rather than elected. However, most Americans would be comfortable with LGBT judges in their community. LGBT representation has also spread out from the west coast and northeast to include states in the upper-Midwest and even in the Deep South. We expect LGBT representation on the bench to continue to increase, just as it has for other government offices in the past thirty years.

Future research should explore the impact of increased LGBT representation on judicial decision-making, court rulings, and public perceptions. We hope that others can build on the data and analysis we have shown here.

REFERENCES

Allen, David W., and Diane E. Wall. 1987. "The Behavior of Women State Supreme Court Justices: Are They Tokens or Outsiders?" *The Justice System Journal* 12: 232–44.

1993. "Role Orientations and Women State Supreme Court Justices." *Judicature* 77(3): 156–65.

Anderson, Susan Heller, and David W. Dunlap. 1985. "NEW YORK DAY BY DAY; Judge Thom Is Reappointed." *The New York Times*. January 15.

Bailey, Mandi Bates, and Steven P. Nawara. 2017. "Gay and Lesbian Candidates, Group Stereotypes, and the News Media: An Experimental Design." In *LGBTQ Politics: A Critical Reader*, eds. Marla Brettschneider, Susan Burgess, and Cricket Keating. New York: New York University Press. pp. 334–50.

Bailey, Robert W. 1999. *Gay Politics, Urban Politics: Identity and Economics in the Urban Setting*. New York: Columbia University Press.

Boyd, Christina L., Lee Epstein, and Andrew D. Martin. 2010. "Untangling the Causal Effects of Sex on Judging." *American Journal of Political Science* 54(2): 389–411.

Brace, Paul, and Brent D. Boyea. 2008. "State Public Opinion, the Death Penalty, and the Practice of Electing Judges." *American Journal of Political Science* 52(2): 360–72.

Bratton, Kathleen A., and Leonard P. Ray. 2002. "Descriptive Representation, Policy Outcomes, and Municipal Day-care Coverage in Norway." *American Journal of Political Science* 46(2): 428–37.

Buhrke, Robin A. 1996. *A Matter of Justice: Lesbians and Gay Men in Law Enforcement*. New York: Routledge.

Button, James W., Kenneth D. Wald, and Barbara A. Rienzo. 1999. "The Election of Openly Gay Officials in American Communities." *Urban Affairs Review* 35(2): 188–209.

Casey, Logan S., and Andrew Reynolds. 2015. *Standing Out: Transgender and Gender Variant Candidates and Elected Officials around the World*. LGBTQ Representation and Rights Research Initiative, University of North Carolina at Chapel Hill.

Clendien, Dudley, and Adam Nagourney. 2001. *Out for Good: The Struggle to Build a Gay Rights Movement in America*. New York: Simon & Schuster.

Collins, Paul M., Jr., Kenneth L. Manning, and Roberta A. Carp. 2010. "Gender, Critical Mass, and Judicial Decision Making." *Law and Policy* 32(2): 260–81.

Corrales, Javier. 2017. "Understanding the Uneven Spread of LGBT Rights in Latin America and the Caribbean, 1999–2013." *Journal of Research in Gender Studies* 7(1): 52–82.

Desert Sun. 2014. "Stephen Lachs Made History as Openly Gay Judge," *Desert Sun* May 9. www.desertsun.com/story/news/nation/lgbt/2014/05/09/stephen-lachs-lgbt-judge-advocate/8900005/.

Everitt, Joanna, and Michael Camp. 2014. "In Versus Out: LGBT Politicians in Canada." *Journal of Canadian Studies* 48(1): 226–51.

Faderman, Lillian, and Stuart Timmons. 2006. *Gay L.A.: A History of Sexual Outlaws, Power Politics, and Lipstick Lesbians*. New York: Basic Books.

Farhang, Sean, and Gregory Wawro. 2004. "Institutional Dynamics on the U.S. Court of Appeals: Minority Representation under Panel Decision Making." *Journal of Law, Economics, & Organization* 20(2): 299–330.

"For Judges in Manhattan and Queens," 1979. *The New York Times*. September 7. p. A24.

Freiberg, Peter. 1985. "Thom Loses Judgeship Bid," *The Advocate*. October 15. p. 11.

Gay, Claudine. 2002. "Spirals of Trust? The Effect of Descriptive Representation on the Relationship between Citizens and Their Government." *American Journal of Political Science* 46(4): 717–32.

Gibson, James L., and Michael J. Nelson. 2017. "Judicial Elections: Judges and Their 'New-Style' Constituencies." In *The Oxford Handbook of US Judicial Behavior*, eds. Lee Epstein and Stefanie A. Lindquist. New York: Oxford University Press. pp. 48–69.

Golebiowska, E. A. 2001. Group Stereotypes and Political Evaluation. *American Politics Research*, 29, 535–65.

2002. Political Implications of Group Stereotypes: Campaign Experiences of Openly Gay Political Candidates. *Journal of Applied Social Psychology* 32: 590–607.

Golebiowska, E. A., and Thomsen, C. J. 1999. "Group Stereotypes of Individuals: The Case of Gay and Lesbian Political Candidates." In *Gays and Lesbians in the Democratic Process: Public Policy, Public Opinion and Political Representation*, eds. E. D. B. Riggle and B. Tadlock. New York: Columbia University Press. pp. 192–219.

Grunwald, Michael. 2016. "Did Obama Win the Judicial Wars?" *Politico*. August 8.

Haider-Markel, Donald P. 1999. "Morality Policy and Individual-Level Political Behavior: The Case of Legislative Voting on Lesbian and Gay Issues." *Policy Studies Journal* 27 (4): 735–49.

2000. "Lesbian and Gay Politics in the States: Interest Groups, Electoral Politics, and Public Policy." In *The Politics of Gay Rights*, eds. Craig A. Rimmerman, Kenneth D. Wald, and Clyde Wilcox. Chicago: University of Chicago Press. pp. 290–346.

2007. "Representation and Backlash: The Positive and Negative Influence of Descriptive Representation." *Legislative Studies Quarterly* 32(1): 107–34.

2010. *Out and Running*. Washington, DC: Georgetown University Press.

Haider-Markel, Donald P., and Chelsie Lynn Moore Bright. 2014. "Lesbian candidates and officeholders." In *Women and Elective Office: Past. Present, and Future*, 3rd ed., eds. Sue Thomas and Clyde Wilcox. Oxford: Oxford University Press. pp. 253–72.

Haider-Markel, Donald P., Mark R. Joslyn, and Chad J. Kniss. 2000. "Minority Group Interests and Political Representation: Gay Elected Officials in the Policy Process." *Journal of Politics* 62 (2): 568–77.

Haider-Markel, Donald P., Patrick R. Miller, Andrew Flores, Daniel Lewis, Barry Tadlock, and Jami Taylor. 2017. "Bringing 'T' to the Table: Understanding Individual Support of Transgender Candidates for Public Office." *Politics, Groups, and Identities* 5(3): 399–417.

Haire, Susan B., and Laura P. Moyer. 2015. *Diversity Matters: Judicial Policy Making in the U.S. Courts of Appeals*. Charlottesville: University of Virginia Press.

Hansen, Eric R., and Sarah A. Treul. 2015. "The Symbolic and Substantive Representation of LGB Americans in the US House." *Journal of Politics* 77(4): 955–67.

Hayes, Danny, and Jennifer L. Lawless. 2016. *Women on the Run: Gender, Media, and Political Campaigns in a Polarized Era*. New York: Cambridge University Press.

Herrick, Rebekah, and Sue Thomas. 1999. "The Effects of Sexual Orientation on Citizen Perceptions of Candidate Viability." In *Gays and Lesbians in the Democratic Process*, eds. Ellen D. B. Riggle and Barry Tadlock. New York: Columbia University Press. pp. 170–91.

Hoekstra, Valerie. 2010. "Increasing the Gender Diversity of High Courts: A Comparative View." *Politics and Gender* 6(03): 474–84.

Jones, Robert P., Daniel Cox, and Elizabeth Cook. 2011. *Generations at Odds: The Millennial Generation and the Future of Gay and Lesbian Rights*. Washington, DC: Public Religion Research Institute. www.prri.org/wp-content/uploads/2011/08/PRRI-Report-on-Millennials-Religion-Gay-and-Lesbian-Issues-Survey.pdf.

Kacprowski, Nick. 2015. "The Pioneer Series: An Interview with Justice Rives Kistler of the Supreme Court of Oregon." *LGBT Litigator*. April 30. http://apps.americanbar.org/litigation/committees/lgbt/articles/spring2015–0415-pioneers-series-interview-justice-kistler-supreme-court-oregon.html.

Kastellec, Jonathan P. 2013. "Racial Diversity and Judicial Influence on Appellate Courts." *American Journal of Political Science* 57(1): 167–83.

Kenney, Sally Jane. 2013. *Gender and Justice: Why Women in the Judiciary Really Matter*. New York: Routledge.

Lambda Legal. 2014. *Protected and Served? A National Survey Exploring Discrimination by Police, Courts, Prisons and Schools against LGBT People and People Living with HIV in the United States*. New York: Lambda Legal. www.lambdalegal.org/protected-and-served.

Lesh, Eric, Anthony Michael Kreis, Ryan Krog, and Allison Trochesset. 2016. *Justice Out of Balance: How the Election of Judges and the Stunning Lack of Diversity on State Courts Threaten LGBT Rights*. New York: Lambda Legal.

McCall, Madhavi, and Michael A. McCall. 2007. "How Far Does the Gender Gap Extend?: Decision Making on State Supreme Courts in Fourth Amendment Cases, 1980–2000." *The Social Science Journal* 44(1): 67–82.

Morin, Jason L. 2014. "The Voting Behavior of Minority Judges in the U.S. Court of Appeals: Does the Race of the Claimant Matter?" *American Politics Research* 42(1): 34–64.

Nash, Tammye. 2008. "Birdwell, State's 1st Gay Judge, Now Mayor of S. Lake Tahoe." *The Dallas Voice*. December 21. https://dallas.edgemedianetwork.com/index.php?ch=news&sc=&sc2=news&sc3=&id=84904.

Neumann, Caryn E. 2015. "Batts, Deborah A." *GLBTQ Encyclopedia Archives*. www.glbtqarchive.com/ssh/batts_da_S.pdf.

Newton, David E. 1994. *Gay and Lesbian Rights: A Reference Handbook*. Santa Barbara, CA: ABC-CLIO.

Perry, Ravi K., and X. Loudon Manley. 2017. "Case Studies of Black, Lesbian and Gay Candidates Winning Identity Politics in the Obama Era." In *LGBTQ Politics: A Critical Reader*, eds. Marla Brettschneider, Susan Burgess, and Cricket Keating. New York: New York University Press. pp. 295–308.

Pitkin, Hanna Fenichel. 1967. *The Concept of Representation*. Oakland: University of California Press.

Preuhs, Robert R. 2006. "The Conditional Effects of Minority Descriptive Representation: Black Legislators and Policy Influence in the American States." *Journal of Politics* 68(3): 585–99.

Rayside, David M. 1998. *On the Fringe: Gays and Lesbians in Politics*. Ithaca, NY: Cornell University Press.

Reske, Henry J. 1994. "Appointment Breaks Barrier." *ABA Journal*. December.

Reynolds, Andrew. 2013. "Representation and Rights: The Impact of LGBT Legislators in Comparative Perspective." *American Political Science Review* 107(2): 259–74.

Riccucci, Norma M., Gregg G. Van Ryzin, and Cecilia F. Lavena. 2014. "Representative Bureaucracy in Policing: Does It Increase Perceived Legitimacy?" *Journal of Public Administration Research and Theory* 24(3): 537–51.

Rocha, Rene R., and Daniel P. Hawes. 2009. "Racial Diversity, Representative Bureaucracy, and Equity in Multiracial School Districts." *Social Science Quarterly* 90(2): 326–44.

Savage, David G. 2013. "Senate Confirms First Openly Gay U.S. Appeals Court Judge." *The Los Angeles Times*. September 24.

Scherer, Nancy, and Brett Curry. 2009. "Does Descriptive Race Representation Enhance Institutional Legitimacy? The Case of the US Courts." *The Journal of Politics* 72(1): 90–104.

Sheridan, Michael. 2011. "California Elects Nation's First Openly Transgender Judge, Victoria Kolakowski." *New York Daily News*. November 17.

Smith, Raymond A., and Donald P. Haider-Markel. 2002. *Gay and Lesbian Americans and Political Participation*. Denver, CO: ABC-CLIO Publishers.

Snell, Paul. 2017. "Equality in the House: The Congressional LGBT Equality Caucus and the Substantive Representation of LGBTQ Interests." In *LGBTQ Politics: A Critical Reader*, eds. Marla Brettschneider, Susan Burgess, and Cricket Keating. New York: New York University Press. pp. 309–33.

Sontag, Deborah. 2015. "Once a Pariah, Now a Judge: The Early Transgender Journey of Phyllis Frye." *The New York Times*. August 29.

Thomas, Sue, and Clyde Wilcox, eds. 2014. *Women and Elective Office: Past. Present, and Future*, 3rd ed. Oxford: Oxford University Press.

Thompson, Mark, ed. 1994. *Long Road to Freedom: The Advocate History of the Gay and Lesbian Movement*. New York: St. Martin's Press.

UPI. 1992. "Appointment of Gay Judge Touches of Uproar." *UPI Archives*. June 3. www.upi.com/Archives/1992/06/03/Appointment-of-gay-judge-touches-off-uproar/9169707544000/.

Vigdor, Neil. 2018. "Opposition to Gay Chief Justice Nominee Sparks Allegations of Bigotry." *CTpost*. January 9. www.ctpost.com/local/article/Opposition-to-gay-chief-justice-nominee-sparks-12485156.php.

Wilson, Janice. 2015. *Interviewed by Heather Oriana Petrocelli*. Portland: Portland State University. https://pdxscholar.library.pdx.edu/cgi/viewcontent.cgi?referer=www.google.com/&httpsredir=1&article=1004&context=pope_oralhist.

Wohlforth, Charles. 2016. "An Anchorage Judge Driven from the Bench for being Gay Questions the Depth of Change." *Anchorage Daily News*. April 18.

Wood, Daniel B. 2011. "Prop. 8 Ruling: Gay Judge Didn't Need to Recuse Himself." *Christian Science Monitor*. June 14. www.csmonitor.com/USA/Justice/2011/0614/Prop.-8-ruling-gay-judge-didn-t-need-to-recuse-himself.

5

Race, Gender, and the Battle to Seat Constance Baker Motley, the First Black Woman Appointed to the Federal Bench

TANEISHA NICOLE MEANS

INTRODUCTION

"I never entertained the thought that I would be appointed to the federal bench. I didn't think they would ever appoint a Black woman to the federal bench. I didn't think that would happen"

(Constance Baker Motley, quoted in Linn Washington 1994, p. 130).

"Mr. President, I cannot approve this nomination. I could not vote for it in the committee"

(Mississippi Senator James O. Eastland, Chairman, Senate Judiciary Committee, quoted in Congressional Record 1966).

Thurgood Marshall, then a judge on the U.S. Courts of Appeals for the Second Circuit (hereinafter called Second Circuit), became U.S. Solicitor General in 1965. Marshall's appointment created a vacancy on the Second Circuit that President Lyndon B. Johnson tried to fill by appointing Constance Baker Motley. Johnson was, however, forced to reconsider and withdraw his nomination of Motley due to identity politics (Nagin-Brown 2017; Salkin 2011; Washington 1994). But on August 30, 1966, the Senate, in a voice vote, confirmed Motley's nomination to one of the nation's busiest federal trial courts – the U.S. District Court for the Southern District of New York. While many saw Motley as remarkably qualified by her educational and career background, and her nominations were viewed as watershed moments in federal judicial selection because she was a woman of color, some wondered if she would ever be successfully appointed to the federal bench given the racial and gender politics that plagued her nominations.

Although the federal bench has diversified in the post-Civil Rights era, court scholars largely agree that a lack of racial and gender diversity continues there, especially when it comes to women of color. For example, while the first black woman was appointed in 1966 (i.e., Motley), only fifty-six black women have ever been appointed to the federal bench. As of December 2017, out of 718 active federal judges, only 39 black women sit on the federal bench, comprising just 5 percent of those judges. The number of black women federal judges has undoubtedly increased in the past fifty years, but black women have historically been and are contemporarily underrepresented given their percentage in the U.S. population (Means and Prado forthcoming). Why have there been so few black women judges on the federal bench? What explains the persistent underrepresentation of this group in the federal judiciary?

Scholars argue that, among other factors, racial and gender politics deeply influence the judicial selection process and therefore the level of judicial diversity on the bench (Asmussen 2011, Means and Prado forthcoming). Race and gender not only influence the applicant pool that presidents tend to draw from to staff the federal bench (i.e., courts, district attorneys' offices, and high-profile law firms), but also whom presidents ultimately decide to nominate and how the Senate handles and acts on those nominations (e.g., Asmussen 2011, Slotnick, Goldman, and Schiavoni 2015).

The struggle to seat black women, and women of color in general, on the federal bench is understudied within law and political science, although diversity on the bench may well influence policy-making in the federal judiciary (Means and Prado forthcoming). While scholars have largely overlooked the nomination of Motley as a potential starting point for exploring whether and how race and gender fundamentally influence the federal judicial selection process, and, therefore, judicial diversity, I contend that Motley's nomination and confirmation undeniably helped pave the way for other black women and women of color who were appointed to the federal judiciary between 1966 and 2017.

This chapter focuses on Motley's ascent and pathway to the federal bench, posing these questions: How did the politics of race and gender influence the appointment of the first black woman federal judge? What lessons can scholars and women of color aspiring to the federal bench learn from Motley's nomination and confirmation? Finally, how do those lessons apply to twenty-first century federal judicial selection politics and processes?

In subsequent pages, I present a brief overview of the scholarship and theories of federal judicial selection. Then, those theories are applied to Motley's appointment using oral history narrative interviews, growing scholarship on Motley, and the Senate Judiciary Committee's historical documents. Using these data, this chapter reveals the politics involved in placing Motley on the federal bench. The historical and qualitative data demonstrate that

Motley's appointment begins a long legacy of women of color being appointed to the federal judiciary. How she, as a potential judicial nominee, was treated and perceived by political elites, including senators, the U.S. president, and sitting federal judges, was deeply influenced by her race and gender. The chapter concludes with evident lessons derived from studying Motley's successful and unsuccessful appointments to the federal bench.

RACE, GENDER, AND THE FEDERAL JUDICIAL SELECTION PROCESS

Article II, Section 2, Clause 2 of the U.S. Constitution outlines the federal judicial selection process. Typically, the president nominates judges only after consultation with the Department of Justice and the attorney general, White House staff, senators, state and local party leaders, and the FBI, which performs a thorough background check. As the president considers potential nominees, interest groups weigh in. Once the nomination is made, the American Bar Association evaluates the nominee's qualifications, and the nomination is sent to the Senate Judiciary Committee for further vetting. If the nominee is viewed favorably by the Senate Judiciary Committee, the nomination goes to the Senate floor where it is approved or rejected by a simple majority vote. Despite increased polarization and bitter confirmation politics, recent presidents have been rather successful in getting their judicial nominations approved (Binder and Maltzman 2009; Steigerwalt 2010). But what factors influence who is nominated and confirmed to the federal bench? These questions are central to judicial politics (Nemacheck 2017; Scherer 2017). Existing literature on the topic points to various factors, with race and gender deeply influencing both nomination and confirmation processes (e.g., Asmussen 2011; Means and Prado forthcoming; Navarro 2013).

Empirical research shows race and gender to be important factors in the selection process, especially when a selection can signal that the courts can be diverse political institutions and inclusive spaces (e.g., Scherer and Curry 2010). Democratic presidents, however, are much more likely to nominate judges from underrepresented groups than are Republican presidents (Asmussen 2011). This is true today when comparing President Barack Obama's nominees to the federal bench with President Donald Trump's nominees (Means and Prado forthcoming); it is particularly true when the vacant seat belonged to a woman or racial minority (Abraham 2008).

Most studies examining federal judicial selection have focused on the Senate's role in the process, specifically the factors that increase or decrease the likelihood of success and the length of time for the Senate to act on a nomination. The results are clear and noncontroversial. While ideology and partisan politics significantly shape the confirmation process, the nominees' race and gender also affects how the Senate acts. A substantial number of scholars demonstrates that gender and/or race can, and often does, affect confirmation politics. Nixon and Goss (2001), for example, find that racial minorities and white women take longer to be confirmed to vacancies on the U.S. Courts of Appeal. Bell (2002) finds that processing the nominations of racial minorities takes longer than the nominations of white and male judges, but this effect for women holds only during divided government. Schraufnagel (2005) and Martinek, Kemper, and Van Winkle (2002) find that racial minorities take longer than white nominees to be confirmed, but that gender did not significantly affect confirmation duration. Finally, Solowiej, Martinek, and Brunell (2005) find that women are most advantaged under conditions of unified Republican control and disadvantaged under conditions of divided control with a Democratic president. They also conclude that minorities are disadvantaged when nominated by a Democratic president facing a Republican-controlled Senate, and even more disadvantaged when nominated under conditions of unified Republican control.

In sum, many factors influence both the nomination and confirmation processes, and it is clear that race and gender have historically been, and remain, important to these processes. Unfortunately, most scholars studying the role of race and gender in judicial selection have focused on the post-1977 period. Indeed, studies have largely ignored the men and women of color, and white women, who were appointed to the federal bench long before 1977 (i.e., when President Jimmy Carter vowed to change the face of the federal judiciary). The present chapter on Constance Baker Motley seeks to repair this lack of historical work by examining whether and how race and gender influenced her appointment to the federal bench.

To do this work, it is important to examine how and why she was nominated and confirmed. Why did President Johnson perceive Motley to be a viable, qualified judicial candidate, and how did U.S. senators and other political elites respond to her nomination? The answers to the questions of this chapter do not appear in any single record or text; answers require us to consult multiple texts. Those most relevant for this chapter are oral history interviews with Motley (Salkin 2011; Washington 1994), scholarship on Motley (Ford 2017; Motley 1998), and records from the U.S. Senate, especially the Senate Judiciary Committee. Together, these texts reveal how Motley's identity as a black woman deeply influenced her ascent to the federal judiciary. Moreover, race and gender affected her in a less-than-straightforward way, for being a black woman both helped and hindered her appointment.

CONSTANCE BAKER MOTLEY BEFORE SHE WAS A FEDERAL JUDGE

Motley was born in 1921 in New Haven, Connecticut, to working-class immigrants from Nevis, a small Eastern Caribbean island. As a teenager, she was politically active – co-founding the New Haven NAACP Youth Council, focused on youth unemployment and employment discrimination, and serving as the secretary of the New Haven Community Council, an organization that promoted civil rights in Connecticut. With the financial support of white philanthropist Clarence Blakeslee, Motley started college at Fisk University in Nashville, Tennessee in 1941. In 1942, she transferred to New York University, graduating in 1943 with a bachelor's degree in economics.

While she was a law student at Columbia University, Thurgood Marshall, then chief counsel of the National Association for the Advancement of Colored People's Legal Defense and Educational Fund (NAACP LDF), hired Motley as a law clerk in the LDF's national office in New York City. After earning her law degree in 1946, Motley stayed on at the LDF for nineteen years, fighting institutionalized segregation and racial discrimination in housing, transportation, and other areas. She was instrumental in the landmark case *Brown v. Board of Education*, which helped her become the chief strategist of most cases litigated by the LDF during the civil rights movement. Motley eventually became the second-highest ranking member of the LDF, as associate counsel. She successfully argued cases in both state and federal courts, as well as important cases before the U.S. Supreme Court, including *Meredith v. Fair* (1962), which made James Meredith the first black student to attend the University of Mississippi (hereinafter Ole Miss, Chin and Chin 2017). Such prominent legal success meant that "everybody in New York, thanks to *The New York Times*, 'knew [her] name,' as they say in politics" (Motley 1998, p. 205). Motley won nine of the ten civil rights cases she argued before the U.S. Supreme Court, and this feat earned her reputation within the legal community.

CONSTANCE BAKER MOTLEY'S FAILED NOMINATION TO THE SECOND CIRCUIT

Motley's nomination to the Second Circuit is little known history. In fact, few books, records, or biographies even mention it, but some do detail this historical event (e.g., Ford 2017; Motley 1998; Nagin-Brown 2017; Washington 1994). One potential reason that scholars have largely overlooked this aspect of her life is that the nomination to the Second Circuit was unsuccessful. Nevertheless, there is much to learn from her failed nomination.

First Nomination

While a civil rights champion in the legal community, Motley never sought a federal judgeship. In fact, she was actively seeking a state court appointment, but could not get one because she had not been deeply involved in city or state politics, and therefore was not well known to the politicos (Washington 1994, p. 131). Meanwhile, U.S. Attorney General Ramsey Clark, the son of U.S. Supreme Court Justice Tom Clark, brought Motley to President Lyndon B. Johnson's attention after he heard her argue a case in the Supreme Court (Motley 1998, p. 213, Nagin-Brown 2017). New York Senator Robert "Bobby" Kennedy, too, reached out to Johnson about the possibility of Motley joining the federal bench (Motley 1998, p. 213).

Seat 9 on the Second Circuit was established on May 19, 1961, by 75 Stat. 80. Thurgood Marshall was appointed to this seat on October 5, 1961, by President John F. Kennedy, and he remained on the Second Circuit until August 23, 1965, when he became the thirty-second U.S. Solicitor General. Marshall's departure from the Second Circuit created a vacancy that Johnson tried to fill with Motley in 1965. However, opposition to that potential nomination was so great that Johnson eventually withdrew her name from consideration (Washington 1994, p. 128). The opposition to her appointment was interesting given that, in many ways, Motley was an obvious replacement for Marshall on the Second Circuit.

Motley was well-qualified and fit most of the informal requirements that determine who ends up on the federal bench, including professional competence and political qualifications. As already mentioned, Motley had been a stellar student her entire life, and had graduated with her bachelor's from New York University and her law degree from Columbia University. Professionally, she had spent twenty years litigating some of the most challenging civil rights cases alongside Thurgood Marshall. Among other implications of her legal career, Motley helped desegregate both K–12 school systems and higher education institutions like Ole Miss. Even using the standards of today that determine how qualified a judicial nominee is for the federal bench, Motley would and should have been seen as well-qualified given her educational background and legal career (Slotnick, Goldman, and Schiavoni 2015).

While Motley's qualifications were important, the political context in which she was being considered was also important. Motley, a champion of civil rights, was being considered for the Second Circuit bench during the height of the black civil rights movement and the movement had just enjoyed a number of legal successes and landmark civil rights laws (e.g., *Brown v. Board of Education*, Voting Rights Act of 1965, and Civil Rights Acts of 1964). In fact, some of these successes were due to Motley's own work at LDF. But, in addition, one of the things the movement argued for was increased racial representation in local, state, and federal political institutions, especially the courts (Morris 1986). This is particularly important because some of the success of the civil rights movement had been accomplished during Johnson's short presidency, and to some extent, Johnson had established himself as committed to a civil rights agenda and diversity. What better way to further cement that commitment in the minds of the public than to increase the representation of African-Americans on the federal bench.

Motley was also a logical nominee given her identity as a black woman. As mentioned previously, the vacancy that Motley would fill was a judicial seat once held by a black jurist (i.e., Marshall). Accordingly, replacing Marshall with another black American makes sense, and in fact, history tells us that this "replacement" tradition operates not just for race (e.g., consider Clarence Thomas replacing Thurgood Marshall when he retired), but for other characteristics including religion and geographic region (Abraham 2008). But Motley was not just a racial minority, she was also a woman, and women were also underrepresented on the federal bench in the mid-twentieth century (Stubbs 2016). To appoint the first black woman to the federal bench would ensure that Johnson would be praised and remembered for diversifying the bench. Furthermore, this appointment would likely not only appeal to African-Americans, but to women of all races as well. We should see that wanting the electorate to view him favorably was most likely a strategy given the fact that Johnson, like most politicians, would seek reelection and would need to garner significant electoral support (Mayhew 1974). Johnson knew that having the support of black Americans and women would be critical to winning any election in the post-Voting Rights Act era. In this vein, Motley being a black woman was absolutely important to her nomination.

In sum, Motley was an obvious replacement for Marshall. She was well-qualified, a black woman, and committed to social justice and civil rights. Moreover, her nomination was intended to fill a vacant seat that was once held by an African-American, and in a political environment that called for the inclusion of historically underrepresented groups into American political institutions. Ultimately, I'd argue that among other things (i.e., qualifications, political context, ideological compatibility), Motley's race and gender helped her nomination prospects.

Opposition to Motley's Almost-Appointment to the Second Circuit

While Motley's race and gender helped her nomination prospects, they also led to much opposition to her nomination to the Second Circuit, which mostly came from the Senate and judges already sitting on the federal bench (Lohier 2017; Motley 1998; Washington 1994). It is important to note that, while I argue that opposition to Motley was influenced by Motley's race and gender, according to Motley herself, opposition to her nomination was based on gender and not race: "This opposition was largely based on my being a woman. I remember how stunned both Johnson and Marshall were by the intensity of the opposition" (Washington 1994, p. 128). Although Motley considered gender more important than race, I argue that women of color are both raced and sexed simultaneously, and it is difficult to say that the responses to her nomination were only or even mostly based on her being a woman and not a black woman. The reality is that it is impossible to separate Motley's race from her gender. This idea is consistent with, and informed by, a large body of work on intersectionality and the simultaneous effects of race and gender in the lives of women of color (Crenshaw 1989, Hancock 2007a, 2007b, Jordan-Zachery 2007, Simien 2007). Nonetheless, many political elites resisted Motley joining the Second Circuit.

J. Edward Lombard, the chief judge of the Second Circuit, led the opposition to her nomination. According to Motley:

> The opposition was great because I was a woman, I can only guess, since Thurgood had been there and he was Black too. But Lombard and others on the Second Circuit didn't want any women in this milieu. New York was the real power center of the whole circuit, which also includes Connecticut and Vermont, because there you had all the great commercial cases and so forth. Their attitude, pure and simple, was that a woman had no business being there. . . . At that time they didn't even have women trying criminal cases in the U.S. Attorney's Office for the Southern District of New York. There was one woman on the civil side, but the feeling was that women couldn't handle criminal cases. So if a woman couldn't handle a criminal case, you know a woman couldn't be appointed as a circuit court judge (Washington 1994, p. 129).

Motley's recollection of the reason why judges sitting on the Second Circuit bench, especially chief judge Lombard, opposed her nomination highlight the role her identities played in her being potentially appointed. At the time she was being considered, and arguably today, the persistent and prevalent (mis)perception that women attorneys' moral perspective constrained their ability to meet the demands of their professional role as lawyers limited women's inclusion in the legal profession (Jack and Jack 1989). The conversation has been, and continues to be, about women's' own personal morality (i.e., perceived femininity, compassion, and sympathy) and less about the biases (i.e., patriarchal, racial, and other) of the legal system. For example, Jack and Jack (1989) write that legal socialization has been instrumental in maintaining bias and bolstering the idea that litigating, especially in cases dealing with criminal law, should be left to men. While Motley had certainly demonstrated that she could successfully litigate challenging cases, she had mostly only focused on civil rights cases with the LDF. She was, therefore, still viewed as ill-equipped to handle the types of cases that would surely come before her as a Second Circuit judge (i.e., cases from Wall Street, criminal cases, etc.).

Influential members of the Senate Judiciary Committee also opposed Motley's appointment to the Second Circuit. The importance of the Senate Judiciary Committee in the appointment process cannot be overstated – it is this committee that vets all nominees for these lifetime appointments, and they set the tone for the confirmation process. The most important member of the Senate Judiciary Committee, the chairperson, can single-handedly derail appointments (i.e., a veto effectively) via their ability to dictate which nominations are discussed and are able to move through the Committee to the Senate floor. When Motley was being considered for appointment to the federal bench, the chairperson of the Senate Judiciary Committee was Mississippi Senator James Oliver Eastland and he led the senatorial opposition to Motley.

"A wealthy Mississippi plantation owner, Senator Eastland was best known nationally as a system of Southern resistance to racial desegregation in most of his years in the Senate" (Hunter 1986). And Motley and Eastland knew (of) each other well – it had been Motley who had argued and won the case that integrated Ole Miss (e.g., *Meredith v. Fair*, Chin and Chin 2017). Moreover, it was Motley who had successfully litigated other desegregation cases and whose work helped dismantle Jim Crow (Motley 1998). The issue(s) Eastland had with Motley were not very clear during her Second Circuit appointment venture, but they would be made very clear when she was appointed to the District Court (see the next section).

Eastland's power in the Senate Judiciary Committee was often leveraged to support or go against judicial nominees, and he himself knew the power he wielded in that position. Eastland made it clear that he would neither support nor move Motley's nomination to the Second Circuit through the Senate Judiciary Committee. Without Eastland putting Motley on the Senate Judiciary Committee's agenda to be discussed and vetted, the Committee could not vote on her nomination and move the nomination out of the committee to the Senate floor. Eastland's obstruction would, therefore, effectively mean defeat for Motley if Johnson were to officially nominate her to the circuit court.

Motley was clearly unwelcome on the Second Circuit bench with the chief judge of the circuit vehemently opposed to her nomination. Moreover, Motley was not viewed favorably by the leading senator in the Senate Judiciary Committee, and with his strong opposition, her nomination would likely not make it out of the Senate committee charged with vetting judicial nominees. While not something to dwell on, it is important to note that Motley was being appointed to the Second Circuit, an appellate court responsible for cases from New York, Connecticut, and Vermont, and for adjudicating important commercial cases. Moreover, the Second Circuit has appellate jurisdiction and can reverse decisions from six district courts. Consequently, in addition to racism and sexism, the power of the Second Circuit was likely an important factor in how both sitting judges and senators responded to the idea that Motley would be appointed to that bench.

Motley knew she faced an uphill battle if she were to be nominated to the Second Circuit: "There was tremendous opposition to my appointment, not only from southern senators but from other federal judges. Some of this opposition was racial, but some of it had to do with my being a woman" (Washington 1994, p. 128). While we cannot know for sure, we can imagine this opposition from both influential senators (i.e., Eastland) and sitting judges (Chief Judge Lombard) to Motley's appointment influenced Johnson's decision to reconsider and withdraw her nomination. Based on the opposition, it is clear that Motley's race and gender hindered her confirmation prospects.

IF AT FIRST YOU DON'T SUCCEED ... CONSTANCE BAKER MOTLEY'S SECOND NOMINATION

Although Motley's first nomination failed, her second nomination was successful, and it is her second nomination that made her the first black woman federal judge. As was the case with the first nomination, racial and gender politics abounded during the appointment process, and I argue that race and gender both helped and hindered her process the second time around as well.

Second Nomination

Motley was serving as President of the Borough of Manhattan when Johnson officially, and finally, announced her nomination to the U.S. District Court for the Southern District of New York (hereinafter SDNY) in January 1966. As mentioned in the previous section, Motley had been first brought to Johnson's attention by U.S. Attorney General Clark after he heard her argue a case in the Supreme Court, and then Kennedy officially asked Johnson to consider Motley for appointment (Nagin-Brown 2017, p. 213). This support that Motley clearly had from the Department of Justice and the New York senator led to Johnson considering Motley as Marshall's replacement on the Second Circuit. Although that nomination had been withdrawn, Johnson took a chance by nominating her again to the federal bench, but this time to a district court.

On January 26, 1966, Motley's nomination was referred to the Senate Judiciary Committee. While Motley was well aware that Johnson found her fit to be a federal judge, and that she had the support of at least some politicos (i.e., Clark and Kennedy), the official district court nomination was a surprise even to her: "When I was called to the White House in January 1966, I did not know that the date on which I was told to appear would be the date on which Johnson would announce my appointment to the federal bench" (Motley 1998, p. 212). Nevertheless, she embraced the opportunity given that she had already thought to "look for other areas in which to practice law or use [her] legal training" (Motley 1998, p. 205).

Motley was well-qualified to join the federal bench, whether that be at the appellate or trial level. This time around, however, because her nomination was formal (i.e., submitted to the Senate), the American Bar Association (ABA) and the New York State Bar Association (NYSBA) were both asked to evaluate Motley and express an opinion pertaining to the nomination. Both the ABA and the NYSBA found Motley qualified for the appointment to the district court. Nevertheless, qualifications and endorsements did not ensure that she would be confirmed this time around – Johnson had just withdrawn her nomination for the Second Circuit and Motley had also just witnessed the hostility around diversifying the federal courts. At the time of her appointment, only four other women and eleven black Americans (read: black men) had been federal judges. Furthermore, she was well aware of the obstacles even Thurgood Marshall faced in being appointed to the federal bench (Washington 1994, p. 128). Nonetheless, Johnson again showed himself to be interested in seating Motley on the federal bench, and while he might have preferred her joining the Second Circuit, he would settle for getting her to the SDNY.

The Confirmation Process and Controversies Surrounding Motley's District Court Appointment

According to Motley, "There had been no opposition to [her] going to the district court" (Salkin 2011, p. 46), and the truth is that she had a lot of support.

Motley had the support of black political leaders and the black masses: "When I went to see Johnson in Washington the day I was appointed, he told me he had called every civil rights leader in the country and every one of them was backing my appointment 100 percent. The power of Black voters and the strength of the civil rights lobby helped me win confirmation" (Washington 1994, p. 129). Motley also had the formal support of Senator Kennedy, as well as liberal Republican New York Senator Jacob K. Javits, whose unwavering support during the confirmation process would prove to be invaluable. Moreover, Motley's nomination was supported by influential members of the Department of Justice (i.e., U.S. Attorney General Clark). While Motley had all of this support, the historical records show that there was still a lot of opposition to her appointment to a district court.

Perhaps unbeknownst to Motley, the Senate Judiciary Committee received over a dozen letters from "concerned" American citizens regarding her SDNY nomination. For example, Fred Meinhart of Rochester, New York, wrote "we have many more people better qualified who will do more for the good of all of the people in the good old U.S.A. and too bad we do not have more real Americans in the U.S. legislative houses" (personal communication, August 3, 1966). Mrs. Myrtle C. Morris wrote "I hope she is NOT nominated as she seems quite worthless in the job she is on – I get this from the newspapers of NYC. Please keep up your good work for our Southern states" (personal communication, August 19, 1966). Although some letters were sent prior to her confirmation by the Senate, most were sent after the approval, and none of the personal letters received and archived by the Senate Judiciary Committee were in support of Motley's nomination. Mr. Edward J. Head of Lebanon, Virginia, wrote "The Executive and Judicial branches of the Government of the United States hit a new LOW-LOW – below the bottom of the barrel – when they appointed Constance Baker Motley U.S. District Judge in New York … Our Country has many well trained, experienced and qualified men who have for years dedicated their talents to serving their Country" (personal communication, August 31, 1966). Similarly, Robert T. Ball from Charleston, South Carolina, wrote that "this appointment is one of the most atrocious ever inflicted on the American Republic" (personal communication, September 13, 1966).

While Motley's nomination was opposed by some members of the American public, most of the opposition to Motley during the confirmation process came from within the Senate, and especially from within the Senate Judiciary Committee. On one hand, the opposition is evident given how long it took for her to be confirmed. She was nominated in January 1966, but not confirmed until August – roughly eight months after her nomination. Although eight months does not seem like a very long time, what scholars now understand is that significant delay on judicial nominations, such as an eight-month delay during this time period, is practically tantamount to defeat (Binder and Maltzman 2009; Steigerwalt 2010).

The opposition to Motley is also clear in the historical records from the U.S. Senate and Motley's own recollection. Motley places the opposition to her nomination in Eastland's hands: "I was nominated in January 1966 but not confirmed until August 1966, thanks to Senator James O. Eastland of Mississippi. Eastland headed the Judiciary Committee and led the opposition. He held up my nomination as well as the nomination of every other African American appointed to the federal bench during the sixties" (Washington 1994, p. 128). Why was Senator Eastland so opposed to seating black Americans on the federal bench? And how had he led the opposition to Motley's district court appointment?

Without a doubt, anti-black racism influenced Eastland's response to the nominations of black judicial appointees during the twentieth century. Eastland, a strict segregationist, felt that black Americans and white Americans should be kept separate in all spheres of life including colleges (Eagles 2009). He had vehemently opposed *Brown v. Board of Education*, found ways to legally drag his feet on implementing the court's decision, and full-heartedly believed black Americans were an inferior race (Annis 2016). In fact, he had earned the reputation of being "The Voice of the White South" (Annis 2016). But Eastland's response to Motley's appointment was probably more personal in nature than that.

As mentioned previously, Motley and Eastland had disagreed over integrating Ole Miss. According to Nagin-Brown (2017), Motley and Eastland

> had been on opposite sides of one of the most consequential and deadly racial conflicts in American history, the battle to desegregate Ole Miss – a beloved white southern institution. Motley had anchored the legal team that represented James Meredith, the prevailing plaintiff in that case. By destroying Jim Crow at the state's flagship institution of higher education, Motley and Meredith had defeated forces of white supremacy in the state – including Senator Eastland and Mississippi's governor, Ross Barnett – vocal opponents of the litigation. (p. 1700)

Despite this history between Eastland and Motley, the senator was not able to defeat her nomination given the support from Senators Javits and Kennedy.

On April 4, 1966, the subcommittee of the Senate Judiciary Committee charged with vetting Motley held a hearing. The subcommittee was composed of Senators Quentin N. Burdick (North Dakota), Philip A. Hart (Michigan), and Jacob K. Javits (New York), but only Senators Burdick and Javits were present during the hearing. New York Senators Javits and Kennedy had already submitted their formal notifications that approved Motley's nomination. This is significant given senatorial courtesy, which restricts a president's ability to appoint district court – and to a lesser extent circuit court – judges because it is an unwritten rule that essentially says local political officials including state senators and local party bosses have a virtual veto over the nomination (Binder and Maltzman 2009; Giles, Hettinger, and Peppers 2001).

It was a good sign that Motley would be confirmed given the support of New York Senators Javits and Kennedy. Their statements to the subcommittee on Motley's behalf were also overwhelmingly positive. Kennedy's statement, which was read to the subcommittee in his absence, explained that Motley had "a long and distinguished record as a lawyer and as a public official," "been counsel in a substantial number of significant cases," and "successfully argued many important appeals before the Supreme Court of the United States," and that "she was most worthy of the President's nomination, and she is most worthy of the favorable action of this Subcommittee" (April 4, 1966). Javits, too, spoke to Motley's qualifications in his statement to the subcommittee, but also spoke to the reputation she had cultivated in the legal community: "the one sterling impression, Mr. Chairman, that I have of Mrs. Motley is an impression of objectivity and steadiness, of a devoted student of public affairs, and especially of how to administer public affairs" (April 4, 1966). Javits went on to talk about Motley's personality: "In addition, she is a woman, with great humanitarian instinct, but I have never seen it to disturb her judgment objectively and on questions of law" (April 4, 1966). Together, Javits and Kennedy made it clear that they were in full agreement with confirming Motley to the district court.

In addition to the statements of Kennedy and Javits, William Higgs, a young white liberal attorney in Washington, DC, from Mississippi, and head of the Students' Legal Research Council, also made a statement in support of Motley's nomination (Motley 1998). In his statement, Higgs shared why he thought Motley would make a fine federal judge:

> I have admired her as a lawyer, for her judicial temperament in court, her ability where many of us might panic in very difficult circumstances, not only in tension in terms of the court but great physical danger. Mrs. Motley has always stood calm, and given reasoned decision. In fact, I have seen her before so many judges that lacked the temperament that she had as a lawyer and, of course, her ability I think is absolutely outstanding, and it is very moving to me to see such a nomination be made because I think it is so eminently proper. (April 4, 1966)

Interestingly, Eastland did not appear at the subcommittee hearing. Moreover, no one opposed her appointment during the hearing either and "no derogatory information was brought forth" (Motley 1998, p. 215). Without substantial opposition, Motley's nomination was approved in the Senate Judiciary Committee, and was sent to the full Senate to be voted on.

While Eastland did not show up to Motley's hearing, he was present during Internal Security Subcommittee meetings, and it was during one of those subcommittee meetings that Eastland claimed he learned Motley had engaged in subversive activities and had ties to communism. In his statement on the Senate floor before the confirmation vote on Motley's nomination, Eastland described bearing witness to testimony by "a very high-class lady" who placed Motley in the Communist Party and said she engaged in subversive activities when she was in her teenage years (Congressional Record 1966). The witness, a high school teacher whom Motley identified in her autobiography as Estelle Segritta of New Haven, said Motley organized a communist study group at New York University, belonged to communist groups such as the Youth Communist League and Connecticut Youth Conference, participated in gatherings of communists in Washington, DC, and New Haven, Connecticut, and was actively being trained for the Red underground (Motley 1998, p. 216). In a memo archived in Senate records by Senator Javits, it becomes clear that this information on Motley was never made available, even after requested, to the Subcommittee on Motley's nomination nor to the entire Senate Judiciary Committee. In this vein, it seems Eastland did not just oppose and want to quash her nomination, but he also wanted to ruin her reputation and career. Motley notes the importance of the venue of Eastland's speech: "In a speech on the Senate floor, where he would be protected from libel and slander suits, Eastland said he opposed my nomination because he believed I was a Communist" (Motley 1998, p. 215–16). At the end of his speech, Eastland made it clear he would never support Motley's bid for federal judge: "Mr. President, I cannot approve this nomination. I could not vote for it in the committee" (Congressional Record 1966).

The allegation that Motley was a communist could have derailed her entire nomination/confirmation. It was only a few years prior to her appointment that there was widespread fear within the United States during the Cold War era about the rise of communism and radicalism worldwide, and it is clear that creating substantial opposition to Motley's appointment that would prevent her from being confirmed via calling her a communist was Eastland's intention. There had already been a precedent of calling individuals struggling for civil rights communists and socialists to discredit and create opposition to their work, especially black civil rights movement activists (Morris 1986). But New York Senator Javits, in his speech on the Senate floor following Eastland's speech, was able to counter the notion that Motley was or had ever been a communist.

In a speech that was interrupted multiple times by Eastland, Javits noted the qualifications of Motley, including her background and career accomplishments. He also addressed Eastland's insinuation that Motley was a communist. Not only did he focus on the fact that the witness against Motley gave "uncorroborated testimony," but that the testimony was gathered in a "totally collateral procedure" (Congressional Record 1966). In Motley's defense, Javits also pointed out that Motley had been in the public eye for all of her career and had been thoroughly vetted prior to her nomination (Congressional Record 1966). Motley had worked with the NAACP LDF for twenty years, and worked as a local and state political official for several years. No claims of communism had been waged against her during that time (Motley 1998). Moreover, as is the case for federal judicial nominees, before Johnson even announced her nomination, the FBI had done a thorough background security check to avoid the embarrassment that would surely happen if he had appointed a less-than-stellar candidate. Finally, Javits highlighted the fact that the witness's own husband denied the accusation entirely (Congressional Record 1966). Javits's statement forcefully discredited and denounced the claims made by Eastland.

After Javits's statement, which he ended by saying, "I urge the confirmation of her nomination," the presiding officer asked would the Senate advise and consent to the nomination. In a voice vote, Motley's nomination was overwhelmingly supported by the senators present, and on August 30, 1966, her nomination was approved. As to how many people opposed her nomination: "two senators, Eastland and John L. McClellan, a segregationist from Arkansas, voted against me" (Motley 1998, p. 215).

Overall, it took eight months for Motley to be confirmed to the federal bench, and most of that time was spent in the Senate Judiciary Committee awaiting action. While there was certainly more support for her nomination to the district court, Motley still faced substantial opposition. Most of this opposition came out in statements made by Eastland, but other senators, such as Javits and Kennedy, were able to refute Eastland's unsubstantiated assertions and advocate on Motley's behalf in the Senate Judiciary Committee and later on the Senate floor. It is this support that helped Motley gain access to the federal judiciary.

SECOND TIME'S THE CHARM?

There had always been hope that Motley would be elevated to the appellate level. When he first nominated her to the district court, Johnson told her, "You take this position on the district court and just work your way up" (Motley 1998, p. 214). Johnson's presidential career was short-lived as he was not re(s)elected in 1968, but presidents succeeding Johnson, such as President Jimmy Carter, still considered Motley for appointment to the Second Circuit. In a recent article, Raymond Lohier (2017), a current judge on the Second Circuit and a former assistant U.S. attorney for the SDNY, describes how Motley was later overlooked for appointment to the appellate level even after having established herself as a federal judge (p. 1807). In his article, Lohier writes that even after spending more than ten years on the federal bench, certain circuit court judges resisted the idea that Motley would join the Second Circuit (p. 1807). While the first time she was considered for the Second Court, resistance from Lombard, for example, stemmed from the fact that she was a black *woman* (Motley 1998), the second time she was considered for the circuit court, opposition claimed she was too liberal and that her high reversal rate as compared to her colleagues indicated her less-than-satisfactory decision-making skills (Lohier 2017, p. 1807; Motley 1998, p. 224–25).

These claims against her proved too much for Carter to overcome, and he never appointed her to an appellate court. In his article, Lohier (2017) analyzed whether Motley's reversal rate was significantly higher than her counterparts' reversal rates. After examining the reversal rates of SDNY judges who were also Democrat-appointees, Lohier found that her rate was not significantly different from the rates of her colleagues (p. 1810). And Lohier (2017) does not fail to point out recent work by political scientist Maya Sen (2015) who found that, in general, black district court judges are significantly more likely to be reversed on appeal than their white district court counterparts. It would appear that, while found worthy of appointment to the appellate level by Carter and perhaps other Democratic presidents, Motley, like many black judges, faced obstacles during judicial selection that are due to race and gender biases (Lohier 2017; Sen 2015). Unfortunately, Motley tried to work her way up the judicial ladder like Johnson told her to, but she was ultimately unable to overcome fierce opposition. But could some other black woman make it to the Second Circuit?

It should be noted that, despite the diversity of the Second Circuit, which again includes New York, Connecticut, and Vermont, there has only ever been one black woman to sit on that bench. Amalya Lyle Kearse, a Carter appointee, was confirmed in June 1979 to a new seat authorized by 92 Stat. 1629 on the Second Circuit and assumed senior status in that position in June 2002. She received her bachelor's degree from Wellesley College and her law degree from the University of Michigan Law School. Unlike Motley's path to the bench, Kearse spent her entire professional career in private practice in New York City, and she also taught at New York University Law School. Why Kearse and not Motley is a good question. It was not necessarily partisanship – like Kearse, Motley was a Democrat. Perhaps it is the career path (i.e., civil rights attorney) that Motley pursued that prevented her from joining the Second Circuit, or the fact that Kearse's work in New York City allowed her to be known in the area that "mattered" most in the circuit. Nevertheless, there is something to be said about the sad fact that with all of the black women living in the Second Circuit's jurisdiction, only one has ever been appointed to that bench.

LESSONS

While there are many lessons that scholars and women of color aspiring to the federal bench can and should take away from the nominations and confirmation of Motley, there are four primary lessons that I consider to be most valuable:

Do your thing. While Motley's background and career propelled her to be nominated to the federal bench, interestingly, it was this background and career as a civil rights lawyer that also made it difficult for her to get confirmed. Consequently, it is clear that from day one, women of color, and others, should do the kind of work that they want to do in this world. Motley did it. As a teenager, she worked on civil rights issues, and she spent most of her adult pre-bench career engaged in this kind of work with the LDF. Undoubtedly, this work made it more difficult for her to become a judge, as she had, along the way, opposed and fought systems of oppression. But her work did not preclude her from becoming a judge. Given this, it is clear that women of color can and should follow the career paths that allow them to do their best work.

Element of Luck. You can do everything right (i.e., be well-qualified, go to the best school, receive support from the legal community and interest groups, be rated qualified by bar associations, etc.) and still not be appointed. Motley recognized the luck factor: "You never have a drive to become a federal judge, because being appointed to the federal judiciary is a matter of sheer, unadulterated luck" (Washington 1994, p. 132). We see this today with some of the most prominent people in the legal profession – attorneys and even law professors such as Devon Carbado, Barbara Arnwine, Kimberle Crenshaw, and countless others who have not yet been appointed to the federal judiciary. While the process is surely political, it is clear that there is an element of luck at work and this luck is completely unpredictable and may or may not lead to a successful appointment to the federal bench.

Opposition. Motley's experiences in being nominated several times and then confirmed finally reveals that there will always be opposition, often times around race and gender, even when you are a stellar nominee like Motley. In her autobiography, Motley (1998) writes about this opposition and does not hold back, naming the people who made it difficult for her to reach the federal bench. But what was not discussed in this chapter due to space, is that the opposition did not go away once she made it to the bench. Also in her autobiography, Motley recalls the continuing opposition once she made it to the bench, and while her approach was to "laugh off the affront[s]," it is incredulous that a sitting federal judge would be disrespected by her colleagues and other political elites (Motley 1998, p. 222). Nonetheless, Motley makes it clear that there was never any shortage of opposition to her as a black woman judicial nominee or sitting federal judge.

Be Sure to Tell Your Story. We all should be incredibly grateful that Motley wrote an autobiography and gave interviews. Without these historical records, we would struggle to make sense and understand her life experiences that had not been described in detail elsewhere. Even the dust jacket on Ford's (2017) recently published book on Motley's life notes that Motley has largely been excluded and marginalized from the narrative surrounding the civil rights movement (Kristen Clark, President and CEO of the Lawyers Committee for Civil Rights under the Law). The same can be said of Motley being overlooked for her work as a federal judge. But beyond the autobiography and interviews, the reality is that a lot of what occurs during the federal judicial selection process happens behind closed doors. Unless people voluntarily share what happens, or nominees themselves speak and publicize their truths, we will not know for at least fifty years. Nomination records, including deliberations in subcommittee and all of the files related to judicial nominees, are closed for fifty years pursuant to Senate Resolution 474. This embargo of files makes it difficult to study how factors, such as race and gender, influence the federal judicial selection process.

In thinking about how these lessons might be applied to twenty-first-century federal judicial selection politics and processes, it is clear that presidents and senators need to reevaluate the metrics they use to appoint federal judges, because it may be disproportionately affecting black women's, and other women of color's, ability to reach the federal bench. Why is it that the career paths most likely to lead to federal judicial appointment – prosecutorial work, being a former state court judge – are careers that have significant histories of racial and gender exclusion? Moreover, why is it that Motley's work was seen as a problem by many senators, and that this work, which is often characterized as too liberal and progressive, often leads to qualified individuals being overlooked for judgeships by both Democratic and Republican presidents, including our nation's first black president? While he had the opportunity to, Obama had a propensity to appoint moderates to the bench, and not more "liberal" social justice–oriented individuals (Kimel and Randazzo 2012). Why is it that federal judges have more often than not gone to Ivy League and public schools for their undergraduate and law school educations, or that their net worth before joining the federal bench was most likely to be over $1 million (Slotnick, Goldman, and Schiavoni 2015)? These background characteristics are not only important for who gets nominated to the federal bench, but who gets confirmed. If we continue to appoint judges the same way we have always appointed them, and select judges from the same pools they have always been selected from, then we will continue to see a federal bench that does not reflect America. And, even if it reflects America by racial and gender standards, if the diversity of experiences of individuals appointed are also not considered, then, while the federal bench might increasingly look like America, it will not contain all of the perspectives that can be found within America. The approach to judicial selection has, whether intentional or not, made it possible to exclude individuals who might transform the federal judicial system, such as women of color, such as Motley.

CONCLUSION

To be clear, it was not just Motley who struggled to be confirmed; obstacles and obstruction in the federal judicial selection process is a longstanding problem (Scherer 2017). In 1959, the Senate Judiciary Committee obstructed Eisenhower's nominations to the federal district and appellate courts (Goldman 1999). Obama faced the most obstruction and struggled to get even his most "agreeable" nominees seated (Goldman, Slotnick, and Schiavoni 2013). But most obstruction has been due to partisan and ideological politics (Binder and Maltzman 2009, Giles, Hettinger, and Peppers 2001), and we saw some of this in the opposition to Motley (i.e., Eastland being a Southern Democrat). Motley's race and gender, however, just added to the typical "drama" in the committee, and we see this more and more with white women, and men and women of color judicial nominees (Asmussen 2011).

While it is not clear where this increased scrutiny comes from, some scholars, and even sitting and former black judges, suggest that black judicial nominees and judges are viewed differently than their white counterparts (Nagin-Brown 2017). There are often concerns about black (potential) judges' qualifications, including legal ability, but more often than not, there is a strong belief that black judges are biased in favor of the legal and policy preferences that they might have advocated for in their pre-bench careers (Ifill 1997). Whether race and gender substantially influence decision-making remains an unsettled topic in both political science and law, with some scholars arguing that identity matters and others finding that identity characteristics do not significantly determine the decisions that judges make (Means and Prado forthcoming; Nagin-Brown 2017; Segal 2000; Steffensmeier and Britt 2001).

Motley is considered a black woman of many firsts (Means forthcoming). While her firsts are great, unfortunately we do not often take the time to think through what being a first meant. As the first black woman federal judge, she experienced disturbing amounts of discrimination and opposition (Lohier 2017; Motley 1998; Nagin-Brown 2017; Washington 1994). But without Motley going through what she went through to get to the judiciary, with as much dignity and resolve as she did, we cannot say when the first black woman would have been appointed to the federal bench. It is clear that Motley partially paved the road faced by judges like Sonia Sotomayor, and more recently, the road faced by all twenty-four black women judges successfully appointed by Obama.

Again, race and gender both helped and hindered Motley's nominations and eventual confirmation to the federal bench. While her race and gender, and other factors led to presidential support, it was her race and gender, and other factors, that also led to senatorial opposition. This is unfortunate, but not completely unexpected given Nicole Asmussen's (2011) work and claim that presidents are often eager to appoint people of color and white women for whatever reason, but that it is hard to get these types of nominees through the Senate Judiciary Committee and confirmed by the Senate.

In conclusion, diversity matters on the federal bench because descriptive representation often leads to symbolic and substantive representation (Means and Prado forthcoming; Scherer and Curry 2010). We can predict that identity politics will continue to plague the federal judicial selection process, especially when it comes to appointing judges who are gender and/or racial minorities. And the stakes are incredibly high for federal judicial appointments. These lifetime appointments ensure that both presidents and senators take them seriously. Until diversity is fully embraced, judges who deviate from the norm (i.e., white male judges) will continue to face opposition, and therefore, we will continue to live in a country where black women are underrepresented on the federal bench and white men are overrepresented.

REFERENCES

Abraham, Henry J. 2008. *Justices, Presidents, and Senators: A History of the U.S. Supreme Court Appointments from Washington to Bush II*. 5th ed. Lanham, MD: Rowman & Littlefield Publishers.

Annis, J. Lee. 2016. *Big Jim Eastland: The Godfather of Mississippi*. Jackson: University Press of Mississippi.

Asmussen, Nicole. 2011. "Female and Minority Judicial Nominees: President's Delight and Senators' Dismay?" *Legislative Studies Quarterly* 36 (4): 591–619.

Bell, Lauren Cohen. 2002. "Senatorial Discourtesy: The Senate's Use of Delay to Shape the Federal Judiciary." *Political Research Quarterly* 55 (3): 589–607.

Binder, Sarah A., and Forrest Maltzman. 2009. *Advice and Dissent: The Struggle to Shape the Federal Judiciary*. Washington, DC: Brookings Institution Press.

Brown-Nagin, Tomiko. 2017. "Identity Matters: The Case of Judge Constance Baker Motley." *Columbia Law Review* 117 (7): 1691–1739.

Chin, Denny, and Kathy Hirata Chin. 2017. "Constance Baker Motley, James Meredith, and the University of Mississippi." *Columbia Law Review* 117 (7): 1741–77.

Congressional Record 20323. 1966.

Crenshaw, Kimberle. 1989. "Demarginalizing the Intersection of Race and Sex: A Black Feminist Critique of Antidiscrimination Doctrine, Feminist Theory and Antiracist Politics." *University of Chicago Legal Forum* 140: 139–68.

Eagles, Charles W. 2009. *The Price of Defiance: James Meredith and the Integration of Ole Miss*. Chapel Hill: University of North Carolina Press.

Ford, Gary L. 2017. *Constance Baker Motley: One Woman's Fight for Civil Rights and Equal Justice under Law*. Tuscaloosa: University of Alabama Press.

Giles, Micheal W., Virginia A. Hettinger, and Todd Peppers. 2001. "Picking Federal Judges: A Note on Policy and Partisan Selection Agendas." *Political Research Quarterly* 54 (3): 623–41.

Goldman, Sheldon. 1999. *Picking Federal Judges: Lower Court Selection from Roosevelt through Reagan*. New Haven, CT: Yale University Press.

Goldman, Sheldon, Elliot Slotnick, and Sara Schiavoni. 2013. "Obama's First Term Judiciary: Picking Judges in the Minefield of Obstructionism." *Judicature* 97 (1): 7–48.

Hancock, Ange-Marie. 2007a. "Intersectionality as a Normative and Empirical Paradigm." *Politics & Gender* 3 (2): 248–54.

2007b. "When Multiplication Doesn't Equal Quick Addition: Examining Intersectionality as a Research Paradigm." *Perspectives on Politics* 5 (1): 63–79.

Hunter, Marjorie. 1986. "James O. Eastland is Dead at 81; Leading Senate FOE of Integration." *The New York Times*. February 20. www.nytimes.com/1986/02/20/obituaries/james-o-eastland-is-dead-at-81-leading-senate-foe-of-integration.html.

Ifill, Sherrilyn A. 1997. "Judging the Judges: Racial Diversity, Impartiality and Representation on State Trial Courts." *BCL Rev.* 39 (1): 95–149.

Jack, Rand, and Dana Crowley Jack. 1989. *Moral Vision and Professional Decisions: The Changing Values of Women and Men Lawyers*. New York: Cambridge University Press.

Jordan-Zachery, Julia S. 2007. "Am I a Black Woman or a Woman Who is Black? A Few Thoughts on the Meaning of Intersectionality." *Politics & Gender* 3 (2): 254–63.

Kimel, T. J., and Kirk A. Randazzo. 2012. "Shaping the Federal Courts: The Obama Nominees." *Social Science Quarterly* 93 (5): 1243–50.

Lohier Jr., Raymond J. 2017. "On Judge Motley and the Second Circuit." *Columbia Law Review* 117 (7): 1803–23.

Martinek, Wendy L., Mark Kemper, and Steven R. Van Winkle. 2002. "To Advise and Consent: The Senate and Lower Federal Court Nominations, 1977–1998." *The Journal of Politics* 64 (2): 337–61.

Mayhew, David R. 1974. *Congress: The Electoral Connection*. New Haven, CT: Yale University Press.

Morris, Aldon D. 1986. *The Origins of the Civil Rights Movement*. New York: Simon and Schuster.

Motley, Constance Baker. 1998. *Equal Justice under Law: An Autobiography*. New York: Farrar, Straus & Giroux.

Navarro, Sharon A. 2013. "Moving On Up: The Political Incorporation of Hispanic Women into the Federal Judiciary of Texas." *Latino Studies* 11 (1): 4–20.

Nemacheck, Christine L. 2017. "Appointing Supreme Court Justices." In *The Oxford Handbook of U.S. Judicial Behavior*, eds. Lee Epstein and Stefanie A. Linquist. New York: Oxford University Press.

Nixon, David C., and David L. Goss. 2001. "Confirmation Delay for Vacancies on the Circuit Courts of Appeals." *American Politics Research* 29 (3): 246–74.

Salkin, Patricia E. 2011. *Pioneering Women Lawyers: From Kate Stoneman to the Present*. Chicago: American Bar Association.

Scherer, Nancy. 2017. "Appointing Federal Judges." In *The Oxford Handbook of U.S. Judicial Behavior*, eds. Lee Epstein and Stefanie A. Linquist. New York: Oxford University Press.

Scherer, Nancy, and Brett Curry. 2010. "Does Descriptive Race Representation Enhance Institutional Legitimacy? The Case of the US Courts." *The Journal of Politics* 72(1): 90–104.

Schraufnagel, Scot. 2005. "Testing the Implications of Incivility in the United States Congress, 1977–2000: The Case of Judicial Confirmation Delay." *The Journal of Legislative Studies* 11 (2): 216–34.

Segal, Jennifer A. 2000. "Representative Decision Making on the Federal Bench: Clinton's District Court Appointees." *Political Research Quarterly* 53 (1): 137–50.

Sen, Maya. 2015. "Is Justice Really Blind? Race and Reversal in US Courts." *The Journal of Legal Studies* 44(1): 187–229.

Simien, Evelyn M. 2007. "Doing Intersectionality Research: From Conceptual Issues to Practical Examples." *Politics & Gender* 3 (2): 264–71.

Slotnick, Elliot, Sheldon Goldman, and Sara Schiavoni. 2015. "Writing the Book of Judges: Part 1: Obama's Judicial Appointments Record after Six Years." *Journal of Law and Courts* 3 (2): 331–67.

Solowiej, Lisa A., Wendy L. Martinek, and Thomas L. Brunell. 2005. "Partisan Politics: The Impact of Party in the Confirmation of Minority and Female Federal Court Nominees." *Party Politics* 11 (5): 557–77.

Steffensmeier, Darrell, and Chester L. Britt. 2001. "Judges' Race and Judicial Decision Making: Do Black Judges Sentence Differently?" *Social Science Quarterly* 82 (4): 749–64.

Steigerwalt, Amy. 2010. *Battle over the Bench: Senators, Interest Groups, and Lower Court Confirmations*. Charlottesville: University of Virginia Press.

Stubbs, Jonathan K. 2016. "Demographic History of Federal Judicial Appointments by Sex and Race: 1789–2016, A." *Berkeley La Raza LJ* 26 (4): 92–128.

Washington, Linn. 1994. *Black Judges on Justice: Perspectives from the Bench*. New York: New Press.

Alexandra Searles, Alexandra Searles Art and Design

6

Diversity Abound

Will Federal Judicial Appointees Mirror a Changing Citizenry?

SHENITA BRAZELTON AND LATASHA CHAFFIN-DEHAAN

In 2009, President Barack Obama made history by nominating the first person of Latin American origin to the U.S. Supreme Court. What made Obama's nomination even more historic was the appointment of a Latina – Judge Sonia Sotomayor of the Second Circuit ascended to the Supreme Court of the United States. However, these firsts are not commonplace: men are not only nominated and confirmed more often than women, the nomination and confirmation is disproportionately lower for Black women and Latinas. As the demographics of the United States change, the federal judiciary has lagged in reflecting these changes, particularly for minority female judges. There are currently 727 active federal district and circuit court judges. Of those judges, 34 percent are women and only 9 percent are women of color (Federal Judicial Center 2017). These statistics are in contrast to an increasingly diverse America. The United States has a population of 51 percent women, comprised of 17 percent Black women and Latinas (U.S. Census Bureau 2017a, 2017b). The federal judiciary continues to lag behind a growing minority population, but gains have been made. In this chapter, we examine the determinants that influence the nomination and confirmation of Black women and Latinas to the federal judiciary.

LITERATURE ON WOMEN AND MINORITIES IN THE FEDERAL JUDICIARY

Due to discrimination, women have trailed men in ascending to the federal bench. The first woman was appointed to the federal bench shortly after the

The author would like to thank Aleah Johnson of the College of Charleston for her interview transcription services.

ratification of the Nineteenth Amendment. Genevieve Cline was appointed to the U.S. Customs Court in 1928 by President Calvin Coolidge. Racial and ethnic minorities have faced even more discrimination. It was ten years later when the first minority judge, William Hastie, was appointed to the federal bench. In 1937, President Franklin D. Roosevelt made history by appointing Hastie as the first African American federal judge (Brazelton and Pinderhughes 2019). However, it would be thirty more years before the first minority female appointment. In 1966, President Lyndon Johnson appointed the first Black woman, Constance Baker Motley, to a federal district court in New York. Even later was the first Latina in 1980 with President Jimmy Carter's appointment of Carmen Cezero to the District Court of Puerto Rico. It was not until Carter's presidency that women of color were appointed in meaningful numbers (see Table 6.1). Even though minority men have made gains in judicial appointments, minority women have lagged behind.

Judicial scholars have conducted a number of studies examining diversity of racial/ethnic minorities and women within the judicial system. Particularly, scholars have assessed the determinants of diversity within the judiciary, examining both federal and state court systems. Scholars have considered a number of explanations. Among these is the "trickle-up" theory. Examined in the context of gender diversity, the theory provides that as the number of women entering the legal profession increases, the number of women attaining seats within the judiciary will also increase. A seat on the federal judiciary is very prestigious, with more prestige for appointments higher in federal judicial hierarchy. Cook (1984) asserts that the "trickle-up" theory is insufficient given the power of "gatekeepers," who have power to fill vacancies and often do so with individuals of "their own kind" (p. 573). Gatekeepers must have positive attitudes toward diversity and must take affirmative steps to diversify a court. She asserts that there are additional factors that must be present for a woman to fill a vacancy. She states that in addition to the number of qualified available women, a larger court for more available seats to fill is necessary. Cook asserts that these gatekeepers more often allow women entry into the less prestigious positions, while maintaining more prestigious positions for men (p. 573–74). Cook's initial observations have been supported by empirical evidence and have endured over time (see Alozie 1996; Hurwitz and Lanier 2003; Kenney 2012; Reddick et al. 2009; Spill and Bratton 2001). These scholars have found that an increase of the percentage of women in the legal profession does not predict an increase in women sitting in the judiciary. More contemporary scholarship provides that the criteria for assessing qualifications of prospective female candidates are biased. Kenney (2012) utilizes a legal concept from employment discrimination law and applies it to explain

TABLE 6.1 *Appointment of minority federal judges*

President	Black Judges (Men/ Women) Total		Latino Judges (Men/ Women) Total		Black Judges (Men/Women) Circuit Courts		Latino Judges (Men/Women) Circuit Courts		Black Judges (Men/ Women) District Courts		Latino Judges (Men/ Women) District Courts	
LBJ	8 (5%)	1 (0.06%)	3 (2%)	–	2 (.05%)	–	–	–	6 (0.05%)	1 (0.01%)	3 (0.02%)	–
Nixon	6 (0.03%)	–	2 (0.01%)	–	–	–	–	–	6 (0.03%)	–	2 (0.01%)	–
Ford	3 (0.05%)	–	1 (0.02%)	–	–	–	–	–	3 (0.06%)	–	1 (0.02%)	–
Carter	30 (12%)	7 (3%)	5 (0.06%)	1 (0.004%)	8 (14%)	1 (2%)	2 (4%)	–	22 (11%)	6 (3%)	13 (6%)	1 (0.005%)
Reagan	6 (2%)	1 (0.003%)	13 (4%)	1 (0.003%)	1 (1%)	–	1 (1%)	–	5 (2%)	1 (.3%)	12 (4%)	1 (0.3%)
Bush I	9 (5%)[1]	2 (1%)	5 (3%)	3 (2%)	2 (5%)	–	2 (5%)	–	8 (5%)	2 (1%)	3 (2%)	3 (2%)
Clinton	46 (13%)	15 (4%)[2]	19 (5%)	6 (2%)	6 (9%)	3 (5%)	5 (8%)	2 (3%)	40 (13%)	13 (4%)	14 (5%)	4 (1%)
Bush II	16 (5%)	8 (3%)	18 (6%)	12 (4%)	4 (6%)	2 (3%)	2 (3%)	1 (2%)	12 (5%)	6 (2%)	16 (6%)	11 (4%)
Obama	35 (11%)[3]	26 (8%)	23 (7%)	11 (3%)[4]	7 (13%)	2 (4%)	4 (7%)	2 (4%)	29 (11%)	24 (9%)	19 (7%)	9 (3%)
Trump	–	–	–	–	–	–	–	–	–	–	–	–
Total[5]	150 (7%)	58 (3%)	92 (4%)	31 (1%)	29 (6%)	8 (2%)	16 (3%)	5 (1%)	131 (7%)	53 (3%)	84 (5%)	29 (2%)

Total percentage of the judiciary are in parenthesis.
Source: Federal Judicial Center (2018)

[1] The total is 9, considering President Bush appointed Timothy Lewis to the District Court and then elevated him to the Third Circuit.
[2] The total is 15, considering President Clinton appointed Johnnie Rawlinson to the District Court and then elevated her to the Ninth Circuit.
[3] The total is 35, considering President Obama appointed Andre Davis to the District Court and then elevated him to the Fourth Circuit.
[4] Judge Analisa Torres of the District Court identifies as African-America and Latina; therefore, totals for the "District Courts" column and overall totals include her identification for both groups.
[5] The total is 150, given that many presidents elevated previously appointed district court judges to the circuit court.

the lack of diversity for women. She discusses how women have been subject to disparate treatment, which is a form of explicit discrimination against women. However, under the theory of disparate impact, seemingly generally applicable rules have a disproportionally discriminatory impact on women. Although there are no constitutional qualifications for attaining a seat on the federal court, the legal profession has developed norms or informal "qualifications" to sit on a federal court. These "norms" (experience as a partner in a large law firm, a U.S. attorney, state court judge, etc.) serve as barriers to restrict women's ability to attain federal judicial appointments because women face barriers to gain positions in these more prestigious positions (p. 1499). Beyond these "norms," governors or presidents who appoint women or minorities to a court often do so when there is absence of a woman or minority sitting on the court. That is, they desire to receive credit for the appointment of a first woman or minority to sit on a bench. At the state level, a governor is more likely to appoint a woman to a state supreme court if there are no women sitting on that court (Bratton and Spill 2002). This research tends to support the notion of tokenism – that is, the woman is a token because the effort to diversify the bench subsides after one woman is appointed to a court (Clark 2004). When a woman retires, another woman is not as likely to replace the female predecessor (Bratton and Spill 2002).

Much of the scholarship that provides explanations and evidence on the lack of diversity on the judiciary provides similar evidence on the dearth of minorities sitting on the bench. The scholarship is promising but still troubling. The likelihood of appointing a Black candidate to a federal court is negatively statistically significant with the number of Black judges who had already been appointed to the court (Solberg and Bratton 2005). This evidence lends to the notion of tokenism insofar as there is a threshold for the number of minorities that a president will appoint.

There are certain factors that increase the likelihood of an appointment of a minority candidate. Examining federal district courts, Solberg and Bratton (2005) find that the greater number of authorized seats within a district court and a larger number of minority attorneys within a state increase the likelihood of an African-American or Latino nomination to the court. A similar effect was found for female candidates. Gryski et al. (1994) likewise examined appointments to the federal district court, finding that the presence of minority judges on state courts of last resort and federal judicial districts with higher minority voting age populations increase the number of Black and Latino federal district court appointees. For Black judges, having a Black U.S. House representative increases the number of Black federal district court judges. The number of Latino businesses increases the percentage of Latino judges.

This literature provides evidence that minority legal communities matter: it shows that having a large population of minority and female attorneys as well as minority judges sitting on state courts increase the likelihood of nominations to the federal bench. The literature also indicates that representation matters. Having higher minority voting age populations and minority representatives in the House also increase the number of Black federal judges. This may provide some support that minority voters assert political pressures on members of the Senate to nominate and confirm minority candidates. This evidence is supported by qualitative albeit anecdotal evidence: Georgia Democratic Senator Wyche Fowler voted to confirm Clarence Thomas to the U.S. Supreme Court in the face of cross pressures between his party and liberal interest groups who opposed Thomas, and his Black constituents who favored the nominee (Asmussen 2011). Although the Congressional Black Caucus has had very few members in the Senate, thus limiting the ability to assert senatorial courtesy for district court nominees, they have influence and are able to successfully advocate for the appointment of Black judges.

However, the literature also provides significant evidence that minorities face more difficulties in the confirmation process, but the scholarship examining confirmation for women varies. Examining both circuit and district court nominees, Schraufnagel (2005) found that minority judges are 25 percent less likely to be confirmed than non-minority judges, but found no effect for gender. Martinek et al. (2002) found longer confirmation times for minority district court nominees but found no similar effect for female district court or circuit court nominees. However, Nixon and Goss (2001) found that both female and minority nominees to the federal circuit court are delayed almost twice as long as male and non-minority nominees. Bell (2002) examined institutional factors of delay in confirmation for both district and circuit court nominees, finding that divided government lengthens delay for both women and minorities, but has no effect under unified government. Solowiej et al. (2005) found an effect based on the party in control of Congress and the presidency, with women benefiting the most under unified Republican control and minorities facing the most resistance under unified Republican control. But some scholarship finds little evidence on delay for women and minorities for district and circuit court nominees (Hartley 2001; Scherer et al. 2008). What is common in the literature is the aggregation of race and gender. That is, these studies aggregate women *and* minorities when conducting empirical tests. The literature fails to parse out the effects for minority women and minority men.

Few scholars have studied the intersectionality of race and gender in the context of the judiciary. One of the early works is that of Kimberle Crenshaw

(1989), a legal scholar who developed a feminist theory on the intersectionality of Black women. Her theory provides that minority women face more discrimination than White women and minority men because the intersection of being a minority woman compounds discrimination. Such intersectionality work has had some scholarship in the context of legislative representation (Brown 2014; Orey et al. 2006; Smooth 2011). Few scholars have examined intersectionality in the judiciary. Among those is the work of Collins and Moyer (2008), who examine the voting behavior of Black women and Latina federal appellate court judges. They find that Black women and Latinas are more likely than White men and minority men to vote in favor of the criminally accused. Haire and Moyer (2015) examine the appointments of Black women and Latina federal circuit court judges. They find that minority women tend to have more prior experience as prosecutors, have either held an elected position or served as their aid, or have served in a cabinet in a state government (p. 63). Most notably, female minority nominees are more likely to hold positions as a judge than White men, who are more likely to work in private practice at the time of their nomination.

The aforementioned studies are limited to minority females within the federal circuit courts. We conduct a qualitative study examining perspectives of diversity on the federal judiciary for Black women and Latina federal judges sitting both on the federal district and circuit courts. Given that the vast majority of literature examines the appointment of women and/or minority judges, we obtain the perspectives of these minority female judges on ways to obtain diversity for women of color on the federal bench. Because minority women face very unique challenges in ways that White women and minority men do not encounter, we set forth a study to provide the unique perspectives of the intersectionality of race and gender for Black women and Latinas sitting on the federal judiciary.

JUDICIAL PIPELINE THEORY

Our theoretical contribution is the judicial pipeline theory. While there has been scholarship on the determinants of judicial selection, we posit that there are four areas of development that are necessary for highly qualified diverse minority and female talent to have inroads into the legal profession and to obtain the opportunity to ascend to the federal bench. First, in order for top legal minds to be nominated to serve on the federal bench there has to be a commitment from political leadership including the sitting U.S. president, senators, and representatives to diversify the bench. We term this *political leaders' commitment to diversity*. Previous scholarship has proffered that having a Black U.S. House Representative, for example, increases the likelihood of Black nominees being confirmed to the federal bench (Asmussen 2011, Gryski et al. 1994). It has also been asserted that the party in power matters, with women faring better under unified Republican control, while minorities fared worse (Solowiej et al. 2005). Secondly, there must be formal and informal institutional mechanisms in place to cultivate the educational background and experience necessary for minorities and women to have inroads into opportunities for legal education and careers. We term this *inroads*. Haire and Moyer (2015) found that minority women tend to have greater experience and in more non-traditional legal backgrounds. Opportunities for traditional pathways to the bench, including federal clerkships, need to be developed, and non-traditional pathways, for example through state trial court experience, recognized as commensurate. Thirdly, once a part of the legal profession, it is essential for attorneys to acquire professional socialization in order to form the social and political networks necessary to receive the support to become nominated to the federal bench. We term this *professional socialization*. It is apparent that systemic discrimination against minorities and women "has been both formal, through decisions by courts, legislatures, law schools, and bar associations to prevent political minorities from entering or engaging in the legal profession" (Graham 1990; Hurwitz and Lanier 2003, p. 329). As a result, both inroads into legal careers and professional socialization once attorneys are members of the legal community are essential to breaking down these discriminatory barriers. Lastly, the American Bar Association (ABA) ratings influence the potential for judicial nominees to be nominated and confirmed to the federal bench. We term this ABA *favorability*. There is evidence of lower ABA ratings for women, Black, and Latino federal judicial nominees that is impactful as it slows the nomination process and can negatively influence confirmation (Sen 2014).

METHODOLOGY

At the time of our research, there were 1,311 sitting federal judges, and of these, 350 or 27 percent were women. Of the 350 appointments of current sitting judges, 257 or 73 percent identify as White, and 93 or 27 percent of the remaining women embody some degree of racial or ethnic diversity. Of these, 12 minority judges have currently earned senior status. To qualify for senior status, a judge's age and years of service must add up to 80, they must be at least 65 or older, and they must be on the bench for 10 years. While the responsibilities of senior status judges are the same as judges that have not earned this status and their salary remains unchanged, they receive a reduced caseload (Cornell University 2017). Of the eighty-eight appointments of Latina and Black women in the history of the United States, 53 or 15 percent Black female judges and 29 or 8.3 percent Latina female judges were currently sitting and serving on the federal bench (Federal Judicial Center 2017).

An anonymous, internet-based survey was sent to seventy-four sitting Black and Latina female federal judges that we were able to identify contact information for in November 2017. The inquiries ranged from questions regarding the judges' qualifications (including the president that nominated them and their ABA ratings) to demographic questions including race, salary, and marital status, and lastly and predominantly questions regarding judicial selection procedures and their professional assessments regarding the diversification of the courts. There were sixteen total respondents yielding a 22 percent response rate. However, the only forced choice questions that existed were ones that qualified the respondents to complete the survey (e.g., "Are you currently a sitting federal judge?") or to respond to specified questions in the survey as a qualifier for the next question (e.g., "Do you qualify for senior status and if so, have you served on senior status?"). As a result, there were judges that opted out of some questions. There was also an opportunity for the respondents to identify themselves through a separate survey in order to be interviewed, of which four sitting federal female Black and Latina judges agreed. Because of the discrete number of female minority judges, the response rate of the survey is commensurable to an already small sample size. Descriptive statistics are provided based on the quantitative small N data collected triangulated with analyses of the qualitative data collected from the internet-based survey and the elite interviews.

Due to the sensitivity of the survey questions asked and the confidential nature of the work that these prestigious judges engage in, all survey and interview participants were advised that conscientious efforts would be made to ensure their anonymity. The federal judges who agreed to elite interviews were advised that their comments would be anonymously reported and that they would be allowed to preview any comments that they individually made that were included prior to publication.

SURVEY AND INTERVIEW FINDINGS

General Background Information

Of the sixteen respondents, twelve identified their race. There were nine Black judges, one Latina, and two judges identified as "other." Overall, for those judges who responded to the survey questions regarding the level of court they sit on and their tenure, 83 percent served as a district court judge and 17 percent served as a circuit court judge. Fifty-four percent of the respondents served as a judge prior to their federal judgeship. The prior service noted was experience as a state trial or appellate court judge, with respondents indicating tenure of between five and twenty years prior to being appointed to the federal bench. This group of esteemed Black and Latina female judges practiced in a variety of areas of law prior to their judgeships, such as such as criminal prosecution and criminal defense, civil litigation, employment and labor law, and family law. When considering geographic diversity, the federal judge respondents sit in courts in the East, Midwest, South, and West.

We additionally interviewed four federal judges, three of whom where district court judges and one a circuit court judge. Of this group, three were Black women and one was a Latina. Three judges had prior experience as a state court judge presiding both on trial and appellate courts. These women all have experience in private practice, with a broad array of practice areas; one judge has experience in academia.

Nominating President, Political Party Affiliation, and Judicial Ideology

Of the Black and Latina survey respondents who indicated the president that nominated them to the federal bench, nine were nominated by President Barack Obama. Of these, six judges identified as Democrats, two identified as Independents, and one judge responded she would rather not disclose her political party affiliation. Only one judge identified herself as judicial restraintist, and the remaining eight respondents to this question indicated that they would rather not disclose their judicial ideology.

Additionally, one federal judge was nominated by President George W. Bush and identified herself as a Democrat, and she was the respondent that also identified as a judicial restraintist. Lastly, one judge was nominated by President Clinton and indicated that she ascribed to no political party affiliation and chose not to disclose her judicial ideology (see Figure 6.1).

Perspectives on Diversity within the Federal Judiciary

The survey and interview questions focused on gaining perspectives on the importance of diversity within the federal judiciary. When asked whether the courts are representative of the demographic makeup of the United States, the comments were sharp and telling (see Figure 6.2). It was expressed that many of these Black and Latina judges are the only minority judges in terms of

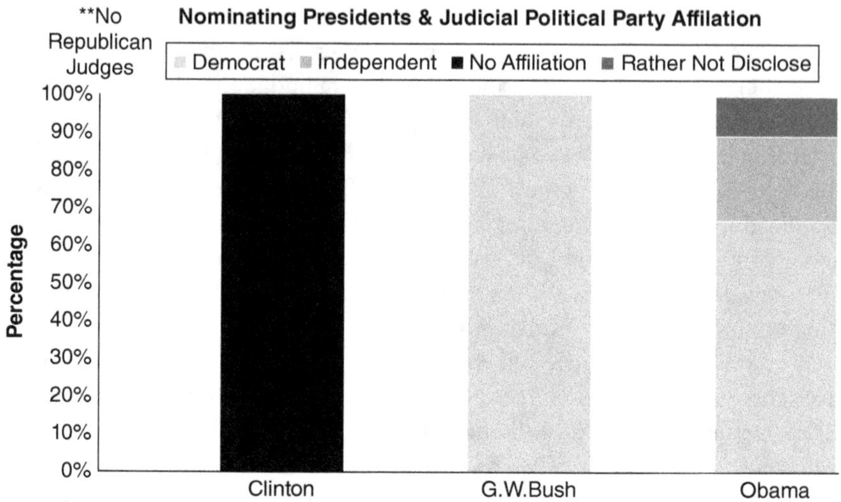

FIGURE 6.1 Nominating presidents and judicial political party affiliation

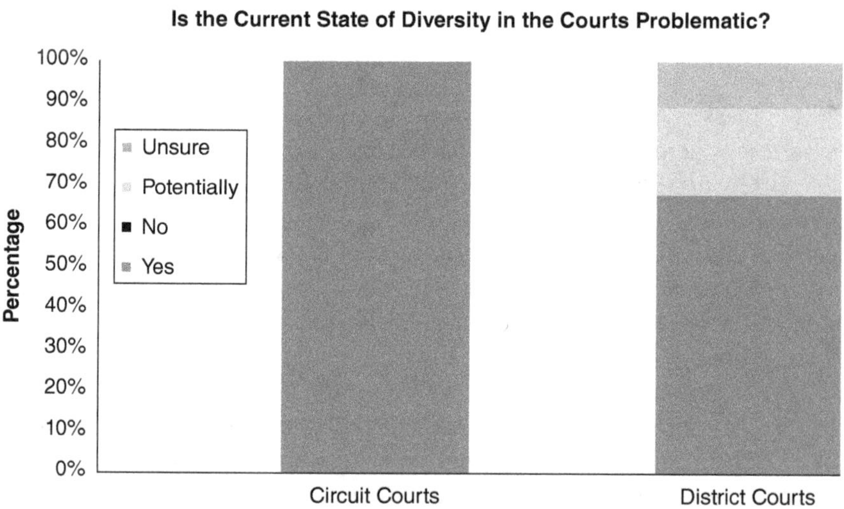

FIGURE 6.2 Is the current state of diversity in the courts problematic?

race and/or gender in their state or court. The comments were deliberative and unambiguous:

- "The faces (and wallets) of our federal Bench fail to reflect the diversity found in America; I wish the process could be made non-partisan and could result in a Bench that looks more like a Naturalization Ceremony and less like a Wall Street luncheon."

- "I was the first and remain the only African American federal judge in the state of _____."
- "The entire federal court system, from judges to clerks to security officers, lacks significant diversity."
- "Greater diversity is needed at each level of the judiciary. Many Circuits have no women of color on Circuit courts. No Circuit has more than one."
- "I work extra hard as the first Latina on the bench .... Just because you have one doesn't mean you've accomplished diversity..."

When asked whether diversity on the federal courts impacts the ability of the courts to equitably represent the interests of the United States, many of the judges affirmatively stated that the justice system is more fair and equitable when there are diverse perspectives on the federal bench:

- "Diversity reflects favorably on the institution because the institutions reflect the demographics of the community."
- "Yes. The public's trust and confidence in the judiciary depends in part on broadly defined diversity."
- "Without question; the closer the Bench's diversity reflects the diversity of the parties that come before the courts (especially the parties facing criminal charges), the better that justice is delivered."
- "Yes. I have encountered situations with my colleagues over the years where my voice and experiences have influenced them."
- "Yes. Although you may not be able to determine whether a decision is made by a male, female or judge of color; diversity on the bench makes the process more just and credible and promotes confidence in the courts."
- "Absolutely. Growing stratification in the legal profession should alarm any person interested in promoting a judicial system that reflects the incredible diversity of our country, as perceptions of inequity necessarily erode the fundamental idea – etched in stone at the entrance to our highest court – that we can all expect 'equal justice under the law.' Because our laws are the glue that makes civilization possible, a legal profession that reflects the great diversity of our communities is critical to the health of our nation."

In response to the question of how diversity on the federal courts can be increased to mirror the changing diversity of the United States, the commentary included:

- "President and Senators must care about promoting diversity."
- "Better selection processes, including more diverse representation on the selection committees."

- "I hope that reducing partisanship in the appointment process might increase diversity."
- "Encourage potential candidates to become involved politically, civically and professionally. Encourage people to seek out an inclusive group of friends, acquaintances, advisors and professional colleagues."
- "By ensuring that youngsters of diverse backgrounds receive a high quality education and access to higher education and graduate education. By ensuring that students from diverse backgrounds are educated about legal opportunities and the necessary qualifications. By ensuring that the cost of education is not a barrier to entering the legal profession. By mentoring lawyers and demystifying the judicial selection process. By using merit selection processes that solicit applications broadly and include merit selection committees from diverse regions and backgrounds."

DISCUSSION AND CONCLUSIONS

History of Black and Latino/a Judicial Appointments

Presidents have the purview to nominate Article III judges who have lifetime appointments to the U.S. Supreme Court, the Court of Appeals, and District Courts. In examining judicial diversity across the federal courts, the nomination and confirmation of diverse Black male and Latino judges became more prevalent during the 1960s during the presidency of Lyndon B. Johnson, with Black male judges receiving 5 percent of the federal judicial appointments, Black female judges receiving 0.6 percent of the appointments, Latino male judges receiving 2 percent of the appointments, and Latino females having no appointees (see Table 6.1). The confirmation of Black and Latino male federal judges continued during the Nixon and Ford administrations yet at a considerably slower pace. Under President Nixon, 0.3 percent and under President Ford 0.5 percent of Black male judges received federal judicial appointments. Under President Nixon, 0.1 percent and under President Ford 0.02 percent of Latino male judges earned federal judgeships again with no Black female or Latina judges confirmed. The diversity of the federal courts began to substantially increase for both Black and Latino/a male and female judges during the Carter administration with 12 percent of the federal judgeships during the Carter administration awarded to Black male judges and 3 percent to Black female judges. In addition to 0.6 percent of federal judicial appointments being awarded to Latino male judges, the first Latina federal judge was confirmed under the Carter administration representing 0.004 percent of the Carter appointments. There were fewer confirmations during the Reagan and G. H. W. Bush administrations relative to the Carter administration, yet minority federal judges were appointed at a steady rate. In the Reagan administration, 2 percent of the appointees, and in the G. H. W. Bush administration 5 percent of the appointees were Black male judges, while only 0.003 percent of judicial confirmations during the Reagan administration went to Black female judges and 1 percent under the G. H. W. Bush administration. Latino judges made some strides during the Reagan and Bush administrations where 4 percent and 3 percent, respectively, of the judicial appointments were earned by Latino male judges and 1 percent and 2 percent, respectively, were earned by Latina female judges.

During the Clinton administration is where the sea change occurred, with the most nominations and confirmations of Black and Latino/a judges up to that point in history, even surpassing the diversity of the courts during the Carter administration, with 13 percent of the federal judgeships acquired by Black male judges and 4 percent by Black female judges. Under the Clinton administration, 5 percent of the federal judgeships were held by Latino judges and 2 percent by Latina judges. The G. W. Bush administration followed with relatively modest minority nominations and confirmations to the bench with 5 percent of federal Black male judges and 3 percent of Black female judges confirmed to the bench. Yet the G. W. Bush administration did further the diversification of the courts as it relates to Latina judges, with 4 percent of its judgeships represented by this demographic and 6 percent represented by Latino judges. President Obama faced opposition from the political right that was impacted by the transition from unified to divided government and had thirty-six of his nominations blocked by Republican Senators. However, the Obama administration still managed to appoint the most diverse total body of Black and Latina judges to the federal bench to date, while keeping pace with previous Democratic administrations in nominating Black and Latino judges to serve on the federal bench. Under the Obama administration, 8 percent of the appointees were Black female judges and 3 percent were Latina judges. Comparable to the Carter and Clinton administrations, 11 percent of federal judgeships under the Obama administration were granted to Black male judges and 7 percent to Latino judges (see Table 6.1).

During the first year of the Trump administration, in a time of unified government, President Trump nominated twenty-three Article III judges as of January 17, 2018, earning him the ranking of six out nineteen presidents appointing the highest number of federal judges during their first year. Even with placing federal judges at this rate, there were 145 vacancies at the beginning of 2018, with 43 nominations pending (Kim 2018). In terms of judicial diversity, while President Clinton's nominees were 72.3 percent White, President G. W. Bush's nominees 86.2 percent White, and President Obama's nominees 48.5 percent White, President Trump's nominees have been 91.2 percent White (Norton Holmes, and Eleanor 2018). During his first year in office, President Trump nominated 19 percent female judges compared to the 42 percent President Obama nominated during his two terms in office, and only 2 percent of President Trump's female nominees during his first year were nonwhite (Anapol 2017). During the first year of the Trump administration, one nominee was Black, one was Hispanic, and four were Asian (Schneier 2018).

Will Diversity in the Courts Mirror a Changing Citizenry?

The United States is projected to be majority-minority by 2043. By 2055, there will be no racial or ethnic majority in the United States (Pew Research Center 2016). In our analysis is a unanimous sentiment by the federal judges interviewed that as the country becomes more diverse it is imperative that qualified female minority federal judges be in contention for federal judicial nominations and confirmed to the federal bench through a largely bipartisan process. This equitable representation in the federal courts is essential as judges from diverse backgrounds are able to relate to the circumstances of a diverse citizenry. In the federal court system, the Black and Latina judges in this study proffered that American citizens benefit from having judges from diverse backgrounds – be it race, gender, religion, socioeconomic status, or diversity of experience and education (along with many other diverse characteristics) – to hear and adjudicate cases that have lasting impacts on their lives.

While other scholars have analyzed the diversification of the courts in relation to minorities or women in the aggregate (e.g., Hurwitz and Lanier 2003; Kenney 2012; Spill and Bratton 2001), this analysis examines the intersectionality of the diversification of Black and Latina judges that are both women and minorities. While this analysis focuses on these judges' perceptions of the courts, it is implausible to posit the causes of the disproportionality of the diversification of the federal courts and its implications on society without a discussion of judicial selection procedures. We introduce the judicial pipeline theory as an extension of previous scholarship, and its theoretical components include commitment to diversity from political leadership, inroads, political socialization, and ABA favorability. This theory is partially derived from comments from the federal Black and Latina judges regarding what they deemed were important determinants of diversity within the judiciary. These judges posited that if the judicial pipeline is developed systemically, then the diversity of the federal courts will increase over time, possibly even one day mirroring the diverse mosaic of the society in which modern day Americans live.

REFERENCES

Allison, G. W. 1996. "Delay in Senate Confirmation of Federal Judicial Nominees." *Judicature* (80), 8.

Alozie, N. O. 1996. "Recruitment of Women to State Courts of Last Resort." *Social Science Quarterly* (77) 110.

Anapol, Avery. 2017. "Trump Picking White Males for the Judiciary at the Highest Rate in 30 Years." *The Hill.* http://thehill.com/homenews/administration/360158-ap-trump-picks-white-males-for-judicial-positions-at-the-highest-rate.

Asmussen, N. 2011. "Female and Minority Judicial Nominees: President's Delight and Senators' Dismay?" *Legislative Studies Quarterly* 36(4): 591–619.

Bell, L. C. 2002. "Senatorial Discourtesy: The Senate's Use of Delay to Shape the Federal Judiciary." *Political Research Quarterly* 55(3): 589–607.

BLS Monthly Labor Review. 2013. "Marriage and Divorce: Patterns by Gender, Race and Educational Attainment." www.bls.gov/opub/mlr/2013/article/marriage-and-divorce-patterns-by-gender-race-and-educational-attainment.htm.

Bratton, K. A., and Spill, R. L. 2002. "Existing Diversity and Judicial Selection: The Role of the Appointment Method in Establishing Gender Diversity in State Supreme Courts." *Social Science Quarterly* 83(2): 504–18.

Brazelton, S., and Pinderhughes, D. 2019. "Black Federal Judges and Civil Rights in the Age of Obama." In *After Obama: African American Politics and a Post-Obama Era*, eds. Todd Shaw, Robert Brown, and Joseph McCormick. New York: NYU Press.

Brown, N. E. 2014. *Sisters in the Statehouse: Black Women and Legislative Decision Making*. Oxford: Oxford University Press.

Clark, M. L. 2004. "One Man's Token Is Another Woman's Breakthrough – The Appointment of the First Women Federal Judges." *Villanova Law Review* 49: 487–550.

Collins, T. and Moyer, L. 2008. "Gender, Race, and Intersectionality on the Federal Appellate Bench." *Political Research Quarterly* 61(2): 219–27.

Cook, B. B. 1984. "Women Judges: A Preface to Their History." *Golden Gate University Law* 14(3): 573–610.

Cornell University. 2017. "What Is Senior Status?" www.lawschool.cornell.edu/careers/judicial-clerkships/What-is-Senior-Status.cfm.

Crenshaw, K. 1989. "Demarginalizing the Intersection of Race and Sex: A Black Feminist Critique of Antidiscrimination Doctrine, Feminist Theory and Antiracist Politics." *The University of Chicago Legal Forum* (1989): 139–67.

Epi.org. 2016. "People of Color Will Be the Majority of the Working Class by 2032." www.epi.org/press/people-of-color-will-be-the-majority-of-the-working-class-by-2032.

Federal Judicial Center. 2017. "Age and Experience of Judges." www.fjc.gov/history/exhibits/graphs-and-maps/age-and-experience-judges.

2018. "Biographical Directory of Federal Judges." www.fjc.gov/servlet/nFormReq.

Graham, Barbara L. 2004. "Toward an Understanding of Judicial Diversity in American Courts." *Michigan Journal of Race and Law* 10: 153–93.

Gryski, G. S., Zuk, G., and Barrow, D. J. 1994. "A Bench That Looks Like America? Representation African Americans and Latinos on the Federal Courts." *The Journal of Politics* 56(4): 1076–86.

Haire, S. B., and Moyer, L. P. 2015. *Diversity Matters: Judicial Policy Making in the US Courts Appeals*. Charlottesville: University of Virginia Press.

Hartley, R. E. 2001. "Senate Delay of Minority Judicial Nominees: A Look at Race, Gender, and Experience." *Judicature* 84(4): 190–97.

Hurwitz, Mark S., and Lanier, Drew Noble. 2003. "Explaining Judicial Diversity: The of Women and Minorities to Attain Seats on State and Federal Appellate Courts." *State and Policy Quarterly* 3 (4): 329–52.

Kenney, S. J. 2012. "Choosing Judges: A Bumpy Road to Women's Equality and a Long Way to Go." *Michigan State Law Review* (2012): 1499–1528.

Kim, Kyle. 2018. "Trump Appointing Judges at Rapid Pace." *The Los Angeles Times.* www.latimes.com/politics/washington/la-na-pol-essential-washington-updates-trump-appointing-judges-at-rapid-pace-1516386665-htmlstory.html.

Martinek, W. L., and Kemper, M. 2002. "To Advise and Consent: The Senate and Lower Federal Court Nominations, 1977–1998." *Journal of Politics* 64(2): 337–61.

Nixon, D. C., and Goss, D. L. 2001. "Confirmation Delay for Vacancies on the Circuit Courts of Appeals." *American Politics Research* 29(3): 246–74.

Norton Holmes, Eleanor. 2018. Press Release. "Norton to Lead CBC Forum on Lack of Diversity in President Trump's Judicial Nominees, Today." https://norton.house.gov/media-center/press-releases/norton-to-lead-cbc-forum-on-lack-of-diversity-in-president-trump-s-1.

Orey, D., Smooth, W., and Adams, K. K. Harris-Clark. 2006. Race and Gender Matter: Refining Models of Legislative Policy Making in State Legislatures. In *Intersectionality and Politics: Recent Research on Gender, Race, and Political Representation*, ed. Carol Hardy-Fanta. New York: Haworth Press. pp. 97–119.

Pew Research Center. 2016. "10 Demographic Trends Shaping the U.S. and the World." March 31. www.pewresearch.org/fact-tank/2016/03/31/10-demographic-trends-that-are-shaping-the-u-s-and-the-world.

Reddick, M., Nelson, M. J., and Caufield, R. P. 2009. "Racial and Gender Diversity on State Courts – An AJS Study." *Judges' Journal* (48): 28.

Scherer, N., Bartels, B. L., and Steigerwalt, A. 2008. "Sounding the Fire Alarm: The Role of Interest Groups in the Lower Federal Court Confirmation Process." *The Journal of Politics* 70(4): 1026–39.

Schneier, C. 2018. "New Additions to Senate Committee Fuel Hope for Greater Diversity in Judicial Nominees." *The National Law Journal.* www.law.com/nationallawjournal/sites/nationallawjournal/2018/01/09/new-additions-to-senate-committee-fuel-hope-for-greater-focus-on-diversity-in-judicial-nominees/?slreturn=20180021131651.

Schraufnagel, S. 2005. "Testing the Implications of Incivility in the United States Congress, 1977–2000: The Case of Judicial Confirmation Delay." *The Journal of Legislative Studies* 11(2): 216–34.

Sen, M. 2014. "How Judicial Qualification Ratings May Disadvantage Minority and Female Candidates." *Journal of Law and Courts* 2(1): 33–65.

Smooth, W. 2011. "Standing For women? Which women? The Substantive Representation of Women's Interests and the Research Imperative of Intersectionality." *Politics & Gender* 7(3): 436–41.

Solberg, R. L. S., and Bratton, K. A. 2005. "Diversifying the Federal Bench: Presidential Patterns." *Justice System Journal* 26(2): 119–33.

Solowiej, L. A., Martinek, W. L., and Brunell, T. L. 2005. "Partisan Politics: The Impact of Party in the Confirmation of Minority and Female Federal Court Nominees." *Party Politics* 11(5): 557–77.

Spill, R. L., and Bratton, K. A. 2001. "Clinton and Diversification of the Federal Judiciary." *Judicature* 84(5): 256–261.

U.S. Census Bureau. 2017a. "Annual Estimates of the Resident Population by Sex, Age, Race Alone or in Combination, and Hispanic Origin for the United States and States: April 1, 2010 to July 1, 2016." https://factfinder.census.gov/faces/tableservices/jsf/pages/productview.xhtml?src=bkmk

2017b. "Sex by Age (Hispanic or Latino) Universe: People Who Are Hispanic or Latino 2011–2015 American Community Survey 5-Year Estimates." https://factfinder.census.gov/faces/tableservices/jsf/pages/productview.xhtml?pid=ACS_15_5YR_B01001I&prodType=table.

7

Marked for Excellence

*Race, Gender, and the Treatment of Supreme Court–Worthy Nominees to the U.S. Courts of Appeals**

LISA M. HOLMES

In April 2013, *The New Yorker* published a short article by Jeffrey Toobin on Sri Srinivasan's hearing before the Senate Judiciary Committee concerning his nomination to the U.S. Court of Appeals for the District of Columbia Circuit (Toobin 2013). The focus of Toobin's article was that Srinivasan's hearing for the current appointment was a trial run for his future nomination to the U.S. Supreme Court. Put succinctly and starkly in the article, Toobin predicted that "if Srinivasan passes this test and wins confirmation [to the DC Circuit], he'll be on the Supreme Court before President Obama's term ends" (Toobin 2013).

Obviously, Toobin's prediction did not come to full fruition. Srinivasan was eventually confirmed to the DC Circuit in 2013, and although Judge Srinivasan was a "leading contender" three years later to be nominated to replace Justice Antonin Scalia in 2016, Judge Merrick Garland got the nod (although ultimately not the seat) instead (Totenberg 2016). Still, the general point raised by Toobin is well taken: certain appointments to the courts of appeals seem to take on added importance given the expectation that the person being nominated is seen as a possible, even likely, future nominee to the U.S. Supreme Court. Srinivasan's appointment to the court of appeals in 2013 is but one recent manifestation of preemptory Supreme Court appointment battles that have played out in recent years. Earlier in President Obama's administration, for example, *The New York Times* ran an editorial (entitled "An Exceptional Nominee") urging the White House and Senate Democrats to fight hard for the confirmation of Goodwin Liu to the U.S. Court of Appeals for the Ninth Circuit over Republican concern that Liu's appointment would place him

* A previous version of this paper was presented at the 2016 Annual Meeting of the Midwest Political Science Association. Many thanks to Brett Curry for his very helpful comments on this previous draft.

directly on the path to a future Supreme Court appointment (*The New York Times* 2010). Seven years previously, on the other hand, the *Times* ran an editorial (entitled "An Unacceptable Nominee") arguing that it was "compelling – indeed necessary" to reject President George W. Bush's nomination of Miguel Estrada to the DC Circuit Court of Appeals, regardless of his "strong legal resume" (*The New York Times* 2003). A key argument against confirmation made in the editorial was the DC Circuit's status as a "traditional feeder to the Supreme Court" (*The New York Times* 2003).

Anecdotally, we know of appointments to the courts of appeals that take on added importance given the prospect of future elevation to the Supreme Court. Furthermore, the Srinivasan, Liu, and Estrada examples also touch on the important question of how a nominee's race, ethnicity, or gender may influence the perception of a court of appeals appointee as a likely future Supreme Court nominee. In the same editorial where the *New York Times* opposed the confirmation of Miguel Estrada to the DC Circuit due to that court's "feeder" position to the Supreme Court, the editors highlighted the "political reasons the [W. Bush] administration would like to name a Hispanic" to the Supreme Court as another point against Estrada's confirmation to the circuit court (*The New York Times* 2003).

Another classic example of the association made between a nominee's race and future potential as a Supreme Court appointee occurred in 1990 when Clarence Thomas was confirmed to the Court of Appeals for the DC Circuit. Many media and academic accounts tied Clarence Thomas's appointment to the circuit court to the seat on the Supreme Court held by aging Justice Thurgood Marshall (see Dewar 1990; Lewis 1990; McAllister 1990; Robinson 1990; Yalof 2005). Leading Senate Democrats at the time were well aware that Thomas's positioning on the DC Circuit may place him in the direct path for elevation to the Supreme Court, and unsuccessfully attempted to distinguish the two jobs, both at the time of Thomas's initial appointment to the DC Circuit (Robinson 1990) and again in 1991 when Thomas was tapped to fill the seat vacated by Justice Marshall (Leahy 1991). This connection was also not lost on other actors interested in Supreme Court appointments, including the Alliance for Justice, a leading liberal umbrella organization focusing on the selection of judges (Lewis 1990; McAllister 1990). In 1990, while Thomas's nomination to the court of appeals was pending before the Senate, Nan Aron, executive director of the Alliance for Justice, acknowledged that it may be impossible to prevent Thomas's appointment to the lower court, but that her intention was to sow seeds of concern about Thomas's suitability for future appointment to the Supreme Court (Lewis 1990; McAllister 1990).

Although all of the anecdotes provided so far have focused on male nominees of color, similar arguments have been made about the placement of women on the courts of appeals as a stepping stone to the Supreme Court. David Yalof (2005), for example, characterized George W. Bush circuit court nominees Priscilla Owen and Janice Rogers Brown as "leading candidates for a future Supreme Court nomination" (pp. 706, 694). Of course, some white, male nominees to the courts of appeals carry with them the expectation that they may as well be particularly appealing as future Supreme Court appointees. The nomination of John Roberts to the DC Circuit Court of Appeals in 2001 serves as but one example (see Miller 2001; Wittes 2002).[1] Still, anecdotal evidence points to differences in how female and minority nominees are viewed as possible future Supreme Court appointees compared to their white, male counterparts.

In this chapter, I provide an assessment of two key issues concerning how future potential for Supreme Court appointment influences the confirmation process for court of appeals nominees. The first issue relates to identifying what factors contribute to a current court of appeals nominee being considered Supreme Court–worthy.[2] It seems unlikely that *all* court of appeals nominees are created equally in terms of the potential for future elevation. Drawing on literature on U.S. Supreme Court appointment politics, I highlight some characteristics that may help distinguish those nominees to the courts of appeals who are considered to be viable future Supreme Court nominees from those who are expected to have less of a chance for further elevation.

The second focus of this paper concerns how consideration as a possible future Supreme Court appointee affects that nominee's current prospects in the lower court confirmation process. In the Estrada and Liu examples, consideration of future Supreme Court appointment further politicized and eventually helped derail their appointments to the court of appeals. Srinivasan, on the other hand, was able to overcome Republican concerns that allowing him to be placed on the court of appeals would pose additional

[1] John Roberts was unsuccessfully nominated to the DC Circuit in the last year of George H.W. Bush's presidency. Roberts was later nominated on May 9, 2001, as part of President George W. Bush's first slate of nominees, and he was confirmed two years later on May 8, 2003.

[2] In this chapter, I refer to "Supreme Court–worthy" or "SCOTUS-worthy" nominees. By this, I do not intend to imply that these court of appeals nominees would be excellent Supreme Court justices or that the remaining nominees would be unsuitable for elevation. Rather, I use this phrase as a way to articulate that some nominees to the courts of appeals are perceived (by those in the political branches, by the legal community, or by the media) to be on something of a possible fast-track to a Supreme Court appointment, whereas others are less likely to be considered for Supreme Court seats in the future.

Supreme Court appointment problems for Republicans down the road. In the second part of this chapter, I provide an assessment of how future Supreme Court appointment viability influences likelihood of confirmation to the courts of appeals from 1977 through 2016. For both parts of this analysis, I pay particular attention to nominee race/ethnicity and gender to determine how future Supreme Court worthiness affects female, minority, and white male nominees to the courts of appeals.

THE CHALLENGE OF DISTINGUISHING POTENTIAL SUPREME COURT NOMINEES FROM OTHER COURT OF APPEALS NOMINEES

Determining in a systematic way why one court of appeals nominee is "Supreme Court–worthy" while another is not is a more complicated task than it may seem at first glance. Falling into the trap of concluding that "I know one when I see one" would be easy, but a more systematic and scientific approach is necessary. Such an approach is also achievable, either through reliance on the determination of other relevant actors as to who is Supreme Court–worthy, or by considering nominee characteristics that differ among those who have a better chance at elevation to the Supreme Court compared to the rest of their court of appeals cohort.

One way to utilize the determination of other actors as to which court of appeals nominees are potential future Supreme Court appointees may be to determine whether media coverage or interest group attention highlights the possibility of a future Supreme Court appointment. Indeed, it is easy to find media coverage of Srinivasan, Estrada, and Liu (and others) that draws a connection between their nomination to the circuit bench and the Supreme Court down the road. However, the existence and extent of media coverage of court of appeals nominees may be influenced by a variety of factors that have little relationship to future Supreme Court potential. For example, although most nominations to the courts of appeals warrant at least some media coverage by statewide newspapers, one factor that appears to depress media coverage of nominees is the regularity with which nominations to the court of appeals are made from that state (Holmes 2016). In other words, circuit court nominees from states where such appointments are relatively common tend to receive less media attention than do nominees from states where these appointments are rare. Measuring Supreme Court worthiness from media coverage that is driven at least in part by such unrelated factors is therefore problematic.

A second option would be to determine whether interest groups opposing nominees discuss the Supreme Court in highlighting their opposition to current court of appeals nominees. This approach, however, would exclude any nominee who does not garner interest group opposition. It is possible that interest groups are more likely to oppose nominees they see as potential Supreme Court threats, of course, but measuring Supreme Court potential by way of interest group behavior risks missing those court of appeals nominees who are Supreme Court–worthy but did not attract interest group opposition at the court of appeals stage for some unrelated reason. For example, interest groups may be less likely to oppose nominees from the home state of key senators (such as the chair of the Senate Judiciary Committee), regardless of their potentiality as future Supreme Court nominees.

A last option for determining which circuit court nominees may be future Supreme Court nominees would be to determine the short list for filling Supreme Court vacancies, as was done by Nemacheck (2007) for her book on the selection of Supreme Court justices. The downside of this approach for my purposes is that it identifies possible Supreme Court candidates well after their previous court of appeals nomination event, which is not ideal for my interest in looking at the perception of nominees at that earlier stage. In addition, this approach narrows the pool of potential Supreme Court nominees based on the ideology, preferences, and party of the person in the Oval Office at the time a Supreme Court vacancy arises. As such, this approach would only identify an incomplete list of Supreme Court–worthy candidates sitting on the courts of appeals at that particular point in time.

Aside from relying on determinations of Supreme Court worthiness made by others, another way – and the approach I use in this chapter – is to identify specific background characteristics that make some nominees more likely for future Supreme Court consideration than others. For example, based on previous research on Supreme Court confirmation politics, successful Supreme Court nominees are those considered highly qualified (or, at the very least, those nominees for whom a lack of qualifications is not an issue) (Epstein et al. 2006; Moraski and Shipan 1999; Shipan 2008). Of course, previous research indicates that general qualifications of court of appeals nominees may be relevant to their confirmation prospects as well. Even so, there is some useful variation in the general qualifications and background of nominees forwarded to the courts of appeals that can be brought to bear in developing a measure of future Supreme Court worthiness.

CREATING A MEASURE OF SUPREME COURT WORTHINESS

This variation in professional backgrounds and qualifications of court of appeals nominees can be harnessed to develop an objective, quantifiable measure of how attractive that nominee would be as a future Supreme Court choice. To develop this, I rely on research on the individual characteristics of successful Supreme Court nominees. More specifically, I am interested in considering what factors appear related to relatively recent success as a Supreme Court nominee. The fact that a substantial minority of Supreme Court justices early in the nation's history had experience as state court judges is less relevant to my endeavor than is the fact that most recent justices have clerkship experience, for instance (Lanier and Hurwitz 2016). Therefore, I now move to an explanation of how factors related to potential future Supreme Court nomination were identified, quantified, and developed into an index of Supreme Court worthiness.

Professional and Educational Background

Previous research points to a variety of factors that may contribute to the perception that a court of appeals nominee today may be a potential Supreme Court nominee tomorrow. These factors relate to a circuit court nominee's educational and professional background, an assessment of their overall temperament and qualifications, the specific circuit court they are being appointed to, and their age. Experience as a U.S. Supreme Court clerk, for example, is a helpful stepping stone for future appointment to the Supreme Court. In a recent study of the evolution of the professional and educational backgrounds of Supreme Court justices and court of appeals judges, Lanier and Hurwitz (2016) found that for justices appointed to the Supreme Court during the most recent period of their analysis (1991–2010), 71.4 percent had a legal clerkship in their background. Although Lanier and Hurwitz do not break these data down into Supreme Court versus lower court clerkships, a Supreme Court clerkship would be the platinum standard for this kind of professional experience. Ward and Weiden (2006) characterize a Supreme Court clerkship as "the most prestigious position a recent law school graduate can attain" (p. 1), while Peppers (2006) concludes that these clerkships "will remain a necessary credential for an elite law school professorship or a high-level position in the Department of Justice" (p. 212). Of the 423 nominees to the courts of appeals made from 1977 through 2016, 57 (or 13.48 percent) had previous experience as a Supreme Court clerk.[3]

[3] Its status as a specialized court, I excluded nominations made to the U.S. Court of Appeals for the Federal Circuit from the analysis (Carp, Stidham, and Manning 2004). From 1977 to 2016, 425 nominees were made to the remaining courts of appeals. Of these, two were dropped due to missing data (on ABA rating or previous experience). Richard W. Arnold was a nominee to the U.S. Court of Appeals for the Eighth Circuit for five days in 1979 and Duncan Getchell was a nominee to the U.S. Court of Appeals for the Fourth Circuit for 139 days late in

Another factor that may contribute to the perception that a court of appeals nominee has future Supreme Court potential is experience as a U.S. Attorney, or other experience within the Department of Justice, including the Office of the Solicitor General. Experience as a prosecutor (or within the federal department responsible for law enforcement generally) may serve to provide nominees with a marker that they are "tough on crime" or are at least on the "right side" of the debate over law and order. By way of contrast, in March of 2016, after the sudden death of Justice Antonin Scalia, the conservative Judicial Crisis Network launched an ad campaign targeting Court of Appeals Judge Jane Kelly's "extreme arguments on behalf of a child predator" in her capacity as an assistant federal public defender in Iowa as a reason why President Obama "should not deny the American people a voice" in selecting Scalia's replacement ("Judicial" 2016). In addition, many of the positions within the Department of Justice held by court of appeals nominees require Senate confirmation. That level of vetting by the U.S. Senate can serve as a valuable test run for Senate confirmation as a court of appeals judge and eventually a Supreme Court justice. Lanier and Hurwitz (2016) find that 28.6 percent of recent Supreme Court appointees have federal prosecutorial experience. Of the 423 court of appeals nominees included in my analysis, 133 (or 31.44 percent) had previous experience in the U.S. Department of Justice. Tellingly, far fewer nominees to the courts of appeals (approximately 5 percent) had previous experience as a public defender or in legal services.

Another background characteristic that may help distinguish viable Supreme Court appointees from other court of appeals nominees relates to educational background. Lanier and Hurwitz (2016) note that in recent decades, although court of appeals judges have come in greater numbers from non-Ivy League and non-elite law schools, all recent Supreme Court appointees received their legal education at Ivy League schools. This contrasts with previous eras when the composition of the court levels was somewhat less distinct in terms of educational background. It is also often repeated that the current Supreme Court is comprised of only those who attended law school at Harvard or Yale.[4] From 1977 through 2016, 108 nominees (or 25.53 percent) to the courts of appeals earned their law degree from Harvard or Yale.

2007–2008. Dropping these two cases results in 423 nominees to the courts of appeals included in this analysis.

4 It is sometimes glossed over that Ruth Bader Ginsburg attended Harvard Law School but earned her LL.B. from Columbia.

American Bar Association (ABA) Rating

Another way in which appointees to the courts of appeals may distinguish themselves as future Supreme Court nominees is in how their professional competence, integrity, and judicial temperament are rated by the American Bar Association Standing Committee on the Federal Judiciary (Goldman 1997; Grossman 1965; Haire 2001; Smelcer, Steigerwalt, and Vining 2012). The ABA gives each nominee a single rating of Well Qualified, Qualified, or Not Qualified, although the committee can split its vote, with a majority (or even a substantial majority) rating the nominee as Well Qualified and a minority giving a rating of Qualified, for instance (Smelcer, Steigerwalt, and Vining 2012). Prior to 1989, the ABA had a fourth rating of Exceptionally Well Qualified; since 1989, the highest rating available is a unanimous rating of Well Qualified (Martinek, Kemper, and Van Winkle 2002; Sen 2014).

The ABA's special role in evaluating judicial candidates has long been criticized, particularly by Republicans, for rating conservative nominees less favorably than liberal nominees. In their analysis of political bias in the ABA ratings given to judicial nominees, Smelcer, Steigerwalt, and Vining (2012) found that although ABA ratings are influenced by professional qualifications (such as previous federal judicial or clerk experience), they also found "strong evidence of systematic bias" in favor of nominees forwarded by Democratic president (p. 836). This bias, however, was detected in terms of the top ratings nominees received, rather than their probability of receiving a rating of Not Qualified (p. 837).

These long-standing criticisms of bias in nominee rating has led to a newly established norm where Republican presidents, starting with George W. Bush, have attempted to remove the ABA's role in the process by refusing to send the names of potential nominees to the ABA early in the selection process (Holmes and Savchak 2003; Liptak 2017). Still, the ABA provides a rating for all nominees, or at least all nominees who remain in the appointment process long enough for the ABA to conduct its assessment. In addition, Haire (2001) found evidence that ABA ratings provide some insight into the quality of the work that judges do once on the bench, at least in the earliest years of their careers as judges. In 2015, Epstein et al. noted that every justice on the Supreme Court at that time earned a rating of Well Qualified by the ABA, with the exception of Clarence Thomas, who was voted as Qualified by twelve members of the committee, with another two voting Not Qualified and a last committee member recusing.[5]

5 The remaining eight members on the Supreme Court in 2015 were all determined to be Well Qualified by the full committee (with one committee member recusing themselves in

A unanimous ABA assessment of a Supreme Court nominee as Well Qualified, then, is the norm for successful nomination to the U.S. Supreme Court in recent decades. A court of appeals nominee unanimously rated as Well Qualified (or above, for those nominated when the Exceptionally Well Qualified rating was still in play) may therefore identify themselves as someone with more potential as a future Supreme Court nominee than is the case for a nominee rated below that highest level.[6] Of those nominated to the courts of appeals from 1977 through 2016, 224 (or 52.96 percent) received a unanimous rating of Well Qualified or above.

The DC Circuit: The Stepping Stone to the Supreme Court

Previous research on judicial selection politics has highlighted the importance of certain "critical nominations" to the bench (see Binder and Maltzman 2002; Holmes, Shomade, and Hartley 2012; Ruckman 1993; Shipan and Shannon 2003). However, the concept of a "critical nomination" in these studies has generally been tied to the partisan or ideological impact of the current nominee on the relevant court. This is not a very helpful factor to consider with respect to determining which court of appeals nominees today may be suitable Supreme Court nominees in the future because of the inherent uncertainty in knowing which justice's seat may be the next to be replaced or the partisan identity of the president nominating the replacement justice.

However, among the various courts of appeals, the Court of Appeals for the District of Columbia Circuit distinguishes itself as a "critical court" because it is a "breeding ground" for future Supreme Court nominees (Banks 1999; Sturgess 1991). Nominees to the DC Circuit would therefore be expected to be more likely to fall into the category of judges considered as future Supreme Court appointees. Of the 423 court of appeals nominees included in this analysis, 34 (or 8.04 percent) were forwarded to the Senate for seats on the DC Circuit.

evaluating Samuel Alito. Neil Gorsuch also received a unanimous rating of Well Qualified when he was nominated to the Supreme Court in 2017 (American Bar Association 2017).

6 It is possible that someone demonstrating exemplary skills, temperament, and ability on the court of appeals could work their way toward a perception of being well qualified for Supreme Court appointment during their years on their circuit court. However, given that I am interested in determining those who are perceived as potential future Supreme Court nominees at the time of their nomination to the court of appeals, it is more appropriate to identify those determined to be the most highly qualified at the time of the circuit court appointment.

Age: The Window of Opportunity for Elevation to the Supreme Court

One last factor relevant to future consideration as a Supreme Court appointee is the court of appeals nominee's age. Relatively younger nominees would simply have more time to serve on the circuit court for an opportunity to have a like-minded president presented with a seat on the Supreme Court to fill. Merrick Garland, for example, has served on the Court of Appeals for the DC Circuit since 1997, having been considered twice previously for elevation to the Supreme Court prior to his unsuccessful nomination in 2016 (Harris 2016). Born in 1952, Garland was in his mid-40s when appointed to the court of appeals, allowing him to watch two Republican appointees and two other Democratic appointees before getting the nod for a Supreme Court nomination himself.[7] Younger nominees at the time of appointment to the court of appeals, therefore, would be expected to be more likely to have long-term opportunity as a future Supreme Court appointee. Nominees to the courts of appeals from 1977 through 2016 have ranged in age from thirty-five to sixty-nine, with 48.23 percent being aged fifty or younger at the time of initial nomination to the circuit court.[8]

AN INDEX OF SUPREME COURT WORTHINESS

Based on the factors discussed in the previous section, I developed an index variable intended to reflect these characteristics relevant to future Supreme Court potential for each nominee to the U.S. courts of appeals from 1977 through 2016. The six factors included in my index of future Supreme Court worthiness were all coded as separate dichotomous variables. Values of "1" were assigned to nominees with Supreme Court clerk experience, U.S.

7 The refusal of Senate Republicans to consider Garland's nomination in 2016 does not detract from the possible relevance of a circuit court nominee's age in determining how long the window of opportunity for future elevation to the Supreme Court will remain open.

8 I have not included perceived ideology as a factor in determining the characteristics that explain why some nominees are considered more Supreme Court worthy at the time of their nomination to the courts of appeals. It is unclear how ideology would play into a nominee's perception as a future Supreme Court appointee. Whether a moderate nominee, a mainstream liberal or conservative, or an ideological firebrand would be a likely future Supreme Court nominee is based on many factors, including the appointment preferences of the president, the composition of the Senate, and even the identities of the Supreme Court justices who may or may not leave the bench for years in the future. As such, a nominee's perceived ideology is not a suitable factor to include for the purposes of developing a measure of future Supreme Court worthiness.

TABLE 7.1 *Descriptive data for SCOTUS-worthy index variable, court of appeals nominees, 1977–2016*

SCOTUS-Worthy Index Score	All Nominees (%)	White Male Nominees (%)	Minority Nominees (%)	Female Nominees (%)
0	40 (9.46)	21 (8.02)	11 (13.75)	10 (10.10)
1	138 (32.62)	78 (29.77)	30 (37.50)	38 (38.38)
2	138 (32.62)	91 (34.73)	22 (27.50)	31 (31.31)
3	78 (18.44)	52 (19.85)	13 (16.25)	14 (14.14)
4	18 (4.26)	14 (5.34)	2 (2.50)	2 (2.02)
5	11 (2.60)	6 (2.29)	2 (2.50)	4 (4.04)
6	0 (0.00)	0 (0.00)	0 (0.00)	0 (0.00)
Column Summary	N = 423 Mean = 1.83	N = 262 Mean = 1.92	N = 80 Mean = 1.64	N = 99 Mean = 1.72

Department of Justice experience, a law degree from Harvard or Yale, and a unanimous ABA rating of Well Qualified or higher. For each of these variables, nominees without that specific background were coded as "0." In addition to these four variables, another dichotomous variable was created labeling nominees to the DC Circuit as "1" (and "0" otherwise) and a sixth variable was created and coded as "1" for all nominees who were fifty years of age or younger at the time of initial nomination to the circuit court, with older nominees coded as "0."

The index of Supreme Court worthiness was then determined based on the simple summation of these six dichotomous variables. The values of this new index variable theoretically ranged from a low of 0 to a high of 6. The actual values for this new variable for those nominated to the courts of appeals from 1977 through 2016 are provided in Table 7.1. No court of appeals nominee in the analysis earned a score of 6. Given my interest in examining how future Supreme Court potential influences how white male, minority, and female nominees are treated in the court of appeals confirmation process, I include descriptive data broken down by racial/ethnic minority status and sex in Table 7.1 as well.[9]

9 Nominees were coded as racial or ethnic minorities if they were identified as African-American, Asian-American, Hispanic/Latinx, Native American, or Arab-American, following previous literature on lower court appointment politics (see Holmes, Shomade, and Hartley 2012; Martinek, Kemper, and Van Winkle 2002). I label as a "white male nominee" anyone who is not identified as a woman or a member of one of these racial or ethnic minority groups.

There is some slight variation among different nominee cohorts with respect to future potential as Supreme Court nominees, as measured by the SCOTUS-worthy index variable. For white male nominees to the courts of appeals, the modal category for the index of Supreme Court worthiness is a "2" whereas the modal category for women and minority nominees is a "1." The mean for the index variable for white men (1.92) is also slightly higher than it is for minorities (1.64) and women (1.72). Aside from that, the general descriptive data are similar across demographic factors, with the vast majority of white men (92.37 percent), racial/ethnic minorities (95.00 percent), and women (93.94 percent) earning index scores of 3 or lower. Only a very few circuit court nominees of any demographic background earned higher scores on this metric.[10]

As noted previously, Clarence Thomas's appointment to the DC Circuit followed quickly by his subsequent appointment to the Supreme Court in 1991 provided a high-profile case study in how the placement of a "non-traditional" (nonwhite male) judge on the court of appeals may particularly pave the way for future appointment to the Supreme Court. Given that Judge Thomas's nomination to the Supreme Court may represent a pivotal moment in the evolution of how "non-traditional" nominees are treated in the court of appeals confirmation process, I examined the influence of Supreme Court worthiness on the court of appeals confirmation process for only those nominated to the circuit courts after 1991. Given that these results were substantively similar to those of all nominees forwarded from 1977 through 2016, I present only the results for the full array of nominees in the analysis.

TREATMENT OF SCOTUS-WORTHY CANDIDATES IN THE COURT OF APPEALS CONFIRMATION PROCESS

My general argument is that court of appeals nominees with Supreme Court potential should garner more attention and controversy in the modern court of appeals confirmation process. This increased attention and controversy could

[10] I am aware that breaking the data down into these three categories (white men, racial/ethnic minorities, women) does not take into consideration any possible intersectional influences for nominees who are both female and identified as members of racial or ethnic minority groups. Only 18 nominees in the analysis fit into this category. This low number created problems for the subsequent statistical analysis, resulting in the decision to code "women of color" as "1" on the race/ethnicity variable and "1" again on the gender variable. This means that female nominees of color are included twice in Table 7.1. They are included in the cells providing descriptive data on minority nominees and again in the cells providing descriptive data on female nominees.

manifest itself in a number of ways. Supreme Court–worthy nominees may attract more media attention or opposition from interest groups compared to other court of appeals nominees. They may take longer to be confirmed by the Senate. Or, they may simply be less likely to be confirmed by the Senate.

For this chapter I have tested the relevance of Supreme Court worthiness to the confirmation success of court of appeals nominees. My expectation is that characteristics that identify a nominee as someone with potential as a future Supreme Court nominee will make it *less* likely that that nominee will be confirmed to the circuit court. I fully realize that this expectation means that court of appeals nominees who are the *most* qualified, who went to the very best law schools, and who have the most impressive experience (say, as Supreme Court clerks) at relatively early stages in their careers are expected to be less likely to be confirmed to the court of appeals. This turns everything we tend to hypothesize about how nominee-specific factors influence the confirmation process on its head. Still, given indications that on some of these measures (such as law school educational background) recent years have seen the experiences of court of appeals judges and Supreme Court justices diverge (see Lanier and Hurwitz 2016), my expectations may be less counterintuitive than they seem at first glance.

For my analysis, I use a simple dichotomous dependent variable of *nominee success* which is coded as "1" for any nominee who is confirmed to the court of appeals, whether the confirmation occurs the first time the nominee is forwarded or after being re-nominated (once or multiple times) by the president, and "0" otherwise. Based on the dichotomous dependent variable, I used a logistic regression model with robust standard errors to measure the influence of political, electoral, and nominee-specific variables on a nominee's likelihood of confirmation to the court of appeals.

Independent Variables

The main independent variable included in the models is the index of Supreme Court worthiness, which is the simple aggregation of six dummy variables measuring nominee characteristics related to professional experience (with nominees earning one point if they have a Supreme Court clerkship and another point if they have U.S. Justice Department experience), educational background (one point for a law degree from Harvard or Yale), ABA rating (one point for a unanimous ABA rating of Well Qualified or above), age (nominees fifty years old or younger earn a point), and nomination to the DC Circuit (one point). This variable varies from a low of 0 to a high of 5, with a mean of 1.83 and a standard deviation of 1.13. Generally, in the judicial appointment politics literature, variables measuring the quality of nominees would be expected to have a positive influence on the likelihood of confirmation success, because nominees with more impressive pedigrees are typically thought to have an easier time in the confirmation process. However, I am interested in whether there is any evidence that nominees who are more likely to be seen as future Supreme Court nominees have relatively *less* success in the court of appeals appointment process compared to nominees with less evidence of future Supreme Court potential. More specifically, I am interested in any notable differences in how Supreme Court worthiness influences the court of appeals confirmation process with respect to a nominee's race, ethnicity, or gender. Therefore, the model was run separately for all nominees, white male nominees, minority nominees, and female nominees.[11]

Nominee-specific factors are only one consideration related to confirmation success in the court of appeals appointment literature. Previous literature on the circuit court confirmation process has generally included variables measuring the political and electoral context surrounding the appointment, as well as the presence or absence of interest group opposition to the appointment. All studies of confirmation politics include one or more measures of the president's relationship to the Senate, with some studies relying on measures of divided government in their analysis (Binder and Maltzman 2002; Solowiej, Martinek, and Brunnell 2005). I included a simple dichotomous variable measuring the presence (coded "1") or absence (coded "0") of *divided government* at the time of initial nomination.

Following the lead of many previous studies, two variables were included to measure the influence of presidential election politics to the likelihood of confirmation success (Binder and Maltzman 2002; Holmes, Shomade, and Hartley 2012; Martinek, Kemper, and Van Winkle 2002; Soloweij, Martinek, and Brunnell 2005). *Presidential year* is a measure from one to four based on the point in the president's term of office that the nomination was forwarded to the Senate. In addition, *second term* is coded "1" for nominations that occurred during the president's second term in office. Given the significance of *interest group opposition* to the confirmation prospects of a court of appeals nominee (see Bell 2002; Scherer 2005; and Scherer, Bartels, and Steigerwalt 2008), I included a dichotomous variable measuring the presence ("1") or absence ("0") of interest group opposition, using the data collection

[11] As noted previously, I ran each of these four models again for nominees forwarded to the courts of appeals after the appointment of Clarence Thomas to the U.S. Supreme Court in 1991 and found little substantive difference between these results and the results of models run for all nominees in the analysis.

TABLE 7.2 *Logistic regression results, confirmation success of court of appeals nominees, 1977–2016*

Variables	All Nominees	White Male Nominees	Minority Nominees	Female Nominees
SCOTUS-worthy index	0.083 (0.136)	0.140 (0.178)	0.035 (0.285)	−0.251 (0.270)
Divided government	−1.549 (0.317)***	−1.526 (0.408)***	−1.710 (0.741)*	−2.337 (0.881)**
Second term	−1.012 (0.281)***	−0.978 (0.375)**	−1.202 (0.669)$^{\#}$	−1.330 (0.709)$^{\#}$
Election year	−1.63 (0.326)***	−1.975 (0.453)***	−0.767 (0.693)	−1.676 (0.638)**
Interest group opposition	−1.433 (0.324)***	−1.438 (0.437)**	−1.487 (0.812)$^{\#}$	−1.747 (0.646)**
Constant	3.396 (0.395)***	3.337 (0.482)***	3.012 (0.878)**	5.409 (1.161)***
N =	423	262	80	99
Log likelihood =	−157.525	−96.553	−32.097	−29.858
Chi-square =	92.27	50.27	21.02	32.57
Probability > chi-square	0.0000	0.0000	0.0008	0.0000

Robust standard errors in parentheses.
$^{\#}p < 0.10$, two-tailed; $^{*}p < 0.05$, two-tailed; $^{*}p < 0.01$, two-tailed; $^{***}p < 0.001$, two-tailed

scheme described in Scherer, Bartels, and Steigerwalt (2008). All four of these variables (*divided government, presidential year, second term,* and *interest group opposition*) are expected to have a negative effect on the likelihood of confirmation success. The results of the logit models are provided in Table 7.2.

The independent variables measuring political climate and interest group opposition are all in the expected (negative) direction, and are typically statistically significant. This is not surprising, given the regularity with which these variables are found to be relevant to confirmation success in the court of appeals confirmation literature. However, my main independent variable (the index of Supreme Court worthiness) fails to achieve statistical significance in any model. What is noteworthy, though, is that while this variable has a positive coefficient in the model including all nominees regardless of demographic cohort, as well as in the models including only white men and only racial/ethnic minorities, in the model including only female nominees the coefficient is negative. This indicates that for female nominees (of any race or ethnicity), a higher score on the measure of future Supreme Court worthiness indicates lower likelihood of confirmation success to the courts of appeals, albeit to a non-statistically significant degree.

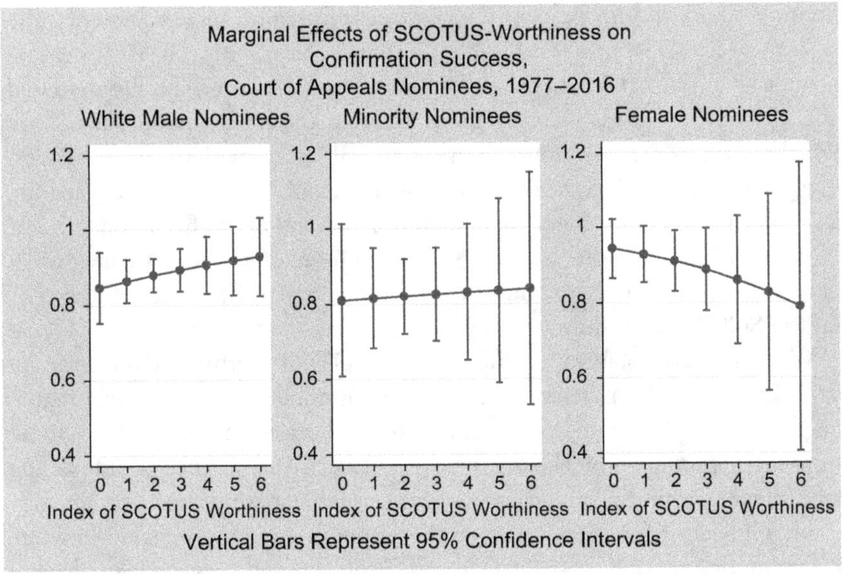

FIGURE 7.1 Marginal effects of SCOTUS worthiness on confirmation success, court of appeals nominees, 1977–2016

Since it is difficult to determine the substantive influence of the independent variables on the dependent variable based on the coefficients from a logit model, I calculated the marginal effects of nominee success for the Supreme Court worthiness variable, holding the other independent variables at their means. These graphs, demonstrating the substantive influence of changes in Supreme Court worthiness on confirmation success for court of appeals nominees from 1977 through 2016 are provided in Figure 7.1.[12]

The substantive influence of the variable measuring SCOTUS worthiness on the likelihood of confirmation success is varied, depending on the demographic cohort to which a nominee belongs. White male nominees scoring a "0" on the SCOTUS-worthy index have a likelihood of confirmation success of 84.7 percent, holding the other independent variables at their means. As white male circuit court nominees become more SCOTUS worthy, the likelihood of confirmation success increases, up to 92.8 percent for the most SCOTUS-worthy nominees (scoring a "6" on this variable). With respect to minority nominees, however, the likelihood of confirmation success changes very little depending on SCOTUS worthiness. The "least" SCOTUS-worthy

[12] I employed Stata 14's "margins, at" command to calculate predicted probabilities at fixed values of the Index variable, holding the remaining covariates at their means.

nominees have an 81.1 percent chance of confirmation success, whereas the "most" SCOTUS-worthy minority nominees have only an 84.1 percent chance of confirmation success. Most interesting, however, are the marginal effects of the SCOTUS-worthy index variable on confirmation success for female nominees. For women, court of appeals confirmation success is most likely when they are the *least* SCOTUS worthy, with female nominees scoring a "0" on this index having a 94.4 percent likelihood of confirmation success. As women become more SCOTUS worthy, on the other hand, their chances of confirmation success go down, to a low of 78.8 percent when scoring a "6" on the SCOTUS-worthiness index.[13]

Why is the substantive influence of SCOTUS worthiness on court of appeals confirmation success different for nominees from different demographic cohorts? As noted previously, anecdotal evidence indicates that those from the opposing political party may be particularly concerned about placing a woman or a minority on the court of appeals if that person would be a readily viable choice for future elevation to the Supreme Court, compared to white male nominees. With respect to the differences seen between female and minority nominees, I can only speculate at this stage. Perhaps senators from the opposing party to the president are less comfortable obstructing highly qualified minority nominees compared to highly qualified female nominees. This may be a particularly problematic dynamic for Democratic senators who may want to oppose a highly qualified minority nominee but may worry about how their base will respond if the Democratic senator regularly obstructs highly qualified nominees of color.

CONCLUSIONS

In this chapter, I develop an index of future Supreme Court potential for nominees to the courts of appeals and use this index to determine what influence SCOTUS worthiness has on court of appeals confirmation success. Although the findings related to the SCOTUS-worthy index fail to achieve statistical significance in any model, there is some evidence that having many characteristics of a potential future Supreme Court appointee substantively

[13] These substantive results were similar for other permutations of the SCOTUS-worthy index variable. For example, I tested a SCOTUS-worthy index variable that only included the measures for law school pedigree, Department of Justice experience, and background as a Supreme Court clerk (dropping the ABA rating, age, and DC Circuit nominee components of the index and including them as separate independent variables instead), with little substantive difference in either the logit models or the marginal effects of the index variable on confirmation success.

influences court of appeals confirmation success differently for women and minority nominees compared to their white male counterparts.

Although my findings are modest, they point to possible differences in how the court of appeals confirmation process treats nominees based on race, ethnicity, and gender in light of future potential as a Supreme Court nominee. Although I only considered the likelihood of confirmation success in this chapter, other measures of confirmation obstruction (such as confirmation delay, or the length and/or content of confirmation hearings) may provide more insight into how the court of appeals confirmation process plays out for nominees of different demographic backgrounds. Avenues of potential future research also include determining whether interest groups are more likely to oppose women or minorities who have more potential as future Supreme Court nominees. In addition, moving forward it will be important to address the treatment of women of color in the confirmation process. The relatively low numbers of women of color who have been nominated to the courts of appeals since 1977, coupled with the fact that only three of the eighteen women of color who have been forwarded were nominated by Republican presidents, makes it difficult to determine how the intersectionality of race/ethnicity and gender play out in the confirmation process. Getting better leverage on questions concerning how women of color fare in the judicial nomination and confirmation process is of course crucial to consider moving forward.

Anecdotally, we know that sometimes court of appeals nominees experience confirmation conflict because of the anticipation that placing them on the court of appeals positions them for future Supreme Court elevation. Although future Supreme Court potential appears to have little influence on court of appeals confirmation success in the model that includes all nominees irrespective of race/ethnicity or gender, there is some evidence that future Supreme Court potential affects women and people of color somewhat differently than it affects white male nominees, to the detriment of the minorities and especially the women who possess more characteristics associated with viable future Supreme Court nomination.

REFERENCES

American Bar Association. 2017. "Statement of Nancy Scott Degan, Standing Committee on the Federal Judiciary, American Bar Association, Concerning the Nomination of The Honorable Neil M. Gorsuch to be Associate Justice of the Supreme Court of the United States." www.americanbar.org/content/dam/aba/uncategorized/GAO/Gorsuch%20Statement%20submitted%203%2019%202017F.authcheckdam.pdf.

Banks, Christopher P. 1999. *Judicial Politics in the D.C. Circuit Court*. Baltimore: The Johns Hopkins University Press.

Bell, Lauren Cohen. 2002. *Warring Factions: Interest Groups, Money, and the New Politics of Senate Confirmation*. Columbus: The Ohio State University Press.

Binder, Sarah A., and Forrest Maltzman. 2002. "Senatorial Delay in Confirming Judges, 1947–1998." *American Journal of Political Science* 46: 190–99.

Carp, Robert A., Ronald Stidham, and Kenneth L. Manning. 2004. *Judicial Process in America*, 6th ed. Washington, DC: CQ Press.

Dewar, Helen. 1990. "Thomas Confirmed by Senate; Two Fault Nominee for Appeals Court." *The Washington Post*. March 7.

Epstein, Lee, Rene Lindstadt, Jeffrey A. Segal, and Chad Westerland. 2006. "The Changing Dynamics of Senate Voting on Supreme Court Nominees." *The Journal of Politics* 68: 296–307.

Epstein, Lee, Jeffrey A. Segal, Harold J. Spaeth, and Thomas G. Walker. 2015. *The Supreme Court Compendium*, 6th ed. Los Angeles: Sage/CQ Press.

Goldman, Sheldon. 1997. *Picking Federal Judges: Lower Court Selection from Roosevelt through Reagan*. New Haven, CT: Yale University Press.

Grossman, Joel B. 1965. *Lawyers and Judges: The ABA and the Politics of Judicial Selection*. New York: John Wiley.

Haire, Susan Brodie. 2001. "Rating the Ratings of the American Bar Association Standing Committee on Federal Judiciary." *Justice System Journal* 22:1–17.

Harris, Gardiner. 2016. "For Garland, Third Time Was Charm." *The New York Times*. March 16.

Holmes, Lisa M. 2016. "The Perils of a Politicized Judicial Appointment Process: Home State Media Coverage of Court of Appeals Nominees." Paper Presented at the Annual Meeting of the Western Political Science Association. San Diego, CA, March 24–26.

Holmes, Lisa M., and Elisha Savchak. 2003. "Judicial Appointment Politics in the 107th Congress." *Judicature* 86:232–39.

Holmes, Lisa M., Salmon A. Shomade, and Roger E. Hartley. 2012. "The Confirmation Obstacle Course: Signaling Obstruction through Delay." *The American Review of Politics* 33:23–49.

"Judicial Crisis Network Launches New Ad Campaign Exposing Potential Obama Supreme Court Nominee Judge Jane Kelly." 2016. March 11. http://judicialnetwork.com/?s=jane+kelly.

Lanier, Drew Noble, and Mark S. Hurwitz. 2016. "Diversity by Other Means: Professional, Educational, and Life Diversity of U.S. Appellate Judges." Paper Presented at the Annual Meeting of the Western Political Science Association, San Diego, CA, March 24–26.

Leahy, Patrick J. 1991. "Opening Statement of Hon. Patrick J. Leahy." *Nomination of Clarence Thomas to be Associate Justice of the Supreme Court of the United States, Hearings before the Committee on the Judiciary*. September 10.

Lewis, Neil A. 1990. "Metzenbaum Weights in against Court Nominee." *The New York Times*. February 21.

Liptak, Adam. 2017. "White House Ends Bar Association's Role in Vetting Judge." *The New York Times*. March 31.

Martinek, Wendy L., Mark Kemper, and Steven R. Van Winkle. 2002. "To Advise and Consent: The Senate and Lower Federal Court Nominations, 1977–2002." *The Journal of Politics* 64: 337–61.

McAllister, Bill. 1990. "Judiciary Panel Votes 12 to 1 to Put Thomas on U.S. Bench; Don't Assume Way is Clear to Supreme Court Seat, Democrats Warn." *The Washington Post*. February 23.

Miller, Bill. 2001. "Appeals Court Nominees Share Conservative Roots; Records of Roberts and Estrada Are Being Studied Closely." *The Washington Post*. May 23.

Moraski, Bryon J., and Charles R. Shipan. 1999. "The Politics of Supreme Court Nominations: A Theory of Institutional Constraints and Choices." *American Journal of Political Science* 43: 1069–95.

Nemacheck, Christine L. 2007. *Strategic Selection: Presidential Nomination of Supreme Court Justices from Herbert Hoover through George W. Bush*. Charlottesville: University of Virginia Press.

The New York Times. 2003. "An Unacceptable Nominee." January 29. www.nytimes.com/2003/01/29/opinion/an-unacceptable-nominee.html.

2010. "An Exceptional Nominee." March 27. www.nytimes.com/2010/03/28/opinion/28sun3.html?ref=topics.

Peppers, Todd C. 2006. *Courtiers of the Marble Palace: The Rise and Influence of the Supreme Court Law Clerk*. Stanford, CA: Stanford University Press.

Robinson, Mike. 1990. "Conservative Black Judicial Candidate Clears Committee Hurdle." *AP Online*. February 22.

Ruckman, P. S. 1993. "The Supreme Court, Critical Nominations, and the Senate Confirmation Process." *Journal of Politics* 55: 793–805.

Scherer, Nancy. 2005. *Scoring Points: Politicians, Activists, and the Lower Federal Court Appointment Process*. Palo Alto, CA: Stanford University Press.

Scherer, Nancy, Brandon L. Bartels, and Amy Steigerwalt. 2008. "Sounding the Fire Alarm: The Role of Interest Groups in the Lower Federal Court Confirmation Process." *The Journal of Politics* 70: 1026–39.

Sen, Maya. 2014. "How Judicial Qualification Ratings May Disadvantage Minority and Female Candidates." *Journal of Law and Courts* 2: 33–65.

Shipan, Charles R. 2008. "Partisanship, Ideology, and Senate Voting on Supreme Court Nominees." *Journal of Empirical Legal Studies* 5: 55–76.

Shipan, Charles, and Megan L. Shannon. 2003. "Delaying Justice(s): A Duration Analysis of Supreme Court Confirmations." *American Journal of Political Science* 47: 654–68.

Smelcer, Susan Navarro, Amy Steigerwalt, and Richard L. Vining, Jr. 2012. "Bias and the Bar: Evaluating the ABA Ratings of Federal Judicial Nominees." *Political Research Quarterly* 65: 827–40.

Solowiej, Lisa A., Wendy L. Martinek, and Thomas L. Brunnell. 2005. "Partisan Politics: The Impact of Party in the Confirmation of Minority and Female Federal Court Nominees." *Party Politics* 11: 557–77.

Sturgess, Garry. 1991. "The Court Also Aches: D.C. Circuit Rocked Again by Nomination Politics." *Legal Times*. October 14.

Toobin, Jeffrey. 2013. "The Supreme Court Nominee-in-Waiting."*The New Yorker*. April 8. www.newyorker.com/news/daily-comment/the-supreme-court-nominee-in-waiting.

Totenberg, Nina. 2016. "President Obama Meets with Supreme Court Candidates." *NPR*. March 8.
Ward, Artemus, and David L. Weiden. *Sorcerers' Apprentices: 100 Years of Law Clerks at the United States Supreme Court*. New York: New York University Press.
Wittes, Benjamin. 2002. "Too Smart to be a Judge." *The Washington Post*. June 11.
Yalof, David A. 2005. "Dress Rehearsal Politics and the Case of Earmarked Judicial Nominees." *Cardozo Law Review* 26: 691–709.

8

Navigating Rising to the Top: Justice Sotomayor

SAMANTHA L. HERNANDEZ

Whether born from experience or inherent physiological or cultural differences, our gender and national origins may and will make a difference in our judging.
– Sonia Sotomayor

In 1789, the first Congress passed legislation creating the federal court system. Since the passing of the Judiciary Act of 1789, the makeup of the courts has greatly changed, not only demographically but also logistically. The number of justices on the Supreme Court fluctuated in the number of seats available until 1869 when Congress authorized the current size of nine members. The lower courts' makeup also changed from needing a Supreme Court justice and two district court justices to hear a case to just one district court judge. Court composition changes would allow for more opportunities for qualified judges to serve on the bench, and as the legal profession grew and diversified, the diversification of the courts would logically follow. However, the courts did not follow the same pattern as the legislative branch. The number of seats, lifetime appointments, and the confirmation process can lead to the lack of diversity on the federal bench, yet the drastic difference between judicial appointments of minorities, women, and women of color to the judiciary compared to the legislative branch raises the question: What will it take to increase diversity?

Since the passing of the Judiciary Act of 1789, one woman of color has been appointed to serve on the highest court. In 2009, President Barack Obama nominated Second Circuit Judge Sonia Sotomayor to serve on the Supreme Court. Sotomayor's nomination went relatively smoothly, with the exception of a comment she made when asked a question a decade prior to her confirmation. Sotomayor was asked how her gender and ethnicity would affect her decision-making. "I would hope that a wise Latina woman with the richness of her experiences would more often than not reach a better conclusion than a white male who hasn't lived that life" (James 2009). The comment created concern that Sotomayor found Latinas superior to all other race and gender groups (James 2009). The scrutiny over these comments brought into question what was the actual problem, Sotomayor's comments or what they represented? The belief that changes in the race and gender makeup of courts could change legal decisions was a very real and still unknown answer. Sotomayor was confirmed 68–31, becoming the third woman to serve on the Supreme Court, the third person of color, and the first Latina.

Effects of having a diverse judiciary are widely unknown, as the increase of women and minorities in the legal profession and the judiciary needs further examination. The case of Justice Sotomayor provides an opportunity to examine how the intersections of race and gender can affect judicial rulings. To better explore this phenomenon, I will first discuss racial threat theory as a means of understanding potential discomfort with a diverse federal bench. Next, I will discuss two key scholars' definitions of descriptive representation. Then, in order to better understand the uniqueness involving Sotomayor's placement on the Court, I will go over the legal and judicial pipelines for women and women of color. Lastly, I will briefly examine statements made by Sotomayor at a talk given at Arizona State University as well as a 2014 ruling on affirmative action to see effects of a Latina on the Supreme Court.

RACIAL THREAT THEORY

Racial threat theory, or in-group theory, has been widely discussed since the 1960s in various fields, but brought to the attention of political scientists in relation to public opinion by Kinder and Cam (2010). Originally discussed as ethnocentrism by Sumner in 1906, and later developed into racial threat theory by Blumer (1958), racial threat theory can be simplified as the limitation of power from the minority group (out group) by the majority group. In this case, the minority group would be Latinos and the majority group would be the largest portion of the American electorate, Whites. The theory holds that the majority group has the one goal of controlling and maintaining power.

Bobo and Hutchings (1996) expanded on this theory by examining how minority groups view one another. They maintain that racial alienation – the measurement of how enfranchised or disenfranchised a group feels given current political, social, and economic conditions – effects views of other groups. The authors findings also highlight that when examining Whites' perceptions of Latinos, negative stereotypes and affect increased the perception of threat from Latinos, whereas a negative affect increases the perception of threat from Latinos towards Blacks and Asians (Bobo and Hutchings, 1996). If affect and perception of threat creates animosity between different racial and ethnic groups, the ability to form coalitions to garner enough votes becomes difficult. When examining political and economic competition, Bobo and Hutchings (1996) found that Whites viewed Latinos as a larger threat than Blacks. In addition, the authors found that the difference in White respondents' perceived threat via political competition between Latinos and Asians was not significant. While Blacks viewed Asians as a larger political and economic threat than Latinos, Asians who were not born in the United States were more likely to view Latinos as a threat (Bobo and Hutchings 1996).

Furthering the findings of Bobo and Hutchings in regard to race relations and coalition-building, political scientists have examined group conflict between Blacks and Latinos or how Blacks and Latinos work together (Hero and Preughs 2013; Sanchez 2007). Work focusing on immigration or housing issues has shown the effect of proximity on reactions towards Latinos (Branton et al. 2007; Rocha and Espino 2009). This resentment towards Latinos leads to covert and overt attempts at excluding Latinos and differential treatment in various aspects of public life, including public service.

While a racial alienation explanation leads to an argument that historical perspective of group standing is important, recent work has shown that demographic projections of minorities surpassing Whites as the largest racial/ethnic group has increased anxiety among Whites (Craig and Richeson 2014). Craig and Richeson conducted three experiments to determine if an increase of exposure to changing minority demographics (i.e, larger African-American, Latino, and Asian-American communities) leads to explicit racial bias increasing among Whites. In the first study, participants were exposed to current census information or the 2042 census projection. After reading the information, respondents were asked questions about whom they preferred to socialize and work with. Those that were exposed to the 2042 census information were more likely to say they preferred associating with people of their same race than those that were exposed to the 2010 census data (Craig and Richeson 2014). In their final experiment, subjects were asked to answer questions to determine which group (Whites, Blacks, Latinos, Asians) they were most hostile to. All groups were more likely to favor Whites and feel the most threatened by Latinos (Craig and Richeson 2014).

Racial threat theory explains potential issues with judicial appointments for people of color, and can be applied to female candidates as well. We do not know the full extent to which this affects appointments; however, given the reaction to Sotomayor's comments on being a wise Latina, the assumption that identity does play a role in how candidates are perceived and how their rulings will be interpreted are clear. In the next section, I discuss how descriptive representation perceptually empowers people of color and women.

DESCRIPTIVE REPRESENTATION

Hanna Pitkin's (1967) seminal work on representation provided a working definition for scholars to work from. For Pitkin, the first step was to actually have members of historically disenfranchised groups involved in government. Having a member of a previously disenfranchised group that simply looked like the group provided a type of representation that had not been experienced before, and was valuable. This definition established the importance of a representative physically matching the group, but did not discuss the role of actual representation. Overall, Pitkin's definition does not account for how a representative from the group acts, leaving the ability for a representative to not act in the group's interests. On the whole, this definition lacks accountability measurements, leaving to question what the actual value is of having someone that looks like a member of a group serving in a political institution. Visibly seeing someone that looks like a disenfranchised group in positions of power can have positive effects; scholars have seen changes in Black attitudes towards the government when a Black person is elected (Gurin, Hatchett and Jackson 1990). Yet, Gay (2002) found that there was no difference in trust of Congress when a Black person was elected. This raises the question of when descriptive representation matters; is there more of an effect at the local level than at the state or federal level? How does Sotomayor's appointment change things for Latino and women youth?

In a 2002 speech, Sotomayor highlighted the importance of seeing changes in the judiciary for both women and Latinos (Sotomayor 2002). While discussing representation, she discussed the improvements that have been made in the judiciary by women, and to a lesser extent Latinos. Noting the 1961 appointment of the first Latino to the federal bench, Sotomayor stated in the same breath that by the time she graduated law school there had still been no woman or Latino appointed to the Supreme Court (Sotomayor 2002). To a young Sotomayor, the number of people that looked like her in the legal profession were minimal, and yet she aspired to keep working and be one of the first. In a 2016 conversation at Arizona State University, she discussed the way attorneys viewed who would be successful. "I realized the difference between the people selected for promotion were the ones who looked and argued like the partners. If you're successful, you will select people that fit that mold, not because you want to exclude people, but because you can see potential success" (Sotomayor 2016).

Sotomayor's comments demonstrate a key point of descriptive representation that Pitkin does not address: what the effects of merely looking like or mimicking a person in power can do. The advantage of descriptive representation does not lie within the concept of having a Black, Latino, Asian, or woman on the bench, but in how it changes the landscape when discussing political elites. By increasing the number of people of color and women in these roles, an increase in clerkships and lower level appointments is possible. Note that the first woman of color appointed to the Supreme Court was nominated by the first Black president. As Sotomayor states, it is having people of color and women presenting arguments, bringing up cases, and mentoring that allows for favorable decisions for their communities (Sotomayor 2002).

Anne Phillips furthers Pitkin's definition and provides four arguments highlighting the importance of descriptive representation, two of which will be discussed here. The first argument discusses the importance of seeing people from disenfranchised groups in positions of power. The role model argument states that seeing a person from a disenfranchised group in a position of power will lead to an increase of self-esteem for members of that group. In essence, by having Sotomayor sit on the Supreme Court, women and Latinos, particularly Latinas, should feel a larger sense of pride than members that are not part of that group.

The second argument Phillips presents is that descriptive representatives are needed to make up for past and continued injustices toward disenfranchised groups. Phillips believes that the presence of these groups facilitates the discussion of their beliefs, opinions, and viewpoints, which otherwise would not be presented. Phillips refers to it as the justice argument, ultimately holding that having these groups at the proverbial political table allows for political trust to be restored. Sotomayor points to this being a key aspect when discussing who actually argues cases in front of the Supreme Court. Sotomayor contends that despite the Court being primarily made up of White males, the attorneys that argued landmark cases included Chief Justice Thurgood Marshall and Justice Carol Motley Brown, the first African-American woman appointed to the federal bench (Sotomayor 2002).

The philosophical underpinnings for descriptive representation demonstrate the importance of having people of color and women in positions of power. Yet the question remains, has this been born out in lower courts? Scherer and Curry (2010) argue that increasing representation on the federal bench increases the legitimization of the courts for Blacks, but simultaneously decreases the level of support from Whites. These findings indicate a level of

TABLE 8.1 *Representation of U.S. federal court women judges*

Type of Court	Total # of Seats	Women	% of Women
United States Supreme Court	9	3	33
Circuit Court of Appeals (Active)	167	60	35.9
Federal District Court Judges (Active) in the United States			33

comfort with how current decisions have been made, but more importantly raises the question of how group threat affects these opinions. In addition to how group threat can affect opinions, it highlights why these resistances can be seen. In the following section, I will look at how diversity in the legal profession and the judiciary has changed over the past decade to better understand where the courts currently sit and why Justice Sotomayor's presence on the Supreme Court has demonstrated the need for descriptive representation.

WOMEN IN THE JUDICIARY AND LEGAL FIELD

For the first 145 years of the judicial system's history, each president appointed and the Senate confirmed 857 White men to the federal courts. Franklin Delano Roosevelt was the first president to appoint a woman and a man of color to the federal bench (Stubbs 2016). Since then, an increase in minorities and women serving as federal judges has occurred. Table 8.1 shows the number of women currently serving in the Judiciary. At this juncture, women compromise roughly one-third of all federal judges in the United States. This increase in women in the judiciary at the federal level is in a large part because of the appointments made by President Obama.

Although improvement has been made, out of the 112 Supreme Court Justices that have been appointed since the founding of the Court, only 4 have been women (nwlc.org 2018). Women make up 35.9 percent of judges on the circuit court of appeals; however, when looking at the Third and Eighth Circuit, women only compromise 17 and 20 percent, respectively. Overall, the increase in women serving as federal judges is important; however, when looking at the circuit level it becomes clear that parity has not been reached. Table 8.2 highlights the number of women serving on federal and state high courts. Similar findings are demonstrated, with women making up about

TABLE 8.2 *Representation of U.S. state court women judges*

Type of Court	Total # of Seats	Women	% of Women
State Final Appellate Jurisdiction Courts	353	122	34.6
State Intermediate Appellate Jurisdiction Courts	991	344	34.7
State General Jurisdiction Courts	11,778	3,502	29.7
State Limited and Special Jurisdiction Courts	4,884	1,628	33.3
All State Court Judges in the United States	18,006	5,596	31.1

one-third of the justices on state-level courts. This indicates that either through the judicial appointment or election process, parity has not been reached for women. Further, the findings are more drastic for women of color. Currently only eighty-two women of color serve as federal judges and twelve serve on the federal circuit court of appeals, with six federal court of appeals having no women of color serving.

Numbers of women in the legal profession are also increasing. In 2016, the number of women graduating from law school was nearly equal to men (americanbar.org 2016). Minority law student graduation rate has fluctuated from 20 to 29 percent (amercianbar.org 2016). As more women and minorities graduate from law school, it should follow that an increase in the number of women and minorities as associates and partners will also increase. The National Association of Law Practitioners found a decrease in women, whereas minorities, in large part due to Asian-American attorneys, have seen a marked increase (NALP 2017). In addition, women of color have also seen an increase at the associate and partner levels. Overall, an increase of women of color in associate and partner levels demonstrates the growth that Sotomayor (2002) hinted towards. This increase would also predict a future increase in judicial appointments. These findings in conjunction with racial threat theory would also provide justification for Scherer and Curry's findings, specifically White reactions towards more Blacks serving as federal judges.

In the next section, I discuss the 2014 affirmative action case, *Schuette v. Coalition to Defend Affirmative Action*, Justice Sotomayor's dissent, and corroborating statements from a 2016 speech at Arizona State university that highlight the justice's stance on the issue.

AFFIRMATIVE ACTION

The 2006 elections in Michigan had a proposition on the ballot that allowed voters to decide whether or not gender and race should be taken into consideration in public education, public employment, and public contracting. The proposition passed, effectively barring affirmative action policies in the state. Exit polls showed that men supported the initiative more than women, and Whites supported it more than Blacks (cnn.com 2006). The clear implication was a decrease in the number of minorities being accepted to universities, in particular the University of Michigan. After the proposition was passed, a coalition was formed among individuals and groups. They immediately sued the governor and Michigan Board of Trustees, arguing that the proposition violated the Equal Protection Clause. The case made its way to the Sixth Court of Appeals, where the ruling that the vote was constitutional was upheld.

In 2013, the Supreme Court heard the case *Schuette v. Coalition to Defend Affirmative Action*. The court did not have a majority decision, as Justice Kegan recused herself because of her involvement in the early stages of the case. The plurality decision was written by Justice Kennedy, with Chief Justice Roberts, Justice Scalia, and Justice Breyer writing concurring opinions. The justices felt that voters, not the courts, should have the final say in what policies are implemented in their states. Additional concerns brought up by the justices include when and how race is used in a policy, and whether or not using affirmative action policies creates more racial tension by bringing attention to race. The dissent was written by Justice Sotomayor and joined by Justice Ginsburg.

SOTOMAYOR'S RESPONSE

Justice Sotomayor wrote a 58-page response detailing her position on affirmative action and how it was in fact the court's duty to protect minority rights. Sotomayor has argued in the past that other programs for college admissions focusing on geographic location or economic status do not perform as they are intended to. Later, in lecture at Arizona State University, Sotomayor made the same argument, citing that universities were able to leave spots available for athletes and musicians to make a well-rounded class and to widen the diversity of its student bodies (Sotomayor 2016).

In her speech, the associate justice also argued that sometimes, working hard was not enough. "You have to work hard, but working hard will not miraculously open doors" (Sotomayor 2016). Citing examples of how people of affluence already knew each other, Sotomayor brought up a children's camp relationship that Justice Ginsburg had with someone at Sotomayor's law firm, stating that when you have social networks and capital, it can be easier for you to improve your life. In her dissent, Sotomayor stated:

> The effect of §26 is that a white graduate of a public Michigan university who wishes to pass his historical privilege on to his children may freely lobby the board of that university in favor of an expanded legacy admissions policy, whereas a black Michigander who was denied the opportunity to attend that very university cannot lobby the board in favor of a policy that might give his children a chance that he never had and that they might never have absent that policy.

The statement pulled from the dissent highlights Sotomayor's concerns for what the ruling will do to people of color. In essence, the argument presented holds that equity cannot be achieved under current guidelines. To bolster her point, Sotomayor used percentages from the University of Michigan's 2012 graduating class, demonstrating the decrease in the number of African-American students at the university (Sotomayor 2006). Using graduation rates to back her belief that affirmative action policies is important; however, it is also a point that anyone in support of affirmative action can make, raising the question: Does race really matter?

Sotomayor's background helped shape her dissenting opinion. Her life experiences colored her belief on the necessity of affirmative action policies, harkening back to her acceptance to Ivy League universities. More telling, however, is her ability to relate to why race matters:

> Race matters to a young woman's sense of self when she states her hometown, and then is pressed, "No, where are you really from?" regardless of how many generations her family has been in the country. Race matters to a young person addressed by a stranger in a foreign language, which he does not understand because only English was spoken at home. Race matters because of the slights, the snickers, the silent judgments that reinforce that most crippling of thoughts: I do not belong here. (Sotomayor 2006)

This statement demonstrates an understanding that Sotomayor's colleagues on the bench, save Thomas, would not understand. She highlights how belonging to a different racial group can lead to stereotypes and assumptions based on perceptions of the group. More importantly, she highlights the isolating feeling that occurs when trying to assimilate in a part of society, regardless if the equal protection clause is in place. Sotomayor's 58-page dissent is more than a dissent because she is arguing from her personal experience, statistics, and the law, whereas the remainder of the justices can only provide reasoning based on the law. The different experiences that Sotomayor has had based on her gender, race, and class allow for a better understanding of how rulings can and will affect people. Thinking back to her "wise Latina" comment, Sotomayor acknowledged this possibility and tempered it with stating that it would not solely be these feelings and experiences that would create her judgement.

CONCLUSION

When Pitkin discussed the role of descriptive representation, the focus was on matching likeness to likeness. Whether or not matching the appearance of a particular group makes a difference in legislative and judicial representation has shown mixed results. However, in the case of the first Latina appointed to the Supreme Court, the evidence suggests that having someone matching your description may play a role in decision-making. Justice Sotomayor is not the only person of color currently sitting on the Court, but she is the first woman of color. It is possible that the intersection of her identities has further shaped her opinions compared to Justice Thomas, or it could be that political ideology plays that significant of a role in changing perceptions. What is certain, though, is that the dissent that Sotomayor wrote in the case *Schuette v. Coalition to Defend Affirmative Action* is not one that could be written without having shared experiences with people that belong to disenfranchised groups.

REFERENCES

2017 Report on Diversity. (n.d.). www.nalp.org.

Barnes, R. 2014. "Justice Sonia Sotomayor Defends Affirmative Action." June 22. www.washingtonpost.com/national/justice-sonia-sotomayor-defends-affirmative-action/2014/06/22/cfdbe774-fa22-11e3-8176-f2c941cf35f1_story.html?utm_term=.c4572a9aae81.

Blumer, H. 1958. "Race Prejudice as a Sense of Group Position." *Pacific Sociological Review* 1(1): 3–7.

Bobo, L., and Hutchings, V. L. 1996. "Perceptions of Racial Group Competition: Extending Blumer's Theory of Group Position to A Multiracial Social Context." *American Sociological Review* 951–972.

Branton, R. P., & Dunaway, J. 2009. "Spatial Proximity to the US–Mexico Border and Newspaper Coverage of Immigration Issues." *Political Research Quarterly* 62(2): 289–302.

Craig, M. A., and Richeson, J. A. 2014. "On the Precipice of a 'Majority-Minority' America: Perceived Status Threat from the Racial Demographic Shift Affects White Americans' Political Ideology." *Psychological Science* 25(6): 1189–97.

Gay, C. 2002. "Spirals of Trust? The Effect of Descriptive Representation on the Relationship between Citizens and Their Government." *American Journal of Political Science* 717–732.

Gurin, P., Hatchett, S., and Jackson, J. S. 1990. *Hope and Independence: Blacks' Response to Electoral and Party Politics*. Washington, DC: Russell Sage Foundation.

Hero, R. E., and Preuhs, R. R. 2013. *Black–Latino Relations in US National Politics: Beyond Conflict or Cooperation*. Cambridge: Cambridge University Press.

James, F. 2009. Sotomayor's 'Wise Latina' Line Maybe Not So Wise. *NPR*, May 27. www.npr.org/sections/thetwo-way/2009/05/sotomayors_wise_latina_line_ma.html

Kinder, D. R., & Kam, C. D. 2010. *Us against Them: Ethnocentric Foundations of American Opinion*. Chicago: University of Chicago Press.

Mears, B. 2014. Michigan's Ban on Affirmative Action Upheld by Supreme Court. April 23. www.cnn.com/2014/04/22/justice/scotus-michigan-affirmative-action/index.html

National Women's Law Center. (n.d.). https://nwlc-ciw49tixgw5lbab.stackpathdns .com.

Phillips, Annne. 1998. "Democracy and Representation: Or Why Should It Matter Who Our Representatives Are?" In *Feminism and Politics*. Oxford: Oxford University Press. pp. 224–40.

Pitkin, H. F. 1967. *The Concept of Representation*. Berkeley: University of California Press.

Rocha, R. R., & Espino, R. 2009. Racial Threat, Residential Segregation, and the Policy Attitudes of Anglos. *Political Research Quarterly* 62(2): 415–426.

Rocha, R. R., Longoria, T., Wrinkle, R. D., Knoll, B. R., Polinard, J. L., and Wenzel, J. 2011. "Ethnic Context and Immigration Policy Preferences Among Latinos and Anglos." *Social Science Quarterly* 92(1): 1–19.

Sanchez, G. R. 2006. "The Role of Group Consciousness in Political Participation among Latinos in the United States." *American Politics Research* 34(4): 427–50.

Scherer, N., and Curry, B. 2010. "Does Descriptive Race Representation Enhance Institutional Legitimacy? The Case of the US Courts." *The Journal of Politics* 72(1): 90–104.

Sotomayor, S. 2002. "A Latina Judge's Voice." *Berkeley La Raza LJ* 13: 87.

Status of Women in Law and the Judiciary. 2017. May. www.americanbar.org.

(2006). Another Historical Moment. *Fed. Law* 53, 29.

(2016). "My Experience on the Bench." Speech given at Arizona State University. April.

Stubbs, J. K. 2016. "Demographic History of Federal Judicial Appointments by Sex and Race: 1789–2016, A." *Berkeley La Raza LJ* 26: 92.

Supreme Court. 2014. *Schuette v. Coalition to Defend Affirmative Action*. 2014.

Concluding Remarks

Without a doubt, securing a judiciary that reflects the diversity of the population it serves is proving more difficult than we thought. So what does judicial diversity encompass? The judiciary should be composed of justices who come from varying backgrounds and have a variety of personal and professional experiences. Diversity is not limited to but reflective of gender, race, ethnicity, national origin, sexual orientation, gender identity, socioeconomic background, and so on. Judicial diversity should be reflective of the diversity of the legal profession. The goal of the chapters in this volume is to address the structural, political, cultural, and intersectional barriers to a more diverse judiciary. Based on what has been put forth by the contributing authors, the struggle for equality of representation is still very clear.

The chapters in this edited volume examine the intersectionality of race, gender, sexuality, and occupation. It is about the symbolic, descriptive, and substantive representation of different identities and experiences in the judiciary. This study is important because diversity on the bench improves the quality of justice, builds confidence in the legitimacy of the courts, and provides decision-making power to formerly disenfranchised populations. One of the primary focuses of this volume is to understand the pipeline, ambition, institutional inclusion, and retention, as well as emphasize the importance of representation by previously excluded groups. This volume aims to identify the institutional and political circumstances in which minority groups are most likely to be selected or elected to the federal and state judiciary.

This volume utilizes both quantitative and qualitative methods to explain the lack of diversity in judiciary. We began our analysis with Nancy Arrington's "Qualifications, Selection, and Retirement Characteristics of Women, Minorities, and Minority-Women State Supreme Court Judges." In this chapter, Arrington identifies the conditions under which characteristics of minority-women state supreme court justices are similar to or different from characteristics of women justices and minority men justices. She finds that there is some evidence that race and gender identity and experiences may affect judging. Moreover, Arrington concludes that minority-women state supreme court justices are more similar to minority men than white women. Minority women are indistinguishable from minority men across six categories (Ivy League education, prior judicial experience, age, selection method, party, and length of tenure). She does find that minority women are indistinguishable from white women in the areas of Ivy League education, selection method, ideology, and tenure.

In Chapter 2, Sharon A. Navarro utilizes standpoint theory to narrate the political trajectory of Hispanic females as they meander their way to becoming sitting justices on the Texas court of appeals. Standpoint theory allows the experiences of a small sample size of individuals to be a legitimate representative of a majority. Navarro describes the way in which intersectionality works to the advantage of sitting Hispanic females in majority-minority Latino districts. She finds that unlike gender – and the continued existence of the "good ol' boy network" – being a Democrat and a minority can be advantageous to winning a seat on the Texas court of appeals.

In Chapter 3, Barbara L. Graham and Adriano Udani demonstrate the relevance of intersectionality of race and gender in state judicial selections. Their findings reveal that partisan effects are important for the ascension of women of color to the state appellate bench. Partisan forces have helped more men of color and white women become appellate judges, and they are also given more opportunity to become appellate judges than women of color.

Donald Haider-Markel and Patrick Gauding, in Chapter 4, argue that LGBT representation in the United States has largely neglected the presence of LGBT judges on the bench. They explore LGBT representation in the American judicial system. The develop and explore a unique database of all openly LGBT judges in the United States since 1979. They find that over time, LGBT representation in the courts will become more common and is enhanced when judges are nominated rather than elected. These authors make it clear that much more research is needed in the areas of judicial decision-making and court rulings.

In Chapter 5, Taneisha Means highlights the way in which race and gender, through a single case study of Constance Baker Motley, not only influences the applicant pool that presidents tend to draw from to staff the federal bench, but also whom presidents nominate and how the Senate approaches and acts on such nominations. Motley's experience confirms that obstacles and obstruction in the federal judicial selection process is a longstanding problem. We learn from Means's chapter that obstructions to higher court positions are dependent upon partisan and ideological politics.

Shenita Brazelton and LaTasha Chaffin, in Chapter 6, purport that Black and Latino male and female judges increased substantially during the Carter administration. There were fewer confirmations during the Reagan and G. H. W. Bush administrations relative to the Carter administration. It was during the Clinton administration where we saw an increase in the nominations and confirmations of Black and Latino/a justices surpassing the appointments under the Carter administration. The G. W. Bush administration's minority appointments were relatively modest, while the Obama administration's Black and Latino/a appointments were on par with the Carter and Clinton administrations. They posit that if a judicial pipeline theory is developed systematically, then diversity of the courts will increase over time.

In Chapter 7, Lisa M. Holmes develops an index of Supreme Court worthiness. Her findings indicate that there is some evidence that certain characteristics of a potential future Supreme Court appointee substantively influence court of appeals confirmation success differently for women and minorities compared to their white male counterparts. Her chapter highlights the fact that nominees are treated differently based on race, ethnicity, and gender when being considered for the Supreme Court.

And, finally, Samantha L. Hernandez examines the effect of having a Latina on the Supreme Court in Chapter 8. Hernandez uses past speeches by Justice Sotomayor and her written dissent in the case *Schuette v. Coalition to Defend Affirmative Action.* She examines the increase of women and minorities in the legal and judicial fields to discuss improvements in descriptive representation and build on the importance of Sotomayor's appointment. By examining Sotomayor's dissent Hernandez argues that the importance of the first Latina on the Supreme Court goes beyond descriptive representation in the traditional sense.

Diversity matters to enriching the judiciary and judicial decision-making. The default image of a justice – as White, male, and heterosexual – should not be the norm. *Who* the judge is matters. *All* justices have different and particular views of what justice requires, what the justice's function is, and so on. What we know is that men, women, those of various racial and ethnic identities, and members of the lesbian, gay, bisexual, and transgender community will introduce different views into their judicial decisions and into the law. But this, far from being a cause for complaint and criticism, provides one of the strongest arguments in favor of judicial diversity.

Diversity is not only a legitimate part of, but is essential to elections and appointments on merit. A judiciary lacking in diversity is one lacking in an essential resource for good decision-making. A diverse judiciary is a better judiciary. It is better not (just) because it is more representative and democratically legitimate, but because it is better positioned to do its job – to deliver justice. The contributors to this edited volume examine the factors that influence *who* is nominated and confirmed to the federal judiciary and *who* is elected and not elected to statewide courts. What we have learned from this edited volume is that race/ethnicity, gender, and sexual orientation matter for the diversity of the courts. Diversity matters because descriptive representation often leads to symbolic and substantive representation. One fact is clear: there needs to be a structural, political, and cultural commitment to diversifying the judiciary.

Index

For EU product safety concerns, contact us at Calle de José Abascal, 56–1°, 28003 Madrid, Spain or eugpsr@cambridge.org.

www.ingramcontent.com/pod-product-compliance
Lightning Source LLC
LaVergne TN
LVHW011521200926
848484LV00001B/95

* 9 7 8 1 1 0 8 4 2 9 8 8 7 *